From Superiority to Parity

From Superiority to Parity

The United States and the Strategic Arms Race, *1961–1971*

Harland B. Moulton

GP

GREENWOOD PRESS, INC.
Westport, Connecticut • London, England

The views expressed in this work are entirely those of the author and do not in any way reflect those of any agency of government with which he has been associated or is presently associated.

Library of Congress Cataloging in Publication Data

Moulton, Harland B
From superiority to parity

Bibliography: p.
1. United States—Military policy. 2. Atomic weapons. 3. Russia—Military policy. I. Title.
UA23.M67 355.03'30046 79-140920
ISNB 0-8371-5822-2

Library of Congress Catalog Card Number: 79–140920
ISBN: 0–8371–5822–2
First published in 1973
GREENWOOD PRESS, INC., PUBLISHING DIVISION
51 Riverside Avenue, Westport, Connecticut 06880
Manufactured in the United States of America
Designed by Christopher Simon

To Patty

Contents

Preface

It may never be known whether John F. Kennedy actually believed there was a missile gap favoring the Soviet Union during the campaign of 1960, or whether he opportunistically exploited the issue against Richard Nixon in his bid to defeat him. Kennedy was aware that the top civilian leadership of the Eisenhower Administration rejected the idea of a missile gap, and it is not known precisely how much information he was given on the highly successful U-2 flights. It is clear that Kennedy was incensed by the low level briefings given him on the strategic nuclear balance at Strategic Air Command Headquarters in August 1960, and it is conceivable that this incident may have influenced his subsequent campaign stance. Secretary McNamara's slip to the press in February 1961 that in his judgment there was no missile gap and never had been one merely fuels greater doubt.

Conceding even a strong commitment to honor this campaign pledge to erase the putative missile gap, and accepting McNamara's and his advisors' fascination with a nuclear strategy of counterforce, it nevertheless seems incredible today (1972) that Kennedy so unabashedly decided to bury the Soviet Union in strategic nuclear inferiority, completely confident after mid-1961 that the Soviet strategic nuclear threat was miniscule, ill protected, and expanding very slowly. Just as grotesque were Kennedy's successful efforts to establish an arms control agency and to pledge his administration to serious discussions with the Soviet Union while at the same time stimulating the arms race to a pace similar to that during the Korean War.

McNamara's flirtation with a nuclear counterforce strategy was brief, and by 1963 he questioned both the credibility and the cost of such a strategy in view of a growing but modest Soviet strategic nuclear threat. Nevertheless, no serious effort was made by either Kennedy or Johnson to slow the pace of strategic weapons deployment in order to test Soviet reactions or to match them in the event they failed to exercise restraint. The fall of Khrushchev in 1964 and the subsequent decision by the new Soviet leaders to accelerate vastly the deployment of strategic missile systems appear to have been triggered by our insistence on gaining and maintaining overwhelming strategic nuclear superiority. Needless to say, arms control negotiations affecting strategic weapons systems were rebuffed by the Soviets until the late 1960s when finally they had achieved a sufficient degree of parity with the United States to permit a comfortable psychological posture from which to engage in the SALT.

To this day (mid-1972) responsible U.S. leaders have eschewed bringing before the bar of American public opinion the argument for and against accepting strategic nuclear parity with the Soviet Union. The fact that an asymmetrical parity exists today between this nation and the Soviet Union is due largely to our heavy commitment after 1965 in the Vietnamese conflict. The controversy surrounding the war and its high costs resulted in the curtailment of new strategic weapons programs in favor of substantial increases in conventional weapons and munitions. The Vietnam conflict in effect allowed the United States to acquiesce in strategic nuclear parity with the Soviet Union without the nation's leaders ever having to justify its wisdom to the American people.

Richard Nixon rode to victory in 1969 on a pledge to maintain this nation's military superiority over China and the Soviet Union. Soon after his inauguration he was pressed by newsmen to explain whether indeed the new administration was prepared to abandon nuclear superiority in favor of parity with the Soviet Union. He finessed the issue by opting for a doctrine of sufficiency which has since been used by the Administration to repel criticism by conservatives demanding superiority, and arms controllers arguing for rough parity. From 1969 to early 1972 Department of Defense officials defined the strategic nuclear balance between the United States and the Soviet Union strictly in quantitative terms, demonstrating the point that the Soviets were rapidly overtaking us in numbers of strategic nuclear vehicles, and appeared to be determined to attain outright superiority. Heavy criticism of the Laird defense programs by the right wing of the Republican party finally induced the Pentagon to acknowledge that the United States enjoyed considerable qualitative superiority over the Soviet Union, was likely to hold on to it in the near future, and that qualitative measurements were indeed significant in computing the strategic balance between the two powers. Having opted for such a stance, the possibility appeared to grow that the Administration might be successful in working out a SALT agreement with the Soviet Union which would allow important numerical asymmetries between the strategic forces of the two superpowers, while permitting the nation's leaders to claim that our qualitative lead was sufficiently offsetting.

As these lines are written, a significant SALT agreement has been concluded with the Soviet Union, which will preclude the possibility of major missile and submarine deployment by that nation during the next several years, and in no way influence this nation's deployment plans, since no new weapon systems could be deployed anyway during the next several years short of a crash program. Both nations have agreed to commence SALT II discussions in the fall, and presumably such issues will be aired as forward deployed tactical air forces, mutual reductions of existing strategic force levels, limitation of future qualitative improvements in existing strategic force levels, and possible restrictions on research and development programs, such as ASW, which would help to insure the long term invulnerability of Polaris-type missile systems and the stability of the nuclear balance. Although optimism may be foolhardy when dealing with the Soviets, it is conceivable that the Moscow summit was an important watershed in our future relations with that nation. There is some evidence suggesting that both superpowers may find their interests better served by achieving a better balance between domestic and defense priorities, by continuing to reduce the possible risks of war between themselves, and by demilitarizing their foreign policies in favor of a more traditional political and economic competition to decide which power will exert the greater influence in the world.

Of those who helped shape my thoughts on the scope and substance of this book, I am most indebted to my long-time advisor and friend, Professor Harold C. Deutsch, of the University of Minnesota, who encouraged me to undertake the study, supported me when my spirit flagged, and challenged me with incisive and timely suggestions for improvement. I wish also to thank Dr. Ralph E. Lapp, physicist and publicist, for affording me frequent access to his probing and capacious mind, as well as his almost limitless source materials. My appreciation is due many of my former colleagues at the U.S. Arms Control and Disarmament Agency who read one of the several manuscripts and whose critical but helpful comments saved me from serious errors of fact and interpretation. I owe an important debt to both the faculty and students at the National War College, who for the past two years have constantly forced me to reexamine my major hypotheses, temper my extremes, and sharpen my conclusions. Above all, I owe unlimited appreciation and gratitude to Patty, my wife, who read and typed every page of every draft I produced, never complaining and constantly a source of inspiration. I would never have completed the book without her assistance.

HARLAND B. MOULTON

June 8, 1972

From Superiority to Parity

CHAPTER 1

Prologue: Nuclear Revolution, the Cold War, and the Strategic Balance of Power, 1945–1960

The Nuclear Age Arrives

In May 1945, when Nazi Germany capitulated to the Allies, the defeat of Japan was also assured. Japan's far-flung wartime empire was steadily collapsing from incessant American air attacks and combined naval and ground assaults. The crucial question facing the Allies was how to end the war quickly while minimizing further casualties. Although opinion varied among American leaders as to the most effective way of achieving Japanese surrender, there was full unanimity among the Allies that Japan must surrender unconditionally and trust its future to the magnanimity of the victors. Lack of decision on the part of a confused and vacillating Japanese leadership reinforced feelings in Washington that the Japanese intended to fight on stubbornly and that an invasion of the home islands would prove costly in American lives. The successful testing of an atomic device in mid-July 1945 appeared to offer the Allies a way out of a serious quandary.

As Winston Churchill reported in his memoirs, whether to use the atomic bomb to compel the surrender of Japan was never an issue among the Allies. A final declaration was issued to Japan in late July calling for the unconditional surrender of all Japanese armed forces and warning that the alternative would be prompt and utter destruction. The Soviet Union gave its assurance that its forces would enter the war against Japan. On August 6, 1945, President Harry S. Truman shocked world sensibilities when he announced on radio that an American bomber had dropped a single and revolutionary bomb on Hiroshima, an important Japanese army base. The President identified the weapon as an atomic bomb containing more power than 20,000 tons of TNT, and he added: "It had more than two thousand times the blast power of the British 'Grand Slam,' which is the largest bomb ever used in the history of warfare."[1]

In a brief but cataclysmic flash an atomic bomb yielding 20 kilotons devastated 4.7 square miles of Hiroshima, killing nearly 80,000 people and wounding thousands more; soon after, Nagasaki felt the searing wrath of the newly born atomic age, suffering over 70,000 casualties from a second atomic weapon yielding approximately 23 kilotons. Stunned and wholly unaware of the nature of the awesome force which had struck her, Japan surrendered unconditionally to the Allies on August 14, thereby ending the hostilities phase of World War II.

The successful atomic bomb literally dwarfed the revolution set in motion by the invention of gunpowder early in the fourteenth century. Five centuries were to pass before the world entered the age of sophisticated modern firearms which included breech loading and rifling and the perfection of explosive projectiles for artillery pieces.[2] The atomic bomb was an unprecedented quantum jump in military fire power, which appeared to challenge fundamentally the validity of past military strategy and tactics. The purpose of this study is, therefore, to examine the impact of the nuclear age on traditional United States attitudes toward war as an instrument of diplomacy, the relevance of the balance of power system, the meaning and consequences of the technological revolution, the maintenance of stable military balances, and the phenomenon of arms races and arms control.

Immediately after World War II, a major debate took place on the question of whether the strategic bombing of Germany and Japan had been decisive in winning the war. The United States Strategic

Bombing Survey produced by a competent staff of American scholars and government officials concluded that strategic bombing had been decisive in the war in Western Europe, but could not be considered decisive in the case of Japan, although it did play a key role in reducing Japan's capability to wage further offensive operations. Because convincing evidence did exist that strategic bombing tended to stiffen morale in both Germany and Japan and because the main thrust of strategic bombing against both nations came late in the war, some critics argued that the repeated defeats inflicted on both adversaries by land and naval forces were the decisive factors in bringing about the collapse of both Germany and Japan. Had the atomic bomb not been perfected at a very crucial time in 1945, it is entirely possible that strategic bombing dependent on high explosive bombs would not have enjoyed so high a priority in the force planning and strategy of the postwar period. A much stronger case could have been made for maintaining a more equal balance among ground, sea, and air forces had not the atomic revolution clinched the case for the decisiveness and the economy of the atomic bomb.

Despite growing signs of deteriorating Soviet-American relations, massive demobilization of American forces commenced in September 1945 in response to restiveness among the troops, Congress, and a large and articulate minority of the American public. Once demobilization gained momentum there was seemingly no way to halt it, and if there was a way, it would have required a blunt warning by the President of the growing threat to the European balance of power from the Soviet Union. The administration refused to act boldly during the winter of 1945–1946, apparently unwilling to risk the displeasure of the Soviet Union with which it still hoped to reach a fair and amicable agreement. The consequence of American temporizing was that during the ensuing eighteen months, the United States almost completely dismantled the greatest military machine ever assembled. Ground, air, and naval units literally melted away until it became virtually impossible to calculate what military forces, if any, the United States could muster in the face of a serious Soviet threat. Thus, the stage was inevitably set for almost total dependence by the United States on the deterrent threat of the atomic bomb to offset the massive superiority of Soviet ground forces which remained in Eastern Europe virtually at wartime strength.

The Cold War

The United States entered the postwar period having failed to learn the main lessons of World Wars I and II. American leaders rejected power politics, spheres of influence, and a restored balance of power in Europe as a basis for securing the peace and banked their hopes for securing peace on the creation of an international authority, the United Nations. This time, the United States was the foremost advocate of collective security and the chief supporter of the concept of providing military forces to an international organization to maintain peace and security. President Roosevelt conceived of the United Nations as a universal organization in which all peace-loving nations would have an opportunity to share.

Unfortunately, however, it soon became apparent that the terms of unconditional surrender had created an enormous power vacuum in Germany. Given the rapid erosion of American military power in Europe, it was unclear what power would emerge to balance the overwhelming strength of the Soviet Union in Eastern Europe. Mutual trust between the United States and the Soviet Union evaporated rapidly after 1945, and American leaders progressively sensed a sinister design in Soviet behavior which no longer seemed aimed purely at protecting commitments in Eastern Europe. An expansionist Soviet Union, operating according to a grand design and motivated ideologically, seemed bent on extending its influence and power into Western Europe.

America's response to assumed Soviet expansionism was the enunciation of the Truman Doctrine and the Marshall Plan, bolstered simultaneously by a rearmament program built upon our atomic monopoly. Soviet response was a decisive move to consolidate its hold on the Eastern and Central European states. Soon, as Louis Halle argues cogently, "the West was governed by the myth of a single conspiracy for world conquest under the direction of a satanic band in the Kremlin, to whom all who called themselves Communists, the world over, gave blind obedience."[3] The advice offered by the State Department's George Kennan against viewing the Soviet threat in military terms and arguing for political containment of a political threat was rejected by the President and his advisors. America's main response to the Soviet challenge was the rapid buildup and deployment of a large and versatile strategic nuclear air force able to strike targets deep in the Soviet Union from an expanding complex of overseas bases. Although for a brief period it appeared that the United States might use nuclear weapons to halt Soviet expansionism, political and moral constraints soon joined with the unexpected achievement of a nuclear capability by the Soviet Union to compel this nation to base its security on a strategy of nuclear deterrence.

After twenty-five years, do interpretations of the origins and evolution of the cold war tend to sustain the conventional wisdom of an aggressive Soviet Union ideologically propelled, or have the historical revisionists succeeded in casting doubt on many premises on which the orthodox case rests? Historians, such as Arthur Schlesinger, Jr., who lately have argued the futility of proving the case for cold war revisionism—even moderate revisionism—have failed notably in persuading the defenders of the new faith.[4] Although strongly indicting both extreme orthodox and revisionist views of the cold war, and embracing a moderately revisionist position similar to that held by such careful interpreters as Louis Halle and Martin Herz, Schlesinger nevertheless concluded: "The Cold War could have been avoided only if the Soviet Union had not been possessed by convictions both of the infallibility of the communist word and of the inevitability of a communist world."[5] Schlesinger marshals no convincing evidence to sustain his main point, and as other scholars have pointed out, sooner or later historians will have to come to serious grips with the cold war. Thus far, the main effort of the orthodox school has been to suppress further serious investigation.

The orthodox view that the origins of the cold war are traceable to historical imperial Russian strategic ambitions or to the imperatives of a militant communist ideology, is less convincing than the thesis advanced by modern scholarship that the cold war had its origins in the events of World War II. On several occasions during World War II, Stalin told Roosevelt and Churchill that any postwar settlement in Eastern Europe must recognize spheres of influence to the extent of insuring pro-Soviet governments along Russia's western periphery. Although Churchill was partly disposed to consider postwar settlements in terms of a realistic balance of power or sphere of influence, Roosevelt was disposed for personal and political reasons to reject power politics, spheres of influence, balances of power, and unilateral action as expedients which had been tried for centuries and failed. In the words of Louis Halle: "The American vision, which was congenial to the British as well, was of a worldwide international community, democratically organized under a sort of parliament of nations, in which all the members enjoyed self-determination by free elections on the Western model."[6]

World War II ended with the Soviet Union militarily in control of Slavic Europe, but as the result of victory over Germany and not of aggression. Allied insistence on unconditional surrender resulted in the total destruction of German power in Europe, leaving a power vacuum in Central Europe, which irresistibly the Soviet Union or the United States would tend to fill. The United States chose to disband its war machine in Europe, creating a void which the British could not fill and conceding the initiative in all of Europe to the Soviet Union. Despite what must have been strong temptations, Stalin's behavior during the immediate aftermath of the war marks him more as a cautious realist and nationalist than as an ideologue bent on opportunistic expansion.

Prior to the final breakdown of the wartime alliance, Stalin's minimum demands appeared to be the achievement of defensible frontiers from the Baltic to the Black Sea which realistically could be controlled from Moscow. As a practitioner of *Realpolitik,* Stalin forcibly imposed communist regimes on Poland, Hungary, Rumania, and Bulgaria, and later repeated it in Czechoslovakia. In part, however, Stalin's tactics in Eastern Europe appear to have been in direct response to Allied insistence on democratic, free elections in Poland. During 1946 and 1947, mutual suspicion of each other's motives grew apace, and "each side felt compelled to adopt policies which the other could not but regard as a threat to the principles of peace. Each then felt compelled to undertake defensive measures."[7]

By the winter of 1947–1948, the whole structure of power that had balanced and contained Soviet power in the West was crumbling, and it appeared that Italy, Greece, and France might well come under communist control. Growing economic chaos from Germany to the British Isles, mounting signs of anarchy in which communism might easily flourish, and the existence of an ideal power vacuum provided the Soviet Union with its greatest expansionist opportunity of the postwar period. Yet the Soviet armies did not move west as so many feared, and the reasons are worth speculating about. The possibility must be admitted that Stalin never did perceive his opportunities in Western Europe in military terms, believing probably that communist electoral successes would ensure strong Soviet influence and block any American efforts to restore the European balance of power. Stalin's ambitions were undoubtedly tempered as well by the sheer size of the reconstruction programs needed in the Soviet Union to eliminate the horrible carnage inflicted by the German armies. Under the circumstances of human suffering and destruction that prevailed in western Russia, it hardly seems probable that Stalin was highly motivated to project his power beyond Eastern Europe which he already dominated but had not yet transformed into communist states on the model of the Soviet Union. Stalin, the realist, would hardly be disposed to undertake risky adventures from such a shaky bastion of power.

Perhaps the strongest curb on Stalin's ambitions by late 1947 and early 1948 was America's growing atomic striking power, which under last-ditch circumstances could have destroyed targets in the Soviet Union from bases in the United Kingdom and the Far East. Thus, the stabilizing effects of nuclear deterrence were already evident. Stalin may have misjudged American moral fibre and commitment to defend its Western European allies, but it was the ominous portent of Soviet military aggression which quickly drew the United States back to the Continent where it inevitably collided with Soviet power and accelerated the pace of the cold war.

For almost two decades after World War II, American strategic planning for general war and rearmament programs was based on the orthodox view of an aggressive, ideologically inspired Soviet challenge, which in due course was viewed in global terms. The current, moderate revisionist interpretation of the cold war, on the other hand, contends that the breakdown in Soviet-American relations was the result of a serious misunderstanding of each other's intentions which intensified mutual suspicions and hardened each other's positions. The moderate revisionists, skirting the pitfalls of historical determinism, hold that American policymakers did have an option of choosing policies different from those embraced and that a more compromising and conciliatory approach to the Soviet Union might have substantially altered the direction and bitter hostility of the cold war. At any rate, the cold war does not appear to have emerged as part of a carefully laid Soviet or Allied plan and was largely improvised by both sides as they confronted each other on what frequently appeared to be a collision course. Stalin, like American and Allied leaders, was a victim of circumstances well beyond his capacity to formulate into any coherent communist scheme.

Historians thus far have failed to challenge fundamentally the basic premises of moderate revisionist scholarship, which appear both conceptually and realistically to offer a more plausible explanation of events during the period of 1944 to 1948 and after. Nevertheless, despite what today appear to be serious inadequacies in the conventional wisdom about the origins and progress of the cold war, orthodoxy prevails widely. If the moderate revisionist interpretation of cold war origins eventually becomes conventional wisdom, the chances will be sharply reduced that the United States and future allies will be condemned to repeat the mistakes of the post-World War II period.

The Strategic Balance

The explosion of two atomic bombs on Japanese cities proved a chastening experience to American leaders and public alike. War, which in the past had been violent, had not become holocaustic and inhuman. Americans were quick to accept the fact that World War III would be intolerable and that the only purpose of military preparedness in the future would be to prevent war from happening. For a brief period, lasting less than a decade, the quantum jump in military power, packaged in the atomic bomb, became a monopoly of the United States. In a burst of characteristic idealism the United States proposed the creation of an International Atomic Development Authority, whose principal purpose was to ensure that atomic energy would be reserved solely for peaceful purposes in order not to condemn mankind to the slavery of fear. The disintegration of friendly wartime relations between the United States and the Soviet

Union into the cold war doomed to early failure the grand design of many American leaders to establish international institutions having a primary responsibility for maintaining the peace and preventing future war. Thus the nations of the world were left with the choice of either learning to live peacefully in a continuing revolution of military power or destroying future civilizations because of failure to impose reason and restraint on inexorable technology.

As the threat from the Soviet Union was perceived by American leaders more and more in military terms beginning in 1946, the only credible threats to the vastly superior Soviet land armies were the atomic bomb and long-range aircraft capable of striking targets in the Soviet Union. A strategy of deterrence, which today is generally acknowledged as having effectively preserved peace during the decades following World War II, was not conceptualized in coherent form at the time the Soviet threat appeared most ominous to the United States and its Allies. Confidence in the efficacy of nuclear deterrence in meeting the challenge of new weapons technology grew slowly during the postwar period, successfully surmounted crises of confidence, and apparently has convinced the two superpowers that continuing to pursue military advantage in arms races is both futile and not worth the formidable price.

This section reviews the strategic nuclear balance between the Soviet Union and the United States from 1945 to 1965 in order to illustrate fundamental American misperceptions of the nature and size of the Soviet threat and why such misperceptions occurred.

In a report to Congress on American foreign policy for the 1970s, President Richard Nixon issued what is undoubtedly the most authoritative and candid historical statement of the relative balance of strategic power between this nation and the Soviet Union: "From 1945 to 1949, we were the only nation in the world possessing an arsenal of atomic weapons. From 1950 to 1966, we possessed an overwhelming superiority in strategic weapons."[8] While only a few unreconstructed skeptics would argue with this assessment today, the issue of the Soviet challenge to America in science, research, and military technology precipitated one of the most bitterly contested debates of the postwar period.

The size and weight of the early atomic bombs and the diminutive size of America's stockpile of operational weapons during the late

1940s, virtually ensured that the B-29s and B-17s of the Air Force's Strategic Air Command (SAC)—created in March 1946—would possess initial monopoly control over the primary deterrent to possible Soviet aggression. In May 1946, the entire atomic capability of SAC resided in the 509th Composite Group located at Roswell Field, New Mexico, and few adequate overseas bases existed from which to operate in an emergency. SAC's atomic-equipped B-29 units expanded substantially during 1947, but it was not until 1948 that the Command received its first improved postwar bombers, the B-50 and B-36, and obtained adequate bases in England and the Far East to which atomic-equipped units regularly rotated. Not until the end of 1948, therefore, was SAC able to pose a substantial strategic nuclear threat to the Soviet Union. Thus for two years, from 1946 through 1948, the deterrent capability of American atomic forces was extremely marginal. Yet contrary to widespread fears among Allied leaders of intended Soviet aggression in Western Europe, Soviet armies were not given orders to advance when their expected gains appeared to outweigh substantially their prospective losses. By the time of the Soviet-generated Berlin Airlift crisis in 1948, it appears that their perceptions of the risks of military adventure militated against a serious test of United States resolve to meet conventional force with atomic force.

The Berlin crisis had barely passed when the Truman administration decided on a far-reaching economy program in the military establishment designed to accommodate pressing domestic programs. The sudden revelation that the Soviet Union had exploded an atomic bomb years in advance of predictions by American scientists, and that China had fallen to the Communists, were decisive influences on the President in reaching his decision to build the hydrogen bomb—partly on the presumption that the Soviets would achieve one first if we did not, and partly because of the enhanced deterrent value it would represent. These two events inspired at the same time the first thorough reexamination of national security policy since the end of the war. The national security document which emerged from six weeks of deliberations by a joint State-Defense ad hoc study group—designated NSC-68—estimated that by 1954 the Soviet Union would have enough atomic bombs and adequate delivery systems to offset substantially the deterrent value of American nuclear weapons. Significantly, the study concluded that the United States could safely afford to devote as much as 20 percent of its GNP to national defense while maintaining economic growth and solvency. Some of the study group members urged that the existing defense spending ceiling be raised from the $13 billion level to a $35 billion to $50 billion level.

A spirited debate ensued within the government over whether one of the primary Soviet aims was world hegemony and the extent to which the United States ought to prepare for the contingency of total war. Key officials, such as Paul Nitze and General Truman H. Landon of the Air Force, argued for giving all-out war the highest priority and urged that greater reliance be put on strategic air power. On the other hand, Charles Bohlen and George Kennan of the State Department argued that the Soviet challenge was more likely to take the form of limited military challenges because of an approaching atomic stalemate and that the highest American military priority should be given to forces capable of fighting conventional limited wars.[9]

The Korean War overcame the reluctance of the Truman administration to embark on a rearmament program of proportions advocated by NSC-68. Without delay the President asked Congress for necessary funds to meet the aggression in Korea, but more importantly, he called for an orderly buildup of military capabilities to deter possible acts of aggression against Western Europe. America still enjoyed its nuclear weapons monopoly in 1950, and the only delivery capability able to strike targets at intercontinental distances resided in the eighteen wings of the Strategic Air Command. Intervention in Korea by the Chinese communist armies in November 1950, followed by the defeat of General MacArthur's American forces, prompted President Truman to announce during a press conference that the use of the atomic bomb was always under active consideration. The invocation of an atomic threat by the President was intended primarily as a deterrent to a possible attack by the Soviet Union on Western Europe. Although many military planners believed in 1950 that the relatively small size of atomic weapons could neither deter nor defeat the vastly superior Soviet land armies in the event of an assault on Western Europe, hindsight strongly suggests that the size and operational readiness status of American strategic forces easily deterred the Soviet Union from contemplating such a risk. Possessing neither operational atomic weapons nor long-range bombers, the Soviets lacked effective means of attacking the United States directly during the Korean War.

At the outset of the Korean War the strategic delivery forces of the Strategic Air Command consisted primarily of World War II B-29 and postwar B-50 medium bombers, although they were steadily augmented by B-36 heavy bombers as the war progressed. After the bars to rearmament were lowered, SAC was permitted to reequip with high performance B-47 jet aircraft, which phased into the first units late in 1951. In April 1952, the first all-jet heavy bomber, the B-52, was flown, and just three years later it began to replace the aging B-36 wings of the Strategic Air Command. The Korean War also provided the impetus to convert naval carrier aircraft and units of the Tactical Air Command into an atomic weapons delivery configuration, particularly as the United States nuclear weapons stockpile grew rapidly in size and versatility from 1951 on. Finally, American fears of a Soviet attack in Europe led to early negotiations for strategic air bases first in Morocco and then in Spain. The Moroccan bases, built on a crash basis, were able to receive SAC bombers by mid-July 1951, and the Spanish bases, built in the atmosphere of a diminished war scare, became operational in 1957. A number of key staging bases were constructed on the Atlantic routes to Europe to service limited-range fighter aircraft, air transports, and SAC air refueling units. By the end of the Korean War, the Strategic Air Command was operating from a global base complex with modern bombers capable of striking targets in the Soviet Union at a range of 3,000 miles, with a single air refueling, and returning to a friendly base.

One of the highest levels of American strategic superiority over the Soviet Union was reached during the years 1953 and 1954. The Soviet Union had acquired only a limited stockpile of atomic weapons and possessed only obsolete bombers of B-29 vintage that did not have adequate range to fly more than one-way missions to the United States.[10] Thus the strategic balance between the two major protagonists consisted of a match between superior land armies conventionally equipped and an increasingly formidable and diversified strategic and tactical atomic capability. The disparity of power between the two nations in the nuclear age was never so stark. Nonetheless, the "intelligence" or "secrecy" gap partially blinded American civilian and military officials, causing them to overestimate both the size and timing of the Soviet threat even during the early 1950s. For example, a meeting during the summer of 1952 of a Summer Study Group of scientists from the newly established Massachusetts Institute of Technology Lincoln Laboratory surveyed the growing Soviet threat and concluded that within two to three years the Soviets would have sufficient long-range strategic air power to enable them to cripple the United States in a surprise attack. This view was also widely shared within both the State and Defense departments.

The explosion by the Soviet Union of a thermonuclear device in August 1953, only a few months after a successful test by the United States, tended to confirm even more the pessimists' view of Soviet progress in overcoming this nation's lead in strategic capabilities. Oddly enough it was not an objective view of the Soviet strategic threat that most influenced the levels of strategic nuclear forces deployed by this nation during the Truman and Eisenhower administrations. Rather it was the fear of both Truman and Eisenhower that excess expenditure on military programs would lead to fiscal insolvency, which dictated restraints on service weapons programs to those that were deemed absolutely essential to meet the rapidly mounting Soviet threat. Granting fiscal restraint, the forces deployed by the United States during the 1950s bore little relationship to the actual Soviet threat, unless one incorrectly assumes that the nation purposely tried to achieve a credible first-strike capability.

One of the key decisions taken by the Eisenhower administration during its first year in office was a decisive shift of United States military strategy away from dependence on balanced conventional and nuclear weapons capabilities. In the name of economic prudence and a more realistic estimate of the Soviet threat, the administration decided in October 1953 that the Joint Chiefs of Staff and the military services could plan on using nuclear weapons, tactical as well as strategic, whenever their use would be desirable from a military standpoint. Henceforth, conventional wars would be limited to "brush fires" and "border skirmishes," and all wars on the scale of Korea or all-out war would be considered nuclear for planning purposes. This decision was clearly the forerunner of the massive retaliation strategy enunciated by Secretary of State John Foster Dulles early in 1954.[11] An inevitable consequence of the so-called New Look strategic appraisal was to accentuate even more the role of the Air Force as the principal arm of American defense.

Secretary Dulles confirmed the administration's decision to rely more heavily on America's rapidly expanding nuclear weapons capabilities during an address to the Council on Foreign Relations on January 12, 1954. He argued that the policy of massive retaliation would enable the President to take initiatives in foreign policy, whereas the Truman policy of containment had forced the United States to react constantly to enemy threats of aggression. Parts of the Secretary's speech were so ambiguous that the new policy was widely construed as meaning that the United States was prepared to use nuclear weapons not only to thwart communist aggression in Western Europe but in the Middle and Far East as well.

The public furor generated by Dulles's speech—which appears to have been written entirely by him with virtually no coordination within the government[12]—prompted an immediate presidential denial that any radically new policy was contemplated and inspired a series of clarifying statements designed to tone down the extremes of the original speech. Thus, the trial balloon named "nuclear panacea" collapsed soon after it was launched.

The Dulles massive retaliation doctrine applied to threats against the security of the United States or Western Europe was in complete harmony with the military strategy for all-out nuclear war embraced by the Truman administration. In this sense massive retaliation prevailed as this nation's primary deterrent strategy throughout the 1950s and the 1960s, even though more palatable terms, such as "unacceptable damage" and "assured destruction," replaced the odious Dulles phrase. Dulles's proposal that local defenses should be reinforced by the further deterrent of massive retaliatory power remained an empty phrase largely because the Soviet Union was already on the threshold of posing a nuclear threat to the United States—a credible threat to Europe already existed—and mutual nuclear deterrence seemed inescapable.

Under such circumstances it was difficult to imagine that future Korea-type conflicts would be declared in the vital national interest of the United States or a threat to use nuclear weapons locally or against a major offending power would be invoked. The dilemma facing the Eisenhower administration was that it was heavily committed to cutbacks in conventional ground and surface forces to allay the risk of economic bankruptcy, and yet such forces were precisely those which might be used in future Korea-type conflicts with acceptable risk. Obviously, America's overwhelming strategic nuclear superiority, retained throughout the 1950s and early 1960s, was extremely effective in preventing challenges to our global presence, which might otherwise have borne the risk of nuclear conflict. At the same time, it was clear that an attack by the Soviet Union on Western Europe would be met by a strategic nuclear response.

The Soviet Union first publicly displayed its long-range turboprop bomber, designated the "Bear," late in 1954. The Bear was the first in a series of strategic aircraft judged by American analysts to be capable of striking targets in the United States with atomic and hydrogen weapons and returning safely to a recovery base. The full impact of emerging Soviet intercontinental aircraft capabilities was not felt until May 1955, when, taken by surprise, American observers, attending the annual Soviet May Day celebration, were shown ten to twelve modern jet engine bombers, designated the "Bison," that appeared to be in a class with this nation's B-52. Administration officials had confidently predicted that American nuclear superiority would not be seriously threatened until 1960. Although the B-52 had been undergoing extensive testing for several years, units of the Strategic Air Command were not scheduled to receive operationally ready aircraft until June 1955.

The so-called bomber gap dispute was precipitated by Congressional critics of the administration who argued, as did most key Air Force leaders, that the Soviet Union was making such rapid strides in the development of new strategic weapon systems that it would likely overtake the United States in numbers of aircraft as well as quality by the late 1950s or early 1960s and proceed to gain a decisive strategic advantage. The picture was confused even more when in late 1955, Premier Bulganin informed the world that the Soviet Union was developing rocket missiles, and in February 1956, Marshal Zhukov spoke of mighty guided missiles.[13]

In retrospect, it seems perfectly clear that the Soviet Union by

1965 possessed only a relatively weak intercontinental nuclear capability and that the May Day fly-by probably displayed the entire inventory of Soviet modern, long-range bombers. This episode marked the beginning of a Soviet strategy of deception which was continued with greater success by Premier Khrushchev during the "missile gap" period. Soviet leaders appear to have been impressed by strong tendencies in the West to exaggerate the U.S.S.R.'s strategic capabilities and to take a pessimistic view of the existing strategic balance. Under Khrushchev's leadership the Soviets appear to have reduced drastically the estimate of the threat to Soviet security posed by superior United States strategic power. American behavior during the Geneva Summit Conference in July 1955 and its moderate reaction during the Hungarian and Suez crises appear to have persuaded Khrushchev to exploit Soviet strategic power to political advantage during the late 1950s. For a brief period the Soviet strategy of deception worked so successfully that America's free world allies generally believed that the balance of strategic nuclear power was inexorably shifting to the Soviet Union and that such a shift might prove decisive in the struggle against communism.[14]

The widely publicized Senate Air Power hearings which opened in April 1956, under the chairmanship of Senator Stuart Symington, provided a number of telling insights into the perceptions of American civilian and military officials of the existing Soviet strategic threat and that expected for the next five years. By and large, those who argued that a serious bomber gap faced the United States by the late 1950s were high-ranking Air Force officials called to testify along with the majority of the Symington committee, who were Democrats. Administration officials, such as Defense Secretary Charles E. Wilson and Deputy Secretary Donald Quarles, denied that a serious gap was likely to occur and strongly refuted the likelihood of an emerging deterrent gap. In support of this view civilian officials pointed out that the units of SAC were beginning to disperse to a large number of bases and that a ground alert program was planned for introduction during 1957, which would permit SAC bombers to react on minimum warning of attack. Secretary Wilson, for example, argued that all comparisons of United States and Soviet military strength tended to ignore our aircraft, carrier task forces, and tactical forces based overseas, all of which had atomic capabilities.

On the pessimistic side, such professional military spokesmen as Generals Nathan Twining, Curtis LeMay, and Thomas White were unanimous in their contention that the Soviets were producing two types of modern long-range bombers at a combined rate higher than the production rate of our B-52. Thus, according to the generals, the Soviet Union would, by 1960, be in position to carry out a surprise attack on the United States with considerable success.[15] Considering the fact that Air Force officers knew they were testifying before a friendly majority on the Symington committee and that appropriations for new weapons systems were at stake, it is difficult to determine whether the unduly pessimistic estimate of the Soviet bomber threat was completely candid, or whether the estimates were colored by other, more overriding considerations. In any event the estimates of the Soviet threat given in public by Air Force military officers during the 1950s were consistently high by wide margins—on both bombers and missiles—and those made by civilian defense officials were more nearly accurate. As is well known today, the mythical bomber gap soon became lost in the noise of the uproar in this nation over the shocking ballistic missile threat with which the Soviet Union seemingly confronted America and its allies after 1957.

The United States did concede several years to the Soviet Union in establishing a high national priority for the development of intermediate-range and intercontinental ballistic missiles. Prior to 1954 and the breakthroughs in missile propellants, survivable reentry vehicles, guidance, and deliverable thermonuclear warheads, this nation chose the air-breathing missile and the manned jet bomber, particularly the B-47, as the surest means of delivering a nuclear weapon to a long-range target. During 1955, there was growing evidence of a Soviet missile test program, soon followed by official Soviet pronouncements of success in solving all of the problems leading to a successful operational missile. Beginning late in 1955, therefore, the United States began intensive development of strategic missiles in an effort to match Soviet progress, or at least to achieve an operational missile in time to deny the Soviet Union any meaningful advantage, in political or military terms, from having succeeded first.

Once again opinion divided sharply among professional military and civilian leaders over this nation's ability to keep pace with the Soviets in advanced missile technology. Top military leaders, with few exceptions, predicted that Soviet technology and productive capacity assured them a substantial lead over the United States in intermediate-range and ICBM missiles by the early 1960s, possibly conveying to the Soviet Union a first-strike capability against soft and warningless SAC air bases. Civilian officials, such as Deputy Secretary Quarles, argued against the probability that the Soviets could solve all of the complicated problems associated with deploying an operational missile and contended that the manned bomber would remain the principal deterrent force for at least another decade. In any event, Quarles argued, it would be a long time before the Soviets were able to deploy sufficient numbers of highly reliable missiles to offset this nation's large bomber force capabilities.[16]

By the end of 1956, the Soviets appeared to have acquired a very modest intercontinental bomber capability, disadvantaged by the lack of good staging bases or any observable in-flight refueling capability. The Soviet air power threat against Western Europe was fairly substantial, and to a degree it complicated American strategic planning. Evidence is lacking, however, that the Soviets had an operational intermediate-range missile capability with which to hold Western Europe hostage. The United States, on the other hand, had virtually completed its B-47 medium bomber program, which at its peak numbered some 1,700-plus aircraft and was fully capable of multiple refuelings en route to and from target areas. The mammoth B-36 had not yet been retired, although the rapid buildup phase of the B-52 program was underway and would be completed during the next several years.

During 1956, as well, the revolutionary Polaris submarine program received its first funds, and, according to Navy spokesmen, early progress on the missile and the submarine indicated that both would be available in time to meet a deployment date in 1960. Projecting to early 1960 from the strategic balance of late 1956, it appeared that the worst situation that might befall the United States could be a temporary missile gap in favor of the Soviet Union, and this only in the event that Soviet missile achievements met the most optimistic forecast given it by American military leaders. Any serious deterrent gap seemed highly unlikely.

The so-called bomber gap interlude failed to shake American confidence in the basic stability of a strategy of deterrence. From time to time, until Sputnik, the American people were given assurances by the administration that the United States held a decisive edge in military technology over the Soviet Union. In the spring of 1957, a study was made of the published or stated views of some 130 international officials, commentators, military scholars, and strategists on the danger of the Soviet threat. The study concluded that the danger of a communist surprise attack with mass destruction weapons appeared to be slight.[17] Secretary of Defense Wilson, apparently in a state of mild euphoria, told Congress in late January 1957 that the smaller atomic weapons, the tactical weapons, had in a real sense become conventional weapons.[18] As the summer of 1957 approached, administration officials appeared uncertain about estimates of Soviet missile strength, although there was clear evidence that the Soviets had developed and deployed ballistic missiles having ranges of several hundreds of miles.

Abruptly, on August 26, 1957, Moscow radio broadcast news of a "super-long-distance intercontinental multistage ballistic missile . . . [which] flew at a very high, unprecedented altitude . . . [and] landed in the target area."[19] Six weeks later, on October 4, the Soviets launched their first satellite, which heralded the dawning of the ballistic missile age and appeared to shift dramatically the technological and possibly the military balance toward the Soviet Union. Pessimists among informed American observers tended to link Soviet space achievements with a simultaneous attainment of an ICBM capability and concluded that the United States was faced with an ominous "missile gap" during the early 1960s which could not be closed until after 1964 when large numbers of Polaris and Minuteman second-generation missiles would enter the United States force. Administration officials, including the President, publicly rejected the notion that Soviet space feats were a convincing indication that they also had solved the rocket engine, guidance, reentry, ground facilities, and training problems prerequisite to the successful deployment of an ICBM.

After recovering from the initial shock of Sputnik, high Defense Department officials explained that a successful Soviet ICBM test was not an adequate basis for predicting when they would have operational units, and Deputy Secretary Quarles, testifying before Congress, argued that overall the United States' long-range missile program appeared to be progressing faster than the Soviets'.[20] While conceding that a small and temporary "missile gap" might occur early in the 1960s, the Eisenhower administration firmly denied that any deterrent gap would result and argued that overall American strategic superiority could deter a rational attack by any aggressor. Key military officials, on the other hand, sided generally with the pessimists who believed that Soviet scientific and technological feats would place United States national security in serious jeopardy during the 1960s.

In retrospect it is quite clear that the Soviet Union procured only a token force of its first-generation ICBMs and that Premier Khrushchev, sometime before Sputnik, decided upon a strategy of deception in order to exploit Soviet strategic power politically.[21] Soviet leaders by the early 1950s appear to have gained confidence that the United States would not initiate nuclear war unless gravely provoked. Also, the "bomber gap" episode of 1955 seemed to have impressed Soviet leaders that the United States was prone to exaggerate the U.S.S.R.'s strategic capabilities and to incline toward pessimism in estimating the strategic balance. During the years 1957 to 1962, therefore, even in the face of growing United States strategic superiority, Khrushchev proceeded to exploit the advantage of Soviet secrecy in an effort to convince the United States, its principal European allies, and the world that the strategic balance which had so heavily favored the United States since the end of the war had now swung dramatically in favor of the Soviet Union. For a brief time the Soviet method of deception did succeed in convincing world public opinion that the strategic nuclear balance had shifted from the free to the communist world. In fact, however, Soviet successes were limited. United States resolve in dealing with successive Berlin crises, penetration of Soviet secrecy by the U-2, and major improvements in the United States strategic force posture—abetted by blatant Soviet military claims—quickly nullified the Soviet political and psychological advantage and spurred the United States and its allies to add new increments to their strategic forces, soon placing the Soviet Union in a position of strategic nuclear inferiority equal to or worse than it had suffered during the years immediately following the Korean War.

Goaded by Khrushchev's calculated campaign to convince the world that the Soviet Union had achieved an exponential breakthrough in the ICBM field, the United States responded by placing one-third of its strategic bomber forces on constant twenty-four-hour alert, by dispersing B-52 and B-47 bombers to additional United States bases, by empowering the President to place a percentage of SAC B-52's on airborne alert during a crisis, and by intensifying efforts to achieve a better warning system against a possible missile attack. More push was put behind the nation's effort to achieve an operational ICBM as early as possible. In mid-December 1957, the first Atlas A ICBM was successfully flight-tested and looking toward a possible operational date of late 1959. The first successful flight of the Titan I took place on February 6, 1959, virtually on schedule. By a supplemental appropriation, three Polaris submarines were authorized in early 1958, and an operational date was set for 1960. Shortly thereafter the Air Force was directed to begin research and development of a second-generation ICBM, the Minuteman, which would use a solid rather than liquid propellant. The first successful firing of a full-scale solid-propellant missile having intercontinental range took place at Cape Canaveral on September 15, 1959, and three years later the first Minuteman missiles were declared operational. Obviously, if the Soviet Union was to attain a significant strategic superiority over this nation during the early 1960s, it would have to exceed even the most optimistic estimates of its capabilities to produce ICBMs, manned bombers, and sea-based missiles. Thus, given the size and variety of nuclear capable forces available to the United States and its allies, it did not seem probable that any reason would induce the Soviet Union to attempt a surprise nuclear attack on this nation.

A new episode in the "missile gap" controversy flared in 1960. Critics contended that if reports of high Soviet ICBM deployment rates were correct and United States warning capabilities remained weak, the Soviet Union might be willing to risk an all-out attack before our superior production capacity closed the gap. The administration response to such renewed attacks was made by Secretary of Defense Thomas S. Gates, Jr., who only recently had succeeded Neil McElroy. During his testimony before the House Appropriations Committee, he revealed for the first time the shift by the administration from basing its estimates of likely Soviet ICBM buildup on theoretical *capabilities* to what was believed the U.S.S.R. *intended* to do. As a consequence of this change, Gates affirmed that the hitherto assumed Soviet superiority in ICBMs on the order of three to one by 1963 had been substantially scaled down.[22] Pressed by congressmen to explain the basis for the new method of estimating Soviet missile buildup, Joint Chiefs of Staff Chairman Nathan Twining was the most forthright: "The basic intelligence principles," he said, "have not been changed at all. This year we had more specific evidence on which we were able to refine our judgment on what the Russians probably have."[23] There seems little doubt that information provided by the U-2 missions over the Soviet Union was beginning to pay off, stripping away (partly at least) the long-persisting veil of secrecy which had provided Khrushchev so much political leverage. It was during this same period also that the United States launched its first surveillance satellites, which within a two-year period permitted the Kennedy administration to label the missile gap as pure myth. As might be expected, the strategic balance between the Soviet Union and the United States became a major issue during the 1960 presidential campaign, and particularly the administration's apparent shift from capabilities to intentions as the basis for estimating the nature of the Soviet strategic threat.

The Eisenhower administration entered the election of 1960 on a platform that ostensibly rejected the estimate by high military officials and many civilian analysts that the Soviet Union had solved the many technical problems of the ICBM and thus could produce sufficient numbers of highly accurate missiles during the 1961 to 1963 period to place the nation's national security in serious jeopardy. While rejecting publicly the thesis that the Soviets were likely to deploy significantly more (if indeed as many) operational ICBMs than this nation during the early 1960s, the administration nevertheless was strongly influenced by the cleverness of Khrushchev's policy of strategic deception and felt compelled to hedge against a "worst case" Soviet threat by substantially accelerating the pace and size of strategic force deployments during 1960. Important new intelligence information gained from the U-2 flights apparently was not yet adequate to give the administration high confidence in its low estimate of Soviet strategic weapons achievement. Faced with a tough political campaign the Republican leadership supported major increases in military programs, especially in the strategic weapons area, in order to remove the preparedness issue from the campaign as far as possible. The very ambivalence of the Republican position on the size and nature of the Soviet threat, however, gave the Democrats a prime issue, which was ably exploited by candidate John F. Kennedy during the campaign.

Strategic Doctrine for the Nuclear Age

Following World War II, Americans were intuitively aware that the United States could not return to a peacetime foreign policy based on isolation and sporadic involvement in world affairs. During two world wars the American tendency to depreciate power and embrace a moralistic approach to foreign policy had made it difficult for the United States to relate the use of power to political aims. With the collapse of the Allied wartime collaboration after 1945 and the coming of the cold war, it soon became clear to American leaders that the threat presented by the Soviet Union required a coherent long-range policy effectively combining the political, military, and economic factors of national power. The advent of the nuclear age reinforced feelings that only a sustained commitment by this nation could succeed in protecting its vital interests against hostile encroachment. Such factors as the precipitous demobilization of American ground forces in Europe, the subsequent collapse of the European balance of power, apparent Soviet intentions to possess all of Europe, and excessive optimism over the likely duration of the American atomic monopoly soon forced the United States to undertake a complete reappraisal of its overall national security position.

American scholars' serious interest in examining the relationship of force to national security did not develop until after World War II. Traditionally, Americans have drawn a sharp distinction between war and peace; peace was regarded as a state of harmony among nations, while power politics and war were considered abnormal. Anti-militarism has long been a hallmark of American liberalism, and the military arm of government has been looked upon as a potential threat to democratic institutions. In the words of one student: "The United States . . . has traditionally rejected the concept of war as a political instrument and the Clausewitzian definition of war as the continuation of politics by other means."[24] Thus, not until American scholars began to comprehend the implications of the nuclear revolution did they begin to explore the close relationship between military policy, foreign policy, fiscal policy, and domestic policy.

The cold war, the end of the American nuclear monopoly, the fall of China to the Communists, the American decision to develop a hydrogen bomb, and the Korean War had profound effects on stimulating scholarly interest in the study of the national security policy process as a separate branch of international relations.

During World War II, thousands of talented scientists and technicians had been enlisted by government and industry to create the weapons necessary to win the war. Although their contributions proved to be decisive, it was only on rare occasions that the scientist or scholar had any impact on either military or political policy and strategy. The acceleration of military technology after the war and the growing complexity of new weapons systems tailored to atomic weapons compelled the government to seek technical assistance from both industry and academic institutions. The result was the emergence of a vast new industry organized and staffed for the express purpose of augmenting the Department of Defense in carrying out its responsibilities for protecting the national security.

Such nonprofit defense research organizations as the RAND Corporation, the Stanford Research Institute, the Research Analysis Corporation, and the Institute for Defense Analyses, staffed by scientists, technologists, and scholars from a wide variety of disciplines, began focusing on the interrelated diplomatic and military-strategic problems stimulated by the cold war.[25] As the defense establishment's dependence on the nongovernmental defense analyst, scientist, and scholar grew during the late 1940s and early 1950s, there slowly developed a highly skilled pool of talent trained in the intricacies of modern weapons systems, nuclear weapons, strategic theory and planning processes, and foreign policy analysis. Concomitantly, proliferation took place within the government, principally in defense-oriented agencies, of highly trained and competent professional military and civilian defense analysts who were fully conversant with the interdependence of military power and political objectives in the national security planning process.

As early as 1946, academicians Bernard Brodie and Arnold Wolfers collaborated on *The Absolute Weapon: Atomic Power and World Order,* a pioneering and unusually perceptive study of the requirements for a strategy of all-out war in the nuclear age. The atomic bomb, the authors argued, represented a true "quantum jump" in the annals of offensive weapons and had removed any remaining doubt about the decisiveness of strategic bombing in future wars. Both Wolfers and Brodie agreed that, whereas in the past the purpose of our military system had been to win wars, in the future, the primary purpose must be to avert them. Thus a strategy based on the threat of retaliation, or a strategy of deterrence, appeared to the authors as offering the greatest promise of avoiding an atomic war as long as the losses each side expected to suffer appeared incommensurate to any prospective gains. In Wolfers' judgment "it would not be surprising . . . if a high degree of Soviet-American 'equality of deterring power' would prove the best guarantee of peace and tend more than anything else to approximate the views and interests of the two countries."[26]

In November 1953, Arnold Wolfers, writing in *The Annals,* expanded his earlier thoughts about the components of a strategy of deterrence and presented the case for a no cities targeting doctrine which was to become an important, although brief, option of the McNamara strategic doctrine of the 1960s.[27] Wolfers exposed the futility of an inferior power's waging nuclear attacks on the cities of a superior power, since it would mean suicide for the inferior power. If it was the intention of the United States to dissuade an enemy from attacking our cities, Wolfers urged that full publicity be given to our willingness to avoid attacking enemy cities, if the enemy refrained from attacks on American cities. He argued, as well, that the optimum targets for either side—regardless of their respective positions of nuclear superiority or inferiority—would be an adversary's nuclear threat targets, i.e., air bases, control networks, defenses. Finally, Wolfers stressed that even though a strategy of deterrence might fail, a superior nuclear power might well destroy a large part of an adversary's strategic nuclear capability, hold his cities hostage, and seek to bargain for a favorable conclusion to hostilities. There is no public evidence that the Eisenhower administration gave serious consideration to a counterforce strategy or a no cities doctrine during the 1950s.

It is not surprising that the decision by the Eisenhower administration in early 1954 to place greater dependence on the threat to use nuclear force evoked a wide ranging, spirited, and scholarly debate over the postulates on which American security policy for all-out war rested. The Soviet Union had successfully tested both an atomic and hydrogen bomb, thus signalling the end of America's nuclear monopoly. At the same time, the increased number of skilled civilian defense analysts and scholars fully conversant with strategic theory, weapons systems, and the war-planning process virtually insured that a debate would be generated by a strategic doctrine as controversial as "massive retaliation." Finally, a growing segment of the American public had become more conversant with the concept of deterrence, nuclear weapons effects, and the consequences of nuclear war for civilized mankind.

The most articulate critique of the Dulles massive retaliation doctrine was made during the summer of 1954 by political scientist William W. Kaufmann, who was then an associate of the Center of International Studies at Princeton University. Kaufmann pointed out that the administration's decision to declare certain areas outside of Western Europe to be vital to United States security interests meant that the main objective of the new policy was clearly "to prevent any further expansion of the Communist empire by giving the Russians and Chinese notice of the losses they may expect to suffer should they attempt to increase their holdings by military means in the Middle East, Southeast Asia and the Far East."[28] The administration did not reveal its intended means of retaliation, but Kaufmann surmised that chief reliance would be placed on the Strategic Air Command and certain naval air forces. Such a policy would presumably reduce the burden of defense expenditures and release energies and resources for other and more congenial tasks of foreign and domestic policy.

In order for a strategy of massive retaliation to appear credible to potential enemies and allies alike, it was essential, wrote Kaufmann, that our expected gains exceed probable losses and that an adversary believe that we would act as we indicated. Although he conceded that the Soviet Union in 1954 could not seriously threaten the United States directly, the time was fast approaching, said Kaufmann, when the Soviet Union would be able to retaliate successfully against the United States no matter how it was attacked. Observable patterns of American crisis behavior during World War II coupled with the inevitable growth of Soviet and Chinese power convinced Kaufmann that the minimum requirements for a credible nuclear defense strategy were not fulfilled in the case of massive retaliation. Therefore, in order to overcome existing deficiencies Kaufmann urged that priority be given to reducing the vulnerability of the nation to atomic attack.

One of the issues exposed by the critics of the Dulles doctrine was the implied need to provide larger and more modern conventional fighting forces which could be deployed rapidly to world trouble spots deemed of significant interest to the United States—in anticipation that conventional limited wars were most likely to be fought in the future under the twin nuclear umbrellas of the United States and the Soviet Union. Missing from the early analysis, however, was the discussion of how a nation prevents a limited war involving two superpowers from escalating up the tactical nuclear ladder to all-out nuclear war and mutual suicide.

Beginning in 1955, defense analysts, both civilian and military, published articles that sought to formulate systematically the elements of an all-out nuclear war strategy preferable to the doctrine of massive retaliation. One commentator, Richard Leghorn, a retired Air Force officer, indicted massive retaliation as primarily a counter-city strategy and argued for a counterforce strategy aimed primarily at an enemy's nuclear weapons systems at H-hour. He argued that the United States could use its advantage in numbers of deliverable nuclear weapons to target them against Soviet military forces. As a corollary, Leghorn supported the no cities doctrine proposed earlier by Arnold Wolfers. A strategy of controlled counterforce for all-out war would in fact be a renunciation of unconditional surrender which the United States mistakenly had insisted upon during two world wars. Such a strategy could offer an important alternative to massive retaliation if, as Leghorn pointed out, sufficient efforts were made to increase the invulnerability of American military forces, to achieve a highly reliable warning system against enemy attack, and to improve the nation's pre- and post-attack intelligence capabilities. Since a counterforce strategy required that the United States maintain a substantial superiority over Soviet strategic forces, it was imperative, if this nation chose to underwrite such a strategy, that intensive research and development efforts be maintained across a broad spectrum of weapons possibilities. Advocates of a counterforce all-out war strategy assumed simplistically that regardless of probable Soviet responses to our bid for significant military superiority, the costs would be economically tolerable and politically acceptable to the American people. No realistic cost estimates of implementing such a strategy were attempted by defense analysts writing in the mid-1950s.

The prime mover in the developing field of military strategy during the period from 1955 to 1960 was the RAND Corporation, located in Santa Monica, California. Organized as a quasi-academic organization able to reconcile the problem of military security, RAND was initially staffed largely by scientists and engineers having broad industrial experience. From the outset RAND devoted high priority to research on a variety of national security problems for the Air Force. After becoming a private, nonprofit organization in 1948, the RAND staff was progressively augmented to include systems analysts, computer experts, mathematicians, economists, and social scientists. With its combination of high salaries, commodious facilities, freedom to publish, and liberal leave and travel privileges, RAND was able to attract a professional staff of exceptional quality. Although RAND received funds under contract to such agencies as the AEC, NASA, and the Office of the Secretary of Defense, the bulk of its work was performed for the Air Force, and that primarily on strategic studies.[29]

During the 1950s the RAND Corporation was able to attract such able military systems analysts and strategists as William W.

Kaufmann, Bernard Brodie, Herman Kahn, Albert Wohlstetter, Daniel Ellsberg, Andrew Marshall, Henry Rowen, Charles Hitch, and Alain Enthoven—all of whom made important contributions in such areas as weapons systems selection, force posturing and techniques of invulnerability, command and control, requirements for future deterrent strategies, politico-military gaming, and enemy capabilities analysis. While adopting such innovations as increased ground alert procedures for SAC bombers, base dispersal concepts, airborne alert, improved warning systems, and tighter command and control procedures, the Eisenhower administration rejected RAND's recommendations for a shift away from a deterrence concept of massive retaliation to one of controlled counterforce. Fundamental change in the nation's all-out nuclear war was destined to await the Kennedy electoral victory of 1960.

Among the more perceptive students of nuclear strategy, such as Paul Nitze, Bernard Brodie, Arnold Wolfers, William Kaufmann, and Henry Rowen (all of whom were writing in public during the 1950s), there was substantial agreement on the essentials of a rational American strategy for deterring all-out nuclear war. All of them attacked the credibility of the strategy of massive retaliation on the grounds that such a threat would probably be interpreted by an enemy as pure bluff. Paul Nitze, a strong advocate of a counterforce strategy, argued that "no rational body of men would initiate a general atomic war unless they believed that the power of their initial atomic attack and its immediate effects on the enemy would be so great as to assure that the subsequent phases of the war would be substantially one-sided."[30] In varying degrees most strategic analysts contended that the United States could and should strive for a meaningful counterforce capability vis-à-vis the Soviet Union, that future wars should be waged for limited political objectives—a rejection of unconditional surrender—and, to the extent that an enemy exercised restraint, all attacks during nuclear war should be directed at purely military targets and away from population centers. Most analysts conceded that the possibility of nuclear war must be entertained, and that the United States should be interested in possible outcomes. As stated by Brodie, almost all outcomes of nuclear war would be bad, but some would be worse than others. Finally, there was an awareness among strategic analysts that as mutual deterrence became a fact of life between the Soviet Union and the United States, the threat of conflict would shift more toward the conventional weapons arena, and it was important that modernization of conventional forces be given higher priority.

Late in 1959, two major congressional committees commissioned extensive studies of the requirements for American security in the 1960s; one was designed to examine national security policy as an element of the budgetary process; the other was an evaluation of anticipated developments in military technology and their impact on American military strategy. Under the direction of such experts as Arnold Wolfers, Paul Nitze, and Henry Rowen, the parallel studies examined the strengths and weaknesses of American all-out nuclear war strategy since World War II and concluded in favor of the adoption by the United States of a nuclear strategy of controlled counterforce based on a secure second-strike posture. Both studies were widely publicized. Each analyzed the latest changes in military technology and their likely implications for the next decade.

The Rowen study, for example, argued that the possibility of nuclear war had to be admitted but questioned whether anyone could "win" such a war in a meaningful sense. It supported a program which would have provided a panoply of American offensive and defensive forces capable of limiting damage to the United States and attaining the best possible outcome. Both studies urged the nation to support early attainment of strategic nuclear forces of sufficient size both to withstand a surprise attack and to destroy an enemy in retaliation, if necessary. Rowen argued for a national program of active and passive civil defense, urging that from such a posture the United States would be able to limit attacks to enemy military targets and permit controlled attacks on enemy civilian targets without abandoning our own cities to unlimited destruction. Finally, both studies recommended a sustained high level of expenditures on military research and development, greater protection of the nation's command and control centers from enemy attack, and improved warning and communications systems to insure that decision-makers would have the right kind of information at critical times.[31] In retrospect it is obvious that all the basic elements of what later became the "McNamara Strategy" were present in the public literature of the mid- and late 1950s. The intellectuals who invented or articulated the new strategic ideas were accessible to an administration which was prepared to liquidate the remaining remnants of massive retaliation in favor of a strategy which balanced conventional and strategic power.

One of the most influential and certainly one of the most prolific analysts of American foreign policy and military strategy during the 1950s was Henry Kissinger, then Associate Director of the Center for International Affairs at Harvard University. Kissinger's books and articles reflect an unusual sensitivity to the inextricable relationship between military and political objectives in a nuclear age. Combining a talent for logical analysis with a provocative writing style, Kissinger rose rapidly to prominence following the publication in 1957 of his book *Nuclear Weapons and Foreign Policy*. His arguments appear to have influenced the Eisenhower administration during 1957 to consider placing greater reliance on tactical nuclear weapons in situations short of all-out nuclear war. The administration rejected a tactical nuclear weapons doctrine on both political and military grounds, and Kissinger recanted his earlier advocacy of tactical nuclear weapons in a subsequent book.[32]

Any future war, said Kissinger, would be in all likelihood a nuclear war. Above all, he stressed, thermonuclear war ought to be avoided except as a last resort. If nuclear war did occur, efforts should be made to avoid all-out nuclear war. What was needed, Kissinger felt, was a doctrine for the graduated employment of force and realistic military capabilities which made limited war possible: "If we build our whole strategy around 'absolute' weapons of megaton size, professions of limited objectives will be meaningless, and any use of nuclear weapons is likely to touch off an all-out war."[33] One of the tasks for American diplomacy, Kissinger declared, was to make clear to an adversary that we do not aim for unconditional surrender and to create a framework in which the question of national survival is not involved in every issue.

The most thorough and systematic presentation of Kissinger's views on the nature of the military threat to the United States and the optimum nuclear war strategy to meet the expected threat were contained in the book *The Necessity for Choice*, published in 1960. Kissinger's assessment of the Soviet threat in the 1960s led him to conclude: "There is no dispute that the 'missile gap' will materialize in the period 1960–1964." He believed that the choices open to the United States lay between a strategy of finite deterrence—a low order of offensive and defensive weapons designed primarily to deter an enemy from attacking—and some degree of counterforce capability. Kissinger rejected a strategy of finite deterrence, because it was based on a requirement for only a small retaliatory force capable primarily of destroying cities or other area targets, which in his judgment would amount to a deliberate United States effort to guarantee the invulnerability of the Soviet retaliatory force. The crucial fallacy of such a strategy, Kissinger pointed out, was that if our deterrent force is designed primarily for a mission of punishment, an aggressor will know that short of the most overriding threat to our existence, and perhaps not even then, the threat of massive retaliation must be bluff.

As to the feasibility of a counterforce strategy, Kissinger argued that it would not solve our basic dilemma either. The dilemma, he said, was how to *win* an all-out war whether the United States struck first or second. He readily conceded that the most desirable strategy for this nation clearly would be based on a capability to win even after suffering a surprise attack. Kissinger argued that the necessary degree of superiority in offensive and defensive forces was almost certainly unattainable under foreseeable conditions. His judgment was that even the effort to achieve such a counterforce—or damage-limiting—capability would involve the nation in a tour de force, and, he said, "It would impose staggering force requirements on us, draining off all other military capabilities." Viewed realistically, Kissinger said, a counterforce strategy designed to win a victory *after* we concede the first blow is an illusion.[34]

Kissinger warned that Americans should have no illusions about what was ahead of them. He predicted that a condition of mutual invulnerability confronted the nation regardless of its preferences. Once this condition was reached by the United States and the Soviet Union, the threat of all-out war would lose its credibility and its strategic meaning. Thus, Kissinger concluded: "The only safe basis for planning strategy is on the assumption of the mutual invulnerability of the retaliatory forces." He supported a requirement for the

United States to maintain a degree of counterforce capability, sufficient, at least, to deter an enemy campaign of attrition against our retaliatory forces, i.e., an assured destruction capability. But, warned Kissinger, even if a high degree of mutual nuclear deterrence is reached, the nation should recognize that the perils of limited aggression must multiply.[35] Viewed in retrospect, it is clear that many of Kissinger's predictions of the late 1950s became the realities of the 1960s.

Election of 1960: Strategic Debate

With the emergence of the cold war almost immediately following World War II, there began a long period during which congressional committees, i.e., Appropriations, Armed Services, Foreign Relations, Joint Atomic Energy, and Congress itself rarely kept an administration from going ahead with a strategic program it deemed essential.[36] In part, congressional abstention from serious opposition to strategies and strategic programs sponsored by the executive branch can be explained on grounds that congressmen were not privy to adequate information and lacked requisite technical competence upon which to make realistic judgments. Traditionally, Congress has shown a strong reluctance to assert its leadership in the determination of the requirements for military security of the nation and has generally recognized and accepted the decisive role of the executive in formulating strategic programs. As Samuel Huntington observed, however, the major reason Congress is unable to play a key role in the strategic planning process is more political than technical. He reasoned:

> The military programs have to be weighed against each other, against conflicting interpretations of the security threats and military requirements, against the needs of domestic and non-military foreign policy programs, and against tax revenues and the requirements of fiscal policy. No congressional committee is competent to do this, not because it lacks the technical knowledge, but because it lacks the legal authority and political capability to bring together all these conflicting interests, balance one off against the other and arrive at a compromise or decision.[37]

Thus, the principal responsibility of Congress tends to be limited to such areas as money, men, materiel, and management.

During the late 1950s, however, there did emerge in the Senate a vocal and perceptive critic of the Eisenhower defense strategy for all-out nuclear war. The critic was the junior Senator from Massachusetts, John F. Kennedy, who, during the years 1958 to 1960, attacked frequently and forcefully what he believed was the dangerous overdependence by the administration on a nuclear strategy for the deterrence and fighting of both limited and all-out wars. In his various speeches on national security policy, one can clearly discern the outlines of the policies for the nation's security he would espouse following his triumphant election in 1960.

As early as 1954, when the Eisenhower administration first publicly announced the "New Look" military strategy, Senator Kennedy firmly opposed cuts in conventional war forces and dependence primarily on a strategy of "massive retaliation." As an alternative, he called for a strengthening of both the nation's nuclear and conventional forces. It was not, however, until the Soviets scored significant missile successes in the fall of 1957 and there was growing awareness that the United States was likely entering a period of national peril that Senator Kennedy decided on the urgent need to assess the full impact of the nation's changed military situation and think through the implications for American policy.[38]

In mid-August of 1958, Kennedy dismayed a Senate audience when he announced: "We are rapidly approaching that dangerous period which General Gavin and others have called the 'gap' or the 'missile-lag period'—a period, in the words of General Gavin, in which our own offensive and defensive missile capabilities will lag so far behind those of the Soviets as to place us in a position of great peril."[39] The Senator stressed that the most critical years appeared to be from 1960 to 1964.

Senator Kennedy's position differed sharply with the Eisenhower strategy which had, Kennedy said, as recently as the 1958 State of the Union message, proclaimed "Our retaliatory power is 'the most powerful deterrent to war in the world today', offering any potential aggressor 'the prospect of virtual annihilation of his own country.' " Such reliance upon massive retaliation not only stultified the development of new policy but encouraged a Maginot Line mentality—"dependence upon a strategy which may collapse or never be used, but which meanwhile prevents the consideration of any alternative." Our missile lag, continued the Senator, is not the cause of the gap—"it is but another symptom of our national complacency, our willingness to confuse the facts as they were with what we hoped they would be, to appeal at the same time to those who wanted a quick solution and those who wanted a less burdensome one." Kennedy was particularly critical of the Eisenhower insistence on placing fiscal security ahead of national security. Reminiscing about post-1960 election statements, Kennedy stressed: "We tailored our strategy and military requirements to fit our budget—instead of fitting our budget to our military requirements strategy."[40]

Moreover, he said:

> The fact of the matter is that during that period when emphasis was laid upon our economic strength instead of our military strength, we were losing the decisive years where we could have maintained a lead against the Soviet Union in our missile capacity. These were the vital years we lost, the years the locusts have eaten, and it is quite obvious we obtained economic security at the expense of military security, and that this policy will bring us into great danger within the next few years.[41]

Thus, said Kennedy, the United States was faced beginning around 1960 with the extremely complex task of maintaining a "deterrent ratio" against the possibility of a Soviet surprise attack which, because of the extreme vulnerability of American worldwide strategic forces, might be so successful that retaliation by our strategic forces against the Soviet Union would be held to very low levels of destruction. "In short," the Senator continued, "the deterrent ratio might well shift to the Soviets so heavily, during the years of the gap, as to open to them a new shortcut to world domination."[42] Senator Kennedy conceded to the Soviets in coming years a substantial edge in missile power—intermediate-range missiles to destroy our European missile and SAC bases and intercontinental missiles to devastate our nation. Thus, the United States would have to rely heavily on manned bombers and face such problems as constant alert, dispersal, and aerial refueling difficulties.

Even on the unlikely assumption that the United States proved able to stalemate Soviet long-range nuclear superiority, Kennedy foresaw that nuclear destruction was not the only way in which the Soviets would be able to use their advantages in striking power. In his view, during the years of the gap "the Soviets may be expected to use their superior striking ability to achieve their objectives . . . through Sputnik diplomacy, limited brush-fire wars, indirect non-overt aggression, intimidation, and subversion, internal revolution, increased prestige or influence, and the vicious blackmail of our allies." In all probability Soviet moves would weaken the West; "but none will seem sufficiently significant by itself to justify our initiating a nuclear war which might destroy us."[43]

In his concluding remarks Kennedy cautioned that to sound the alarm was not to panic. Time may be running out, he said, but complacency or hysteria will not help. Nor would he advocate, as the Romans were said to have done, that if a nation wants to maintain peace it must constantly prepare for war. But, said Kennedy, "We should certainly use all elements of national policy—economic, diplomatic, and military—in order to prepare us for the most serious test in our nation's history, which will be impending in the next five years."[44]

Despite Kennedy's pessimistic predictions about the likely plight of the United States in the early 1960s because of growing Soviet long-range nuclear power and a manifestly belligerent foreign policy, he nevertheless prescribed positive steps aimed at strengthening the national security. In public speeches and interviews during late 1959 and early 1960 Kennedy argued:

> We must make invulnerable a nuclear retaliatory power second to none—by making possible now a stop-gap air alert and base dispersal program—and by stepping up developments and production of the ultimate missiles that can close the gap and will not be wiped out in a surprise attack—Polaris, Minuteman and long-range air-to-ground missiles—meanwhile increasing our production of Atlas missiles, hardening our bases, and improving our continental defense and warning systems. As a power which will never strike first, we require a retaliatory capacity based on hidden, moving, or invulnerable weapons in such force as to deter any aggressor from threatening an attack he knows could not destroy enough of our force to prevent his own destruction.[45]

Senator Kennedy did not concede to the Soviets overall military superiority, but acknowledged that in late 1959 the United States had fallen behind the Soviet Union in the production of ballistic missiles (both intercontinental and intermediate range), modernized submarines, and air defenses. He admitted, as well, that the nation may be falling behind in the numbers of long-range jet bombers having a nuclear bomb capacity. In the opinion of the Senator, "We [the United States] won't have security until we have either Polaris submarines widely dispersed and constantly at sea, or fully protected intercontinental ballistic missiles in hardened bases here in the United States which can be defended. Until we have these, we're not really going to have security against the ultimate weapon."[46] Kennedy also strongly favored accelerating production of the Atlas missile on a high priority basis. Along with such substantial increases in nuclear deterrent capabilities, Kennedy urged that parallel efforts be made to provide the nation's armed forces with modern conventional weapons and effective and versatile firepower in order to avoid being put in a position of being prepared to fight a war we least want to fight and are least likely to fight. In Senator Kennedy's remarks are the clear outlines of a strategy of flexible response which was quickly embraced by the Kennedy defense team following the presidential victory of 1960.

While Senator Kennedy in his writings and speeches of the late 1950s did not spell out in detail a new strategy for all-out nuclear war, he did nevertheless stake out a position on national defense clearly opposed to that of the Eisenhower administration. Thus, the stage for the 1960 campaign was set.

The status of United States defense preparedness inevitably became a major issue during the 1960 presidential campaign. During the late 1950s, prominent Democratic congressmen, including Senators John F. Kennedy and Lyndon Johnson, led attacks on the Eisenhower administration's alleged inadequate preparations for the contingency of either all-out or limited war. The Democrats attacked what they believed to be the Republicans' extremely heavy emphasis on economic solvency, which they felt necessarily led to the perpetuation of a strategy of massive retaliation long after the growth of Soviet power indicated a situation of mutual nuclear deterrence. Democrats, like John F. Kennedy and others within the Democratic Advisory Council, called for a shift to a strategy based on a controlled and flexible response, graduated to meet a variety of levels and forms of aggression. Democratic alarms about the seriousness of an approaching missile gap were sounded frequently during the campaign and promises were made by Senator Kennedy to bolster America's strategic nuclear defenses.[47]

The move by the Republican administration during 1960 to downgrade the missile gap issue by shifting to a new but not clearly defined method of estimating Soviet capabilities tended to sow more suspicion than it relieved. The revelation of the U-2 flights in May 1960 raised serious doubts in the minds of many Americans about the degree of confidence administration officials placed in their estimates of Soviet strategic missile strength. Nonetheless, Richard Nixon was able to avoid a strong commitment to existing Eisenhower defense policies, and the Republican platform pledged the party to accelerate missile and other defense programs to insure that the United States remained militarily the strongest nation in the world. In the summer of 1960, the administration announced a number of significant increases it was making to further improve the nation's all-out and limited war defenses.[48] All in all, the gap separating the Republican and Democratic parties on questions of military preparedness seemed to narrow sharply during the campaign as both candidates moved closer together on most key issues.

Based on the available evidence it does appear that the missile gap controversy during the 1960 campaign was the result of honest conviction and best estimates of intelligence available to the Democratic candidate and his advisors. In his account of the campaign, Theodore Sorensen states:

> All of the evidence available to Kennedy and to those Senators on whose efforts he drew, indicated a dangerous situation. In his primary and fall campaigns he [Kennedy] referred sparingly and for the most part cautiously to the Soviet missile "advantage" avoiding precise dates and numbers, quoting nonpartisan experts and emphasizing that the United States was still the stronger military power although danger lay ahead.[49]

An important issue raised during the 1960 campaign was the extent to which the Eisenhower administration was confident that the Soviet Union was not building and deploying ICBMs at a high rate, as assumed by the Democratic opposition, on the basis of its assessment of the U-2 intelligence data. Sorensen believed that "all the U-2 evidence was in before the Kennedy-Nixon campaign began," and he concluded that the photographic evidence clearly indicated that Khrushchev was bluffing on the missile threat issue. He stated that Kennedy was not given available evidence during the briefings given him by the CIA and military officials. Late in August, Kennedy flew to Strategic Air Command Headquarters at Omaha, Nebraska, for a briefing arranged for him by the administration. According to Sorensen's account of the visit, "almost immediately it was apparent that he [Kennedy] was not to be given a full-scale Top Secret fill-in on Soviet–American missile and bomber strength."[50] Kennedy was visibly upset by the "sanitized" briefings given him and informed his hosts that he had more access to information as a member of the Senate Foreign Relations Committee. The experiences during the campaign involving the missile gap issue prompted President-elect Kennedy to initiate a thorough study of the entire issue in order to resolve it once and for all.

Prior to the transfer of power to the incoming Democratic administration, President Eisenhower in defense of the soundness of his own military preparedness policies cited a number of recent achievements. He pointed to the approaching operational status of the first of a substantial number of ballistic missile-carrying Polaris submarines; the attainment of operational readiness of the liquid-fueled Atlas ICBM missile; the progress toward the hardening of ICBM sites; the substantial improvement in the capability of Strategic Air Command bombers to penetrate enemy air defenses; the development of air-launched ballistic missiles for strategic bombers; and finally, the forecast deployment and full operational readiness during 1961 of a new long-range ballistics missile early warning system (BMEWS).

In his final State of the Union message in January 1961, the retiring President declared: "The 'bomber gap' of several years ago was always a fiction and the 'missile gap' shows every sign of being the same."[51] This judgment, however, was not to end the controversy over the existence or nonexistence of the so-called missile gap; the issue was not finally resolved until the middle of 1961 when it was declared officially nonexistent by the newly installed Kennedy administration.

NOTES

1. Eugene M. Emme, *The Impact of Air Power* (Princeton: D. Van Nostrand Co., 1959), p. 83.

2. Bernard Brodie, *Strategy in the Missile Age* (Princeton: Princeton University Press, 1959), p. 148.

3. Louis J. Halle, *The Cold War as History* (New York: Harper and Row, 1967), p. 414.

4. See his curious and unconvincing indictment of the revisionist school in *Foreign Affairs* (October 1967), entitled, "Origins of the Cold War," pp. 22–52.

5. Ibid., p. 52.

6. Halle, *Cold War*, p. 69.

7. Schlesinger, "Origins of Cold War," p. 45.

8. Richard Nixon, "U.S. Foreign Policy for the 1970s: A New Strategy for Peace," A Report to the Congress, February 18, 1970 (Washington, D.C.: U.S. Government Printing Office).

9. Warner R. Schilling, Paul Y. Hammond, and Glenn H. Snyder, *Strategy, Politics, and Defense Budgets* (New York: Columbia University Press, 1962), pp. 313– 314.

10. Arnold L. Horelick and Myron Rush, *Strategic Power and Soviet Foreign Policy* (Santa Monica: RAND Corporation, 1965), p. 25.

11. Warner R. Schilling, Paul Y. Hammond, and Glenn H. Snyder, *Strategy, Politics and Defense Budgets* (New York: Columbia University Press, 1962), pp. 433–437.

12. Halle, *Cold War*, p. 281.

13. U.S., Congress, Senate, Subcommittee on the Air Force of the Committee on Armed Services, *Study of Air Power*, 84th Cong., 2d sess., 1956, II.

14. For a fuller explication of this thesis, see Horelick and Rush, *Strategic Power*.

15. Senate, Subcommittee, *Study of Air Power*, I, 104–105, 175, 213.

16. U.S., Congress, House, Subcommittee of the Committee on Appropriations, *Department of Defense Appropriations for 1957*, 84th Cong., 2d sess., 1956, pp. 787, 790, 793–794.

17. Charles H. Donnelly, *United States Defense Policies in 1957* (Washington, D.C.: Government Printing Office, 1958), p. 12.

18. Quoted in ibid., p. 14.

19. Charles H. Donnelly, *The United States Guided Missile Program* (Washington, D.C.: Government Printing Office, 1959), p. 9.

20. U.S., Congress, Senate, Preparedness Investigating Subcommittee of the Committee on Armed Services, *Hearings, Inquiry Into Satellite and Missile Programs*, 85th Cong., 1st and 2d sess., 1957 and 1958, Part 1, p. 265.

21. For detail, see the scholarly and imaginative account by Horelick and Rush, *Strategic Power,* chapters 3, 4, and 5.

22. U.S., Congress, House, Subcommittee of the Committee on Appropriations, *Hearings on Department of Defense Appropriations for 1961,* 86th Cong., 2d sess., 1960, Part I, pp. 23, 25.

23. U.S., Congress, Senate, Preparedness Investigating Subcommittee of the Committee on Armed Services and Committee on Aeronautical and Space Sciences, *Joint Hearing on Missile and Space Activities,* 86th Cong., 1st sess., 1959, p. 371.

24. John Spanier, *American Foreign Policy Since World War II* (New York: Frederick A. Praeger, 1965), p. 15.

25. See Richard H. Rovere, "Letter from Washington," *The New Yorker,* February 27, 1960; Edward L. Katzenbach, Jr., "Ideas: A New Defense Industry," *The Reporter,* March 2, 1961.

26. Bernard Brodie and Arnold Wolfers, eds., *The Absolute Weapon: Atomic Power and World Order* (New York: Harcourt, Brace and Co., 1946), p. 136.

27. Arnold Wolfers, "Superiority in Nuclear Weapons: Advantages and Limitations," *The Annals* 290 (November 1953): 7–15.

28. William W. Kaufmann, "The Requirements of Deterrence," Memorandum No. 7, Center of International Studies (Princeton: Princeton Univeristy Press, 1954), p. 5.

29. Gene M. Lyons and Louis Morton, *Schools for Strategy: Education and Research in National Security Affairs* (New York: Frederick A. Praeger, 1965), pp. 246–252.

30. Paul Nitze, "Atoms, Strategy and Policy," *Foreign Affairs* 34 (January 1956), p. 195.

31. U.S., Congress, Senate, Committee on Foreign Relations, *Developments in Military Technology and Their Impact on United States Strategy and Foreign Policy,* prepared on request by the Washington Center of Foreign Policy Research, Johns Hopkins University, pursuant to S. Res. 336, 85th Cong. and S. Res. 31, 86th Cong., December 6, 1959; U.S., Congress, Joint Economic Committee, *National Security and the American Economy in the 1960's,* by Henry Rowen, 86th Cong., 2d sess., January 30, 1960.

32. Henry A. Kissinger, *The Necessity for Choice* (New York: Doubleday and Co., 1960), pp. 59–101.

33. Henry A. Kissinger, "Force and Diplomacy in the Nuclear Age," *Foreign Affairs* (April 1956).

34. Henry A. Kissinger, *The Necessity for Choice* (New York: Harper and Row, 1960), pp. 36–39.

35. Ibid., pp. 39–40.

36. See Samuel P. Huntington, *The Common Defense* (New York: Columbia University Press, 1961), pp. 130–135, for an assessment of this phenomenon.

37. Ibid., p. 131.

38. John F. Kennedy, *The Strategy of Peace* (New York: Popular Library, 1961), pp. 226 and 59.

39. Ibid., pp. 61–62.

40. Ibid., pp. 61, 66–68.

41. Ibid., p. 69.

42. Ibid., p. 64.

43. Ibid., p. 65.

44. Ibid., p. 75.

45. Ibid., p. ix. The quotation is taken from Kennedy's June 14, 1960, statement in the Senate.

46. Ibid., pp. 236, 258.

47. Arthur M. Schlesinger, Jr., *A Thousand Days* (Boston: Houghton Mifflin Co., 1965), pp. 310–315 and 317; Theodore C. Sorensen, *Kennedy* (New York: Harper and Row, 1965), pp. 610–611.

48. Huntington, *Common Defense*, pp. 263–264.

49. Sorensen, *Kennedy*, p. 612.

50. Ibid., pp. 611–612.

51. *Public Papers of the Presidents of the United States: Dwight D. Eisenhower, 1960–1961* (Washington, D.C.: Government Printing Office, 1961).

CHAPTER 2

A Strategy of Controlled Nuclear Response

When the results of the presidential election of November 1960 were tabulated, President-elect John F. Kennedy received 303 electoral votes to 219 for Richard Nixon. Of the total number of Americans eligible to vote, 64.5 percent (68,832,818) went to the polls. John F. Kennedy received 49.7 percent of the popular vote to 49.6 percent for Mr. Nixon, and the election was decided by a slim margin of 112,881 votes. One authority on the election observed cogently: "If only 4,500 voters in Illinois and 28,000 voters in Texas had changed their minds, the sum of their 32,500 votes would have moved both those states with their combined fifty-one electoral votes, into the Nixon column. Thus, giving him an electoral majority of two, these 32,500 votes would have made Richard M. Nixon President of the United States."[1]

Narrow margin of victory to the contrary, John Kennedy was determined to be a strong executive. He believed the office demanded that he place himself in the thick of battle, that he care compassionately about the fate of the people he was to lead, and that he be prepared to exercise the fullest powers of his office. Jubilant about his victory, but exhausted by the heavy demands of the campaign,

Kennedy nevertheless realized there were only a short seventy-two days until inauguration. Determined to avoid the pre-inaugural chaos and confusion of 1932 and 1952, the President-elect set out immediately to surround himself with a "ministry of talent." He asked brother-in-law Sargent Shriver to lead the search for talent. The task of finding and selecting competent and experienced men to fill the key cabinet posts of State, Defense, and Treasury proved the most difficult for the President-elect, especially since he wanted new faces in these offices. Very early in his quest for talent, Kennedy was deeply impressed both by the credentials and personal charm of Robert A. Lovett, a leader of the American establishment, and was prepared to offer him any one of the three top cabinet posts. At one point he tried to get Lovett to accept the Defense post, if only for a year, along with Robert Kennedy as Deputy Secretary. Lovett declined all offers on grounds that his health would not withstand the strain.[2] He did, however, figure prominently in the Kennedy choice for Secretary of Defense.

Soon after the election, at a luncheon in downtown Georgetown attended by Lovett and Kennedy, discussion focused on candidates for the Defense post. The name of Robert S. McNamara had been mentioned by Lovett to Clark Clifford during a conversation in New York. McNamara, a year older than Kennedy, had been elected president of the Ford Motor Company the day after Kennedy was elected President of the United States. As it happened, during World War II when Lovett was Assistant Secretary of War for Air, he brought to the Pentagon a team of management specialists from the Harvard Business School. According to Schlesinger's account, Lovett told Clifford that McNamara "was the prize of the lot" and should be considered for either Defense or Treasury.[3] Despite Kennedy's skepticism about the effectiveness of former presidents of motor companies as Secretary of Defense, he asked Sargent Shriver to check McNamara's credentials.

Shriver's investigation revealed Robert McNamara as a man of exceptional talent. From high school McNamara went to the University of California and was elected to Phi Beta Kappa while a junior. In 1937 he entered Harvard Business School and performed so well that he was retained on the faculty as an Assistant Professor of Business Administration. During World War II McNamara rose to the rank of lieutenant colonel in the Army Air Force, while teaching his specialty, statistical control, to Army Air Force officers at Harvard; in 1943, he put his talents to work in the Pentagon helping to make logistics decisions based on calculations involving thousands of miles, millions of human beings, and billions of gallons of gasoline.

When the war ended, McNamara and nine of his Army Air Force colleagues were invited by the ailing Ford Motor Company to apply their skills toward restoring the company to a healthy profit footing. In fourteen years McNamara rose to the presidency of the Ford Motor Company which, during the year of his departure, earned a net profit of $427 million. While in Michigan, McNamara preferred to live in Ann Arbor some thirty miles from Detroit where he was a contributor to the National Association for the Advancement of Colored People and the American Civil Liberties Union and was a recognized "egghead" in the university community. McNamara could not be typed readily as a Republican or a Democrat, frequently contributing selectively to the candidates of both parties. In 1960 he voted for Senator John F. Kennedy, Democratic candidate for the presidency.

One day in late November 1960, Robert Kennedy telephoned McNamara and asked if he would see Sargent Shriver. McNamara agreed to see Shriver but was not told the purpose of the latter's visit. Shriver flew to Michigan the first week of December and immediately informed McNamara that the President-elect was prepared to offer him an appointment as Secretary of Defense or Secretary of the Treasury. Shriver was impressed by a number of things: "The matter-of-fact way that McNamara moved to a discussion of the post—without surprise, or arrogance, or false modesty, or self-depreciation; the ease with which he could rattle off the three or four main problems of both the Treasury and Defense; his worry about deserting the Fords, who had just made him president, and his total indifference to money."[4] McNamara quickly declined the Treasury declaring that he did not have the necessary experience in banking and fiscal affairs. As for the Defense post, McNamara reminded Shriver that his experience in national security affairs was fifteen years out-of-date. Shriver asked McNamara whether he would agree to meet personally with the President-elect before finally making up his mind. Out of courtesy McNamara agreed to fly to Washington the next day.[5]

In Washington, McNamara repeated to the President-elect his doubts about his qualifications to be Secretary of Defense. Kennedy is said to have replied that he was unaware that there was a school for cabinet officers. McNamara named several other people whom he considered better qualified, but Kennedy rejected them all for reasons McNamara could accept. At one point in the conversation McNamara sought to put Kennedy on the defensive when he asked the President-elect whether he had actually written *Profiles in Courage*. Kennedy rejoined that he had. McNamara, according to Sorensen, "reconsidered, obtained the President-elect's assurance that he would not be bound by either the Symington task force on Pentagon reorganization or by any political commitments on the choice of his subordinates, and decided that one could not say 'no' to a President."[6]

In early December Robert McNamara came to Washington, opened an office in the Shoreham Hotel and by telephone began an intensive country-wide search for the key civilian staff to run the Pentagon. McNamara chose as Deputy Secretary, Roswell Gilpatric, who had been recommended to him by Sargent Shriver and President-elect Kennedy. Gilpatric, a New York lawyer and a Democrat, had served as Under Secretary of the Air Force during the Truman administration. For the position which McNamara believed to be crucial to the management of the vast Pentagon sprawl —the Comptroller—he chose Charles Hitch, a Rhodes scholar and economist whose work in operational analysis at the RAND Corporation in California revealed an ability to break down complex problems into their essential parts with both speed and exactness. With Hitch came another RAND economist and Rhodes scholar, Alain C. Enthoven, who completed an imaginative and indefatigable team able to apply the techniques of systems analysis to the broad range of defense problems. For the highly important office of Assistant Secretary for International Security Affairs, McNamara selected Paul Nitze, a man of high intellect and long experience in dealing with all aspects of national security and nuclear age strategy.[7]

Late in December 1960, President-elect Kennedy gave his new

Secretary of Defense a list of questions which asked, for example, whether there should be a supplemental defense budget; whether additional funds were needed now for Polaris, Minuteman, and Atlas missiles; whether a basic reevaluation of the nation's defense strategy, targets, and capability was needed; and what was the role of manned bombers and aircraft carriers. In addition, McNamara was given his first basic policy change. No longer, said Kennedy, should a predetermined arbitrary financial limit be allowed to establish either strategy or force levels. The nation's strategy would be determined by the objectives of foreign policy, and force levels in support of those objectives would be determined by the needs of our safety and commitments.[8]

Less than a week after the inauguration of President Kennedy, Secretary of Defense McNamara reported his preliminary findings on defense preparedness to the cabinet and then in detail to the President. The Pentagon, said the Secretary, supported "a strategy of massive nuclear retaliation as the answer to all military and political aggression, a strategy believed by few of our friends and none of our enemies and resulting in serious weaknesses in our conventional forces." He found, he said, financial ceilings imposed on national security, "making military strategy the stepchild of a predetermined budget." McNamara also reported that the nation possessed a strategic nuclear force highly vulnerable to surprise missile attack. As a consequence of these findings, the Secretary informed President Kennedy that he would be unable to answer all of the questions asked of him until a number of basic analyses were performed.[9]

The first public indication of the President's intent to reexamine thoroughly the nation's existing general war strategy was given during his State of the Union message to Congress on January 30, 1961.[10] The nation, he said, was " . . . moving into a period of uncertain risk in which both the military and diplomatic possibilities require a Free World force so powerful as to make any aggression clearly futile." Alluding to the post-World War II period the President said: " . . . in the past, lack of consistent, coherent military strategy, the absence of basic assumptions about our national requirements, and the faulty estimates and duplication arising from inter-service rivalries have all made it difficult to assess accurately how adequate—or inadequate—our defenses really are." Because of these inadequacies, the President concluded: "I have . . . instructed the Secretary of Defense to reappraise our entire defense strategy—our ability to fulfill our commitments—the effectiveness, vulnerability, and dispersal of our strategic bases, forces and warning systems. . . ." Congress heard from the President that he was asking for preliminary conclusions by the end of February, following which he would recommend, as appropriate, needed legislative, budgetary, or executive action.[11]

In order to strengthen further the nation's military posture the President asked the Secretary of Defense to implement three measures immediately. First, he asked for action to increase the nation's airlift capability in order to obtain greater mobility. Second, prompt action was needed to step up the Polaris submarine program in order to place on station nine months sooner a substantially greater capability. Finally, Kennedy ordered a speedup in the nation's entire missile program, because "we need an invulnerable missile force powerful enough to deter any aggressor from even threatening an attack he would know could not destroy enough of our force to prevent his own destruction."[12]

In an unprecedented move to reappraise the nation's entire defense strategy in less than a month, Secretary McNamara directed the Joint Chiefs of Staff to provide detailed answers to ninety-six questions (known notoriously as McNamara's ninety-six trombones) bearing on all aspects of national military capabilities, commitments, and strategy. Sorensen writes: "No incoming President had ever undertaken a more searching reexamination of the defense establishment. . . ."[13] And Secretary McNamara is reported to have said that he was attempting to telescope a lifetime's work into twenty days.

Before the end of February the Secretary had at least preliminary replies to all of his questions. A succession of meetings was held with the civilian and military staffs in the White House, Department of Defense, and Bureau of the Budget in order to put in shape a number of major revisions to the defense budget for fiscal year 1962.

The Kennedy Defense Strategy, 1961

On March 28, 1961, President Kennedy sent his first major defense message to Congress outlining important changes he intended to make in the nation's defense strategy, capacities, commitments, and needs. In his opening remarks the President said: ". . . no single question of policy has concerned me more since entering upon these responsibilities than the adequacy of our present and planned military forces to accomplish our major national security objectives."[14] He conceded that a full appraisal of the nation's defense policy would take months; nevertheless, he said, there were some urgent and obvious recommendations which could be presented for inclusion in the fiscal 1962 budget.

The keystone of our defense policy the President stated was peace, not war—"to deter all wars, general or limited, nuclear or conventional, large or small." Moreover, he stated, "The basic problems facing the world today are not susceptible to a military solution." Noting the nation's determination to be strong and yet always ready to negotiate to reduce tensions and seek reduced levels of arms, he emphasized: "Our arms will never be used to strike the first blow in any attack. This is not a confession of weakness but a statement of strength. It is our national tradition." With respect to general war strategy, the President continued, "this doctrine means that such capability must rest with that portion of our forces which would survive the initial attack. We are not creating forces for a first strike against any other nation. We shall never threaten, provoke or initiate aggression—but if aggression should come, our response will be swift and effective."[15] Kennedy enunciated the primary objective of our strategy as the maintenance of sufficient retaliatory forces capable of inflicting unacceptable losses upon any enemy which had attacked the United States.

The President went on to elaborate some of the key elements of the new strategy he was proposing. For one, he said, "our arms must be subject to ultimate civilian control and command at all times, in war as well as peace." Second, our arms must be adequate to meet national commitments and insure American security, without being bound by arbitrary budget ceilings. Third, our defense posture must be both flexible and determined, so that a potential aggressor contemplating an attack on any part of the free world must know that our response will be suitable, selective, swift, and effective. Fourth, our defenses must be secure against prolonged reattack as well as a surprise attack. Fifth, improvements are needed in the command and control capabilities of our strategic deterrent—more flexible, more selective, more deliberate, better protected, and under ultimate civilian authority at all times. Finally, the nation's defense posture must be designed to reduce the danger of irrational or unpremeditated general war—the danger of an unnecessary escalation of a small war into a large one.[16]

Placing special emphasis on strengthening and protecting American strategic deterrent forces, President Kennedy recommended increased land- and sea-based missiles which come from hidden, moving, or invulnerable bases incapable of being wiped out by a surprise attack. In view of the success attained to date in the Polaris program, the President urged funds for the construction of ten more Polaris submarines for fiscal year 1962, making a total of twenty-nine. Production would be expanded from five to twelve submarines a year in order that twenty-nine Polaris submarines could be completed and at sea several months ahead of the existing program calling for nineteen boats. Because the President envisaged a major deterrent role for the solid-fuel Minuteman missile, he recommended the addition of three more fixed-base squadrons—postponing three mobile Minuteman squadrons funded in the January budget and increasing the total number of missiles added by two-thirds. Production capacity for Minuteman missiles should, he said, be doubled as a hedge against the future requirement to move swiftly to higher levels if events required it.[17]

In view of plans to expand the nation's missile forces, the President proposed no funds for the procurement of additional B-52 and B-58 strategic aircraft. He acknowledged that the nation's strategic bomber forces constituted the best hope of deterring attack during the period prior to the completion of our missile expansion, and recommended, therefore, funds to complete the standby capacity and matériel support to place one-eighth of our entire heavy bomber force on airborne alert at any time an emergency warranted it. He also urged that ground alert for both medium and heavy bomber forces be increased from 33⅓ percent to 50 percent.[18]

The supplemental defense programs recommended by President Kennedy amounted to $1.5 billion in new obligational authority. Determined that the Defense establishment should be "lean and fit, efficient and effective," the President stressed, "it is the national interest that calls upon us to cut our losses and cut back those programs in which a very dim promise no longer justifies a very large cost." Accordingly, he announced a decision to eliminate the last two squadrons of Titans originally contemplated, to accelerate the phaseout of a number of B-47 wings already planned, to phase out the obsolete subsonic Snark airbreathing missile, to suspend the development of the B-70 mach 3 manned bomber as a full weapons system, while preserving the option to develop the weapons system at a later date if needed, and, finally, to terminate the expensive ($1 billion) developmental program to achieve a militarily useful nuclear-powered aircraft.[19]

The President concluded his message on a somewhat optimistic note, stressing, "Our military position today is strong." But, he cautioned, positive action must be taken now if we are to have the kind of forces we will need for our security in the future. Kennedy affirmed that the nation's interest lay in peaceful solutions, in reducing tensions, and in settling disputes at the conference table and not on the battlefield.[20]

Early in April 1961, Secretary McNamara made his first appearance in public session before the Defense Appropriations Subcommittee of the House Appropriations Committee.[21] In his opening statement, the Secretary stressed the importance of particular weapon systems capable of deterring general nuclear war and in this context told the Senate Armed Services Committee:

> Only a year or so ago the principal general war threat to our security was a surprise attack by large numbers of nuclear-armed manned bombers. A year or two from now our principal concern will be a surprise attack by large numbers of nuclear-armed ICBMs.

Therefore, in reevaluating our general war position, McNamara continued:

> Our major concern was to reduce our dependence on deterrent forces which are highly vulnerable to ballistic missile attack or which rely for their survival on a hair-trigger response to the first indications of such an attack.[22]

Greater emphasis, he said, was being placed on kinds of forces capable of riding out a massive nuclear attack and those which could be deliberately applied while always remaining under complete control of constituted authorities.

Addressing himself specifically to the strategic missile program, McNamara said: " . . . it is our conclusion that emphasis must be shifted more rapidly from the first generation, liquid-fuel Atlas and Titan programs to the second generation solid-fuel Polaris and Minuteman programs. The second generation missile systems would lend themselves far more to a calculated and deliberate response. On this basis the President recommended an increase in Polaris and Minuteman missiles over those programmed in the 1961 budget by 160 and 60, respectively.[23]

Then the Secretary turned his attention to the manned bomber force with a look into the future, "In the era which lies ahead when our potential adversary could launch a heavy ICBM attack with little warning, the number of bombers on an alert status and capable of immediate launching is much more important than the total number of bombers available in the inventory."[24] Studies performed for McNamara had indicated that about one-half of the total strategic bomber force could be maintained on ground alert and launched within fifteen minutes—the warning time that could be expected from the Ballistic Missile Early Warning System (BMEWS). In addition, McNamara continued, a much larger proportion of the bomber force could be brought to an alert status and held there for a relatively short period of time during an emergency.

During the cross-questioning of McNamara by both the Mahon Appropriations Subcommittee and Senate Armed Services Committee, several aspects of defense policy were pursued which illustrate well the extreme complexity of determining an optimum strategy and correctly ascertaining all of the requirements in support of such a strategy. Secretary McNamara was asked by the Chairman of the Mahon Subcommittee whether in fact the administration was contemplating major changes to existing strategy. He replied that the term "basic change" did not exactly apply, but it was true, as the President had earlier stated, that considerable attention was being directed to (a) the appropriate level of strategic delivery power; (b) the survivability of that power; (c) and the appropriate command and control of that power, all in relation to our strategic aims. McNamara was emphatic, however, that "there is no change in our policy regarding the use of nuclear weapons."[25]

At one point Mahon asked the Secretary whether "we have a definite idea of how much we need in the way of prepared and protected offensive capability in order to ride out a massive nuclear attack and still retaliate with assured effectiveness." McNamara's reply was particularly forthright and revealing:

> Yes. I have directed a great deal of my personal attention to exactly that question you have raised. I think it is fundamental to a determination of our strategic delivery requirements particularly, involving missiles, aircraft, heavy bomber aircraft, and items of that type.
>
> I will answer the question in two or three steps.
>
> First, I do not believe we have an adequate statement of our requirements at the present time. We are undertaking a development of just exactly that as a foundation for the fiscal year 1963 budget proposals.
>
> Secondly, I do not believe we will ever be able to develop such a statement of requirements with such precision as to yield a definite answer which can be presented without qualification.
>
> I say that because there are parts of the question to which we will never have the final answers.[26]

Because it would be most difficult, for example, to estimate the damage which our forces would suffer from an enemy first strike, or to gauge fully the impact of new weapons systems, the Secretary emphasized that it would always be necessary to "inject judgment into the equations" on which we would depend for answers.

During his appearance before the Senate Armed Services Committee, Chairman Russell asked McNamara whether it was possible for him to define a saturation point in our requirements for ICBMs in terms of numbers and time period. The Secretary replied:

Mr. Chairman, I cannot answer that question, and this is a most important matter. It is one that the Joint Chiefs of Staff have discussed, and I have discussed, and we have set up a working group to prepare a comprehensive study of this problem for the preparation and foundation for the 1963 budget. The question is should we have 1,300, 700, or 10,000, and I just cannot answer the question.[27]

Having acknowledged the growing Soviet threat which he said was based on a large and ready force of ICBMs capable of being launched with little or no warning, McNamara assessed the nation's general war capabilities as follows, "Today, we believe our strategic forces are fully adequate to carry out their assigned tasks."[28] Presumably, the Secretary meant that the nation's strategic nuclear forces were fully capable of carrying out their assigned missions under conditions of either a first or second strike.

During the Eisenhower administrations, the critics of "massive retaliation" had taken sharp issue with the reputed first-strike implications of the nation's general war strategy. Since the hint of a possible preemptive nuclear attack against the Soviet Union, under several imaginable circumstances, was considered by defense officials to be a deterrence-reinforcing measure, the ambiguity of whether the United States would actually strike first or respond only to an enemy attack was deliberately never fully clarified. Recall, however, that President Kennedy in his now-famous budget message of March 28, 1961 had stated unequivocally that the United States would not strike first in a nuclear war and had directed the Defense Department to design its strategy and forces solely for a retaliatory role.

During Secretary McNamara's testimony before the Mahon Subcommittee, Representative Gerald Ford raised the first-strike issue anew by alluding to a statement allegedly made by Deputy Secretary of Defense, Roswell Gilpatric, which purportedly encouraged a belief that under some circumstances the United States might strike first. Mr. McNamara rejoined pointedly, "The alleged statement attributed to Mr. Gilpatric is inaccurate. Mr. Gilpatric has talked privately on the subject and has always, when the first-strike question arose, clearly stated that the United States position is never to strike first, and this is the basic philosophy of the President.[29]

As the Kennedy-McNamara approach to a strategy of controlled and flexible response continued to unfold during 1961 and 1962, the categoric denial that the United States would under any circumstances use nuclear weapons first in war tended to become less and less credible. As we shall see, the administration's decision to place maximum emphasis on deterring war and winning such a war if necessary, evoked a requirement for a possible strategy of preemption the effect of which would further reinforce deterrence or permit greater effort to limit damage to the United States if nuclear war resulted.

When the Kennedy administration took office in 1961 the nation's general war strategy was based on a war plan characterized as containing an "optimum mix" of targets. Strategic nuclear forces were procured according to a requirement to destroy simultaneously, if required, Soviet society and nuclear bombers and missiles in one massive attack. Other strategic options open to the administration were, first, a minimum deterrent, consisting of a small highly invulnerable force of several hundred missiles whose prime purpose was to deter war. If war should occur, such a force would not be large enough to limit damage to the United States and would be limited in its employment largely to attacks on Soviet cities.

The second option was known variously as the strategy of flexible or controlled response and counterforce. Such a strategy rested on several important premises. First, it was assumed that despite the best efforts to make deterrence effective, it might not work. Second, the fatalities occurring in a general war could vary significantly depending, for example, on the types of targets attacked by both sides. Third, efforts to limit damage to the United States and its allies were worthwhile wartime objectives and might best be accomplished by attacking an enemy's bombers and missile sites and providing active and civil defenses for American and allied populations. Fourth, and a kind of corollary to the preceding premise, by avoiding deliberate attacks on enemy cities and holding forces in reserve, an enemy would have an incentive to confine his attacks to American nuclear threat targets, thus, possibly further limiting damage. Finally, it was assumed that even though general nuclear war might occur it would not end the nation's interest in the nature of the postwar world. It would be desirable, therefore, to retain sufficient forces to eliminate or neutralize residual enemy forces, terminate the war, and provide some protection thereafter.

The decision confronting Secretary McNamara between competing strategies was, according to one defense analyst, "a choice between a deterrent capability of high quality with a range of options built into it, and a deterrent of lesser quality, greatly dependent on Soviet restraint for its effectiveness. . . ."[30] The Secretary apparently gravitated readily to a strategy based on flexible response which presupposed forces adequate to weather a massive enemy nuclear attack, even under conditions of little or no warning, and able to respond with sufficient strength to strike a decisive counterblow. This force, McNamara insisted, must be of such character that even in the face of attack it could be employed in a cool and deliberate fashion always under the complete control of the constituted authority.[31]

As part of the job of making a strategy of flexible response meaningful and especially as a means of seeking to limit fatalities and damage during a nuclear war which the Secretary deemed possible, it was thought necessary by many defense analysts to make fallout shelters an essential component of a capability for flexible response. President Kennedy apparently had given little thought to the need for a major nationwide fallout shelter program up to the time of the Bay of Pigs fiasco in April 1961.[32] A study performed by Carl Kaysen of the White House staff concluded that existing civil defense efforts were based on outmoded ideas and that the United States should either face up to the problem in a serious way or forget it. President Kennedy, when presented with the choice of protecting the nation's weapons of war but not the nation's population, decided to acknowledge the problem and bring it to Congress's attention in a sober but urgent appeal.

In his second State of the Union address, delivered to Congress on May 25, 1961, President Kennedy said:

> One major element of the national security program which this nation has never squarely faced up to is civil defense. This problem arises not from present trends but from national inaction in which most of us have participated. In the past decade we have intermittently considered a variety of programs, but we have never adopted a consistent policy. Public considerations have been largely characterized by apathy,

> indifference, and skepticism, while, at the same time, many of the civil defense plans have been so far-reaching and unrealistic that they have not gained essential support.[33]

The President went on to explain that a civil defense program could not be obtained cheaply, nor could it deter enemy attack or protect against blast effects from thermonuclear attack. He was particularly concerned that the lessons of history "remind us of the possibilities of an irrational attack, a miscalculation, an accidental war, or a war of escalation in which the stakes by each side gradually increase to the point of maximum danger which cannot be either foreseen or deterred."[34] Thus, said the President, civil defense was justifiable as insurance for the civilian population in case of an enemy miscalculation. And if Congress recognized the validity of this concept, a nationwide long-range program of identifying present fallout shelter capacity and providing shelter in new and existing structures could be initiated without delay. The President believed such a program would protect millions of people against the hazards of fallout in the event of a major nuclear attack.

Kennedy's plea in May for a federally sponsored civil defense effort was cautiously worded. In July, however, when he addressed the nation on the Berlin crisis, his speech "was delivered in a context of clear and present danger. It had the anxious attention of the nation to a far greater degree. It was concerned with a possible nuclear war over Berlin that very year, not simply an accidental attack at some speculative time."[35] Speaking with Berlin clearly uppermost in mind, the President said:

> In the event of an attack, the lives of those families which are not hit in a nuclear blast and fire can still be saved—*if* they can be warned to take shelter and *if* that shelter is available. We owe that kind of insurance to our families—and to our country. . . . But the time to start is now. In the coming months I hope to let every citizen know what steps he can take without delay to protect his family in case of attack. I know that you will want to do no less.[36]

Public confusion and near-hysteria greeted the President's urgings for a national civil defense program. A hitherto apathetic populace was suddenly bestirred far beyond anyone's expectations, and during the summer and early fall of 1961, fallout shelter fever gripped thousands of Americans. Thousands of home shelters were sold, many at exorbitant prices. Civil defense officials everywhere were besieged with inquiries, and debates were held in church, scientific, and public forums on all aspects and implications of survival in nuclear war.

Much of the consternation and confusion was attributable to the Kennedy administration's lack of a comprehensive shelter program, a well-defined shelter policy, or even a public leader able to lend authority and direction to the effort. According to Theodore Sorensen, the President himself was uncertain and his chief advisors were divided on the issues. Controversy raged over whether emphasis should be placed on family shelters or community shelter programs. What priority should an agreed program be given, and should it be under federal or local control? The President was urged to hold another "fireside chat" and take his case to the American people. He refused because no acceptable program was ready with which he could agree.

As a consequence, the administration in 1962 began to tone down the whole issue. Proposed legislation called for a long-range program of federal incentives for the construction of community shelters in schools, hospitals, libraries, and similar public structures. Finally, in 1963 the shelter bill was not given high priority and was reduced from the level of a major presidential message to a departmental request. From that time on, the fallout shelter issue failed to generate much administration or public interest, and congressional hostility to any federally sponsored program whatever grew apace.

The "Missile Gap"

It was early in 1961 when the new administration became embroiled in its first major controversy with the Republican party on the issue of relative missile strength between this nation and the Soviet Union. In fact, hardly a month had passed since President Eisenhower debunked the idea of a "missile gap" in his farewell speech to the nation. Partisan political feelings had not ceased to run hot because of vivid campaign memories of Democratic attacks on the Eisenhower administration as led by Senator Symington, which charged, "A very substantial missile gap does exist and the Eisenhower administration apparently is going to permit this gap to increase."[37] Presidential candidate Kennedy, according to Senator Symington's own account, had "warned of the missile gap in no less than nine campaign speeches just among those which have been reprinted."[38]

The latently explosive "missile gap" issue emerged out of a press background briefing called by Secretary McNamara during the second week of February 1961, at which he sought to explain "that merely counting missiles is not the way to assess United States or Russian military strength. All other weapons must be taken into account." Later in his impromptu remarks, the Secretary contended that the most important thing was that no "destruction gap"—that is, a superior Soviet capability to deliver destruction with nuclear weapons—existed. Then he is reported to have said rather casually, "that today the Russians probably have no more intercontinental ballistic missiles than the United States."[39] Because of the partisan uproar that immediately followed, presidential Press Secretary Pierre Salinger issued a statement which said that since an administration study underway had not been completed, it was premature to conclude that the "missile gap" had disappeared. The very next day, President Kennedy himself told reporters that until his audit of United States defense forces was completed, he would make no further comment on the "missile gap."[40]

Reviewing briefly the events preceding the "flap" over the existence or nonexistence of the "missile gap" in 1961, it is useful to recall that during late 1959 the intelligence ground rules for estimating Soviet ICBM capability had been changed so that Soviet intentions—or what he probably will do—replaced capabilities—or what his productive plant is capable of producing—as the basis for making the all-important estimates.[41] This issue involved not only the credibility of American intelligence but brought into sharp focus and under debate the policy position of the United States that it would not strike first since it had chosen to design and deploy a retaliatory force capable of surviving any predictable Soviet sneak attack.

The question of how United States officials estimated Soviet capabilities became a major issue for the first time in February 1960 when the estimates of Soviet long-range missile strength were reduced 66 percent from that announced just two months before. Despite this downward revision, however, the Soviets were expected to have many times more ICBMs deployed by 1961 than would the United States. Then in August 1960, American estimates of Soviet ICBMs for the mid-1961 time period were again revised downward to 30 percent of the 1959 base level. Yet, even with this reduction, it was estimated that the Soviet Union would possess a substantial ICBM margin over the United States a year later.[42]

Testifying in April 1961 before the House Appropriations Subcommittee, Secretary McNamara was asked by Representative Mahon whether, according to intelligence estimates, there was a missile gap. The Secretary responded: "Based on intelligence estimates available to me, yes."[43] Pursuing the same line of questioning, Mr. Mahon asked McNamara whether in his view there had been a missile gap in existence or anticipated in 1960. The Secretary replied that his reading of the estimates would indicate a probable missile gap both then and for the current period. Pressed further as to how long the missile gap was likely to last, McNamara said: "... there is evidence that a missile gap may exist up to and through 1963." He qualified his statement importantly, however, by indicating that our missile inventory at the end of FY 1963, or at the end of calendar year 1963, may exceed that of the Soviet Union.[44] Toward the end of his extensive testimony before the House Appropriations Subcommittee, McNamara was asked by a committee member whether, in the event it was determined that our estimates of the Soviet missile threat were high by something on the order of 25 percent, it would have a material impact on the program he, the Secretary, was presenting to the committee? To this, the Secretary replied: "It would have some but not much."[45]

Congressman Mahon asked McNamara whether in his judgment the nation was presently the victim of a "deterrent gap." The Secretary replied: "I do not believe there is a deterrent gap today." Asked by Mahon whether in his judgment the deterrent gap issue was more significant than the question of a missile gap, McNamara stated, "Yes, sir, I do." And when asked whether the nation was equally as strong or stronger militarily than the Soviet Union, the Secretary said cautiously: "I do believe we are strong relative to the Soviet Union today."[46]

In June 1961, the national intelligence estimate of Soviet ICBM strength was again revised downward, this time to only 15 percent of the figure estimated in December 1959 for July 1961. Finally, in September 1961, the estimate went down once again. Senator Symington, writing in *The Reporter,* drew this conclusion, "At that time, [September] it was estimated that Soviet ICBM strength was exactly 3.5 percent of the original 1959 estimate; a reduction of 96.5 percent in less than two years. Thus, the missile gap vanished."[47] To clear up a possible public impression that considerable legerdemain was employed by the administration in making the "missile gap" disappear, Secretary McNamara came to the administration's defense during his appearance before the Senate Armed Services Committee in April 1962 and stated, "I would say that those who discussed the missile gap and who based their statements on information from the national intelligence estimates were speaking of the missile gap in good faith."[48]

In retrospect it seems perfectly clear that John F. Kennedy and Secretary of Defense-designate, Robert McNamara, were briefed by outgoing administration officials on the nonexistent missile gap, probably sometime late in 1960. By early 1961, at least McNamara, and probably Kennedy, appears to have accepted the position held by President Eisenhower and his top civilian defense officials that evidence derived from U-2 flights refuted widely held beliefs that the Soviets were rapidly deploying an operational first generation ICBM. In fact, Soviet missile testing had slackened and there was virtually no evidence to support the contentions that significant deployment was taking place.

The furor generated by Secretary McNamara's almost offhand remark in mid-February suggests that the Kennedy administration did not want the missile gap issue before the public until after the bitter feelings generated during the recent campaign had simmered down. By claiming to have the missile gap issue under thorough review, Kennedy was able to buy time and to reinforce an already convincing case with additional evidence. As events turned out, the President was able to turn the missile gap issue into a considerable advantage at a time when public memories of the 1960 campaign had faded, and new issues claimed primary attention.

In the fall of 1961, the Kennedy administration took a major initiative designed to convince the American public, allies, neutrals, and adversaries throughout the world of the preponderance of this nation's strategic nuclear power. The Berlin crisis was uppermost in the mind of Deputy Secretary of Defense Roswell Gilpatric as he addressed the Business Council at Hot Springs, Virginia, on October 21, 1961. Gilpatric said he would not dwell on the many problems of government–business relations which needed resolving; rather, he said, it would be more profitable to try to develop further the thinking behind our present defense policies and programs. Somewhat plaintively the Deputy Secretary said, "I am convinced that we [the administration] have not yet succeeded in getting across to the public at large a full understanding of the defense policies we are now pursuing." Mr. Gilpatric quickly reviewed the primary defense policy changes made by the administration since January, stressing that "the President was determined that our strategic power must be sufficient to deter any deliberate nuclear attack on this country or its allies by being able to survive a first strike by the enemy with sufficient arms to penetrate his defenses and inflict unacceptable losses upon him."[49]

Gilpatric emphasized that the Berlin crisis had reached emergency proportions and accused the Soviets of having made it so. He noted the various quick-fix measures which had been taken to improve the Western tactical position in Berlin and then stressed that our real strength in Berlin was much more broadly based. Specifically, said the Deputy Secretary, "Our confidence in our ability to deter Communist action, or resist Communist blackmail, is based upon a sober appreciation of the relative military power of the two sides."[50] He doubted that the Soviets had any less realistic views despite their proclivity for extravagant claims. And, he said, despite Soviet efforts to protect the secrecy of their military deployments, "their Iron Curtain is not so impenetrable as to force us to accept at face value the Kremlin's boast."[51]

Then in remarkably candid and comprehensive terms, Gilpatric reviewed the existing status of United States military power and its meaning for potential aggressors:

> The fact is that this nation has a nuclear retaliatory force of such lethal power that an enemy move which brought it into play would

be an act of self-destruction on his part. The U.S. has today hundreds of manned intercontinental bombers capable of reaching the Soviet Union, including 600 heavy bombers and many more medium bombers equally capable of intercontinental operations because of our highly developed in-flight refueling techniques and worldwide base structure. The U.S. also has 6 Polaris submarines at sea carrying a total of 96 missiles, and dozens of intercontinental ballistic missiles. Our carrier strike forces and land-based theater forces could deliver additional hundreds of megatons. The total number of our delivery vehicles, tactical as well as strategic, is in the tens of thousands; and, of course, we have more than one warhead for each vehicle.

Furthermore, he continued:

Our forces are so deployed and protected that a sneak attack could not effectively disarm us. The destructive power which the United States could bring to bear even after a Soviet surprise attack upon our forces would be as great as—perhaps greater than—the total undamaged force which the enemy can threaten to launch against the United States in a first strike. In short, we have a second-strike capability which is at least as extensive as what the Soviets can deliver by striking first. Therefore, we are confident that the Soviets will not provoke a major nuclear conflict.[52]

In his concluding remarks, Secretary Gilpatric reiterated for the world public and Soviet leadership to hear, "Although we are confident that we would ultimately prevail in a test of strength no matter at what level conflict might be initiated by the Soviet Union, this does not alter our determination to seek a peaceful solution to the world's problems.[53]

While attending a meeting in London at the Institute for Strategic Studies, the Defense Department's Paul Nitze sought to allay any remaining fears about the credibility of the West's nuclear deterrent. He addressed the missile gap issue forthrightly:

There was always a certain degree of misunderstanding concerning the so-called missile gap. The question was not so much one of relative numbers but one of the potential vulnerability of our strategic deterrent. Much has been and is being done to reduce that vulnerability. Furthermore, it appears to be the consensus of the intelligence community,

> both in the United States and in the United Kingdom, that the Soviet deployment of ICBMs has proceeded less rapidly than it was once feared it might. There has never been any doubt that the West possesses by far the greater nuclear force, including delivery capability, than does the U.S.S.R. Now that the problems of vulnerability, dispersal and command and control have become manageable, we believe that this force, including the U.K. nuclear forces and the NATO forces deployed on the Continent, give the West a definite nuclear superiority. We further believe this superiority can be maintained into the future as improved weapons systems are developed and deployed by both sides.[54]

Three weeks after Deputy Secretary Gilpatric confidently asserted the superiority of American nuclear power over the Soviet Union, Secretary McNamara elaborated further some of the details of the nation's strategic nuclear capabilities. Speaking in Atlanta on November 11, 1961, at a dinner honoring Senator Russell and Congressman Vinson, the Secretary said the United States currently possessed nearly 1,700 intercontinental bombers including 630 B-52s, 55 B-58s and 1,000 B-47s. We can, said McNamara, count eighty Polaris missiles deployed at sea in nuclear-powered submarines and several dozen operational Atlas intercontinental ballistic missiles ready on launchers in the United States. In addition to these forces, the Secretary reminded his audience that the Navy was capable of launching fifty attack aircraft carrying megaton weapons from the decks of each Forrestal class carrier, six of which were deployed in the oceans worldwide.[55]

By the end of 1961, the Kennedy administration had taken a major stride toward restoring public and allied confidence in the military superiority of the United States relative to the Soviet Union and, in particular, in its strategic nuclear superiority. Unquestionably, the worsening Berlin crisis spurred administration efforts to convince Premier Khrushchev that to risk nuclear war over Berlin would surely result in the destruction of the Soviet Union. At the same time, President Kennedy was deeply concerned that dissension among the Western allies might prevent them from maintaining a solid front against the Soviet threat to the vulnerable position in Berlin. Despite what appeared to be a crisis building toward an inevitable confrontation over Berlin, the December 1961 deadline passed with no agreement and the crisis atmosphere slowly faded away.

It was not until late in 1962, however, that the final official postmortem was made on, and a postscript written to, the controversial "missile gap." The occasion was an interview between Stewart Alsop and Secretary McNamara which appeared in the December 1 issue of the *Saturday Evening Post.* Alsop queried the Secretary about the near-dramatic shift in our military position from one of presumed inferiority to one of unquestioned superiority. McNamara replied: "This nation created a myth of its own weakness. . . . The myth was the result of incomplete intelligence; although it was created by intelligence analysts acting in good faith, it was a myth all the same." When asked how confident he was of his information, the Secretary said, "Absolutely confident. Of course, there is a margin of error. There always is. But the margin of error is much less than the margin of our superiority."[56] Put in more specific terms the meaning of all the hubbub about the missile gap could best be explained, said McNamara, as follows:

> The Soviets simply did not build the kind of long-range missile force they were expected to build. According to the intelligence estimates current three or four years ago, the Soviets were expected by this time to have between 600 and 800 intercontinental missiles. According to the current estimates their 100th long-range missile became operational only a few weeks ago.[57]

During its first six months the Kennedy administration made significant progress toward strengthening and protecting the nation's nuclear strength. Of a total $6 billion budgetary increase, more than $2 billion went directly toward increasing the ability of our nuclear forces to survive a surprise nuclear attack and launch an effective counterstrike. Among the more significant actions taken were the increase in the rate of Polaris submarine construction by approximately 50 percent, the increase in the ground alert of the strategic bomber force to 50 percent, the retention in operational readiness of some 270 B-47 bombers which had been scheduled for early retirement, and an increase of 100 percent in the plant capacity to produce Minuteman missiles. According to Secretary McNamara, the administration's procurement objectives had been increased for the current fiscal year by 200 Polaris and Minuteman missiles.[58]

NOTES

1. Theodore H. White, *The Making of the President 1960* (New York: Atheneum Publishers, 1961), p. 420.

2. Arthur M. Schlesinger, Jr., *A Thousand Days* (Boston: Houghton Mifflin Co., 1965), pp. 120, 129.

3. Ibid., p. 131.

4. The foregoing background on Robert S. McNamara is drawn largely from Theodore H. White, "Revolution in the Pentagon," *Look*, April 23, 1963, as reprinted in the *Congressional Record*, Senate, April 11, 1963, pp. 6130–6135; Theodore C. Sorensen, *Kennedy* (New York: Harper and Row, 1965), pp. 269–270; Schlesinger, *A Thousand Days*, pp. 131–133.

5. Schlesinger's account of the meeting with Shriver appears consistent with other informed accounts and is in some respects more detailed. See *A Thousand Days*, p. 132.

6. Sorensen, *Kennedy*, p. 269.

7. The author has drawn heavily for the preceding on Schlesinger, *A Thousand Days*, pp. 152–153, since the treatment seems to be quite balanced.

8. Sorensen, *Kennedy*, p. 603.

9. Ibid.

10. The term "general war strategy" is used consistently in this book during the period from 1961 to 1965 since it was the preferred term for all-out or strategic nuclear war. During the period from 1949 through the Eisenhower administration the term "all-out war" or "all-out nuclear war" has been consistently employed since it was used most frequently by high government officials and students of military strategy.

11. John F. Kennedy, State of the Union Message, *Documents on Disarmament* (U.S. Arms Control and Disarmament Agency, Washington, D.C.: Government Printing Office, 1962), pp. 16–20.

12. Ibid.

13. Sorensen, *Kennedy*, p. 603.

14. John F. Kennedy, Special Defense Budget Message, March 28, 1961, reprinted in *Congressional Record*, Senate, March 28, 1961, pp. 4652–4657.

15. Ibid., p. 4653. So direct and unambiguous a statement should have put to rest the controversy over United States first-strike policies which were fostered during the Eisenhower administration and never emphatically denied. However, the

Kennedy administration did not long adhere to so cut-and-dried a position with regard to preemptive nuclear attack against the Soviet Union under conditions of a massive attack against NATO forces in Central Europe and in the event of unimpeachable evidence of an imminent Soviet nuclear attack on the United States. Apparently the administration took the position that an open-and-shut position on second-strike strategy only tended to weaken the effectiveness of deterrence and provide the Soviet Union too easy a basis for planning its own strategy and tactics.

16. Ibid., pp. 4653–4654.

17. Ibid., p. 4654.

18. Ibid., pp. 4654–4655.

19. Ibid., p. 4656.

20. Ibid., p. 4657.

21. U.S., Congress, House, Subcommittee of the Committee on Appropriations, *Hearings on Department of Defense Appropriations for 1962*, 87th Cong., 1st sess., 1961, p. 4.

22. Ibid.

23. Ibid., pp. 5, 8.

24. Ibid., p. 9.

25. House Subcommittee, *DOD Appropriations, 1962*, p. 143. On May 22, 1962, addressing the White House Conference on National Economic Issues, Secretary McNamara speaking about the severely limited range of possible responses by the United States and its allies to Soviet aggression in Europe, said, "We recognized from the beginning that we must always be prepared to use our nuclear weapons. But it was also evident that our position throughout the world would be greatly strengthened if we were not forced to choose between doing nothing as deliberately initiating nuclear war." See William W. Kaufmann, *The McNamara Strategy* (New York: Harper and Row, 1964), p. 68.

26. Ibid., p. 137.

27. U.S., Congress, Senate, Committee on Armed Services, Hearings, *Defense Appropriations for 1962*, 87th Cong., 1st sess., 1961, p. 32.

28. U.S., Congress, House, Subcommittee of the Committee on Appropriations, Hearings, *Department of Defense Appropriations for 1962*, 87th Cong., 1st sess., 1961, p. 4.

29. Ibid., p. 80.

30. Kaufmann, *McNamara Strategy*, p. 53.

31. U.S., Congress, House, Committee on Armed Services, testimony by Robert S. McNamara, 87th Cong., 1st sess., 1961.

32. Sorensen, *Kennedy*, p. 613.

33. John F. Kennedy, Address to Congress, "Urgent National Needs," May

25, 1961, reprinted in *Documents on Disarmament, 1961* (Washington, D.C.: Government Printing Office, 1962), p. 156.

34. Ibid.

35. Sorensen, *Kennedy*, p. 614.

36. *Documents on Disarmament, 1961*, p. 263.

37. *Time*, February 17, 1961, p. 12; also, Hanson W. Baldwin, "Missile Controversy," *New York Times*, February 12, 1961.

38. Stuart Symington, "Where the Missile Gap Went," *The Reporter*, February 15, 1962, p. 21.

39. *Time*, February 17, 1961, p. 12.

40. Ibid.

41. Symington, "Missile Gap," p. 22.

42. Ibid.

43. House, Subcommittee, *DOD Appropriations, 1962*, p. 60.

44. Ibid.

45. Ibid., p. 112.

46. Ibid., p. 61.

47. Symington, "Missile Gap," p. 22.

48. U.S., Congress, Senate, Committee on Armed Services, *Department of Defense Programs and Authorization of Appropriations for Procurement of Aircraft, Missiles, and Naval Vessels by the Armed Forces*, 87th Cong., 2d sess., 1962, p. 50.

49. Roswell L. Gilpatric, Speech before the Business Council, Hot Springs, Virginia, October 21, 1961 (Department of Defense, Office of Public Affairs, Release No. 1173–61), pp. 1–2.

50. Ibid., pp. 2–3.

51. Ibid., p. 3. Mr. Gilpatric's allusion here seems clearly to the success of the U-2 flights—terminated in May 1960—the results of which, when fully assessed, clearly indicated that the Soviets were largely bluffing in asserting claims to have hundreds of ICBMs deployed throughout the Soviet Union.

52. Ibid.

53. Ibid., p. 7.

54. Quoted in Kaufmann, *McNamara Strategy*, pp. 108–109.

55. Michael Brower, "Nuclear Strategy of the Kennedy Administration," *Bulletin of the Atomic Scientists* 18 (October 1962); p. 1 of reprint; P.M.S. Blackett, "Steps Toward Disarmament," *Scientific American*, April, 1962, p. 3.

56. Stewart Alsop, "McNamara Thinks the Unthinkable," *Saturday Evening Post*, December 1, 1962, p. 18.

57. Ibid., p. 16.

58. Kaufmann, *McNamara Strategy*, p. 69.

CHAPTER 3

Controlled Nuclear Response Challenged

In his State of the Union message to Congress on January 11, 1962, President Kennedy affirmed that "in the past 12 months our military posture has steadily improved." He pointed to a 15 percent increase in the defense budget over the previous year, to a more than doubled acquisition rate of Polaris submarines, and a doubled production capacity for Minuteman missiles. For the coming year, the force levels planned under the new defense budget included nearly 300 additional Polaris and Minuteman missiles to insure the continued strength of our nuclear deterrent. Echoing the new general war strategy of flexible response the President said, "We have rejected any all-or-nothing posture which would leave no choice but inglorious retreat or unlimited retaliation."[1]

When Secretary McNamara appeared before the House Subcommittee on Department of Defense Appropriations in late January he came prepared to present the first defense budget put together wholly by the Kennedy administration. In his explanatory remarks about the new programming and budgeting procedure the Secretary stated that the defense program was developed in relation to the principal military missions of the Defense establishment and not by organizational (service) components as in the past. Committee chairman, George Mahon of Texas, indicated that the proposed new approach to the costing of defense programs had interested the committee for some time. McNamara strongly endorsed the new approach as an essential management tool and described its underlying philosophy this way:

> Because of the great technical complexity of modern day weapons, their lengthy period of development, their tremendous combat power, and their enormous cost, sound choices of major weapon systems in relation to military tasks and missions have become the key decisions around which much else of the defense program revolves. But the full cost implications of these decisions, present and future, cannot be ascertained unless both the programs and their cost are projected over a period of years, ideally over the entire life cycle of the weapon system. Since such long-term projections are very difficult to make with any degree of precision, we have fixed on a 5-year period, which is short enough to assure reasonably accurate estimates and long enough to provide a good approximation of the full cost.[2]

Having explained the rationale for the new defense programming and budgeting procedure, Secretary McNamara turned to a consideration of specific problems in the international situation which related importantly to a determination of the nation's military policies and programs. The outcome of the Berlin situation, he said, was still in doubt, but, "what is at stake there is not only the territory of that city or the freedom of its 2 million people, but even more important, the ability of the free world alliance to continue to be master of its own destiny."[3] The Soviet Union, the Secretary said, appeared to be embarked on a policy designed to divide and weaken the NATO alliance and to produce a loss of confidence in the strength and purpose of the United States everywhere. Pointing to the communist challenge to freedom in South Vietnam, Laos, the Congo, and Cuba, McNamara reasoned that the safety of the United States depended on our willingness to defend the outposts of freedom around the world. Our allies, he said, have great and growing economic and military strength. What is needed, therefore, is a unity of purpose—a common determination to use this strength effectively in the collective defense of the free world alliance.

In this alliance envisaged by the Secretary, NATO played a very special role. In his estimation, "There is no question but that NATO represents the balance of power in the struggle against communism. The loss or neutralization of this area would be a disastrous blow to our own security."[4] If for no other reason than self-interest, America must maintain the closest cooperation at all levels with its NATO partners, no matter what the difficulties. Thus, in planning the nation's military forces the Secretary affirmed that it was essential to take into account the plans of the other free-world nations, particularly our NATO partners and to continue to plan for the collective defense with each alliance member contributing those forces best suited to his capabilities.

McNamara turned next to a detailed discussion of the strategic retaliatory forces that the administration was recommending for fiscal year 1963 and planning through fiscal year 1967. He summarized the current capabilities of the nation's strategic retaliatory forces in this manner:

> There is no question but that today our strategic retaliatory forces are fully capable of destroying the Soviet target system, even after absorbing an initial nuclear surprise attack.[5]

Answering his own question as to how large a strategic retaliatory force and what combination of weapons systems we would need over the next several years in order to deter the Soviet Union successfully, or if deterrence failed, to strike back decisively, Secretary McNamara stated that it would depend in large measure on the size and kind of long-range nuclear forces the Soviets could bring to bear against the United States and its allies and on the effectiveness of their defensive systems. We must assume, said the Secretary, that the Soviet Union will ultimately build a large ICBM force. As far as our own forces are concerned, the Secretary affirmed, "the requirement for strategic retaliatory forces lends itself rather well to reasonably precise calculation." Given the types of weapons available to the United States, "this task presents a problem of reasonably finite dimensions, which are measurable in terms of the number and type of targets or aiming points which must be destroyed and the number and types of weapon delivery systems required to do the job under various sets of conditions."[6]

Our calculations, McNamara stressed, must take into account a possible enemy first strike, and thus must consider the losses which our forces would likely suffer from the initial enemy attack. Thus, in determining our force deployments, such factors as the size of the enemy offensive forces, attacking warhead yields, and assumed reliability and accuracy of the weapons system must be carefully considered. McNamara acknowledged that each of these crucial factors introduced varying degrees of uncertainty into the calculations, but that these uncertainties were not completely unmanageable. "By postulating various sets of assumptions, ranging from optimistic to pessimistic, it is possible," he said, "to introduce into our calculations reasonable allowances for these uncertainties."[7]

Explained another way, Secretary McNamara told the Mahon committee, "We have adopted the philosophy [that] we must take account of even the most pessimistic of conditions and provide sufficient power to achieve our objectives under those circumstances which automatically means, that under less extreme circumstances, we would have more power than we require."[8] After carefully weighing all of these factors, Secretary McNamara said he came to the conclusion that the strategic force structure for the next five years would continue to consist of a mixed force of missiles and manned bombers.

Secretary McNamara reviewed for the committee the highlights of the improvements the administration was recommending in its strategic retaliatory forces for fiscal year 1963. First, he said, the planned buildup of the B-52 force to fourteen wings would be completed by the end of 1962. The Secretary emphasized that he was not prepared to procure another wing of B-52s, as urged by the Air Force and Congress, partly because it did not represent a significant added increment of capability. Even more important was the fact that manned bombers present soft and concentrated targets and they depend upon warning and quick response for their survival under nuclear attack. Hardening, dispersal, and mobility were preferable to warning and quick response, McNamara explained, and he disagreed with the requirement to commit bombers very early in a war rather than being able to hold them in reserve to be used in a controlled and deliberate way. Finally, McNamara pointed out, bombers were expensive; for the cost of $1 billion to deploy fully a wing of B-52s, 250 hardened and dispersed Minuteman missiles or six Polaris submarines could be purchased.[9] In addition to the B-52 fleet, the Secretary announced that by the end of the year two wings of B-58 supersonic medium bombers were to be operational. Finally, he announced that with the progressive buildup of the missile force the number of B-47 bombers in the fleet would be progressively reduced. McNamara saw no reason to request a further increase in the percentage (50 percent) of manned bombers on constant ground alert, nor did he recommend any change in the authorization for an airborne alert program over that of the previous year.

Continuing his prepared statement, McNamara announced that 12 squadrons of hardened and dispersed Minuteman missiles, totalling 600, were funded through the fiscal year ending in July 1962. The administration, he said, was requesting funds for four more squadrons in subsequent years. After considerable analysis of the rail-mobile Minuteman concept, the Secretary concluded that the costs outweighed its potential benefits and he would cancel further development. Through fiscal year 1962 a total of twenty-nine Polaris submarines were fully funded. McNamara proposed to add six more submarines in fiscal year 1963 and an additional six the following year, bringing the total to forty-one. He added: "Considering the number of Minuteman missiles and other strategic delivery vehicles which will be available over the next few years, it is difficult to justify a Polaris force of more than forty-one submarines. Finally, he added, the first six Polaris submarines would be equipped with A-1 missiles having an effective range of 1,500 nautical miles: the seventh through the nineteenth submarines would be equipped with the Polaris A-2; the twentieth and all subsequent submarines would be equipped with A-3 missiles with an effective range of 2,500 nautical miles.[10]

The essential superstructure of the Kennedy administration's strategy of controlled counterforce response in general war became clearer during a speech by Secretary McNamara to the American Bar Foundation in Chicago on February 17, 1962. The Secretary referred in his opening remarks to a speech delivered by Chairman Khrushchev in January 1961 at a meeting of the Soviet Communist party organization which was, in his judgment, "one of the most significant speeches of the past year, and it may prove to be one of the most important statements made by a world leader in the decade of the 60's."[11] The Soviet Premier had warned in his speech that a world war would be a rocket and nuclear war, the most destructive war in history. Even local wars were too dangerous, Khrushchev had continued, because they might grow into a thermonuclear rocket war. Only liberation wars and popular uprisings were admissible, and the Soviet leader strongly espoused their support. Clearly, declared Secretary McNamara, the Soviet decision to concentrate on wars of covert aggression was not taken in a power vacuum. Rather, he said, "It rests on the fact of United States nuclear power, which is able to survive a nuclear surprise attack and strike back with sufficient power to destroy the enemy target system."[12]

The Secretary conceded that within several years the growth of a Soviet intercontinental missile force would further complicate United States defense planning. However, he said, today not even the most boastful Russian rocket rattler asserts that the Soviet Union has the nuclear power to destroy the United States.

> It does have the power today to damage severely the nations of Western Europe, and we must anticipate that over the years the Soviets can, and undoubtedly will, produce weapons with sufficient range and destructive power to inflict increasingly severe damage on the United States, even while we ourselves retain a substantial margin of strategic power.[13]

What then, McNamara asked, should our military policy be in order to meet effectively the growing Soviet threat? Clearly, he stated, we must maintain our nuclear striking power as a realistic, effective deterrent against Soviet initiation of major wars. But, the Secretary emphasized, "We can no longer hope to have such a deterrent merely by maintaining a larger stockpile of nuclear weapons. Our weapons must be hardened, dispersed, and mobile so they can survive an enemy attack, and they must be equipped with the most sophisticated devices necessary to penetrate enemy defenses.[14]

Reviewing the increases in the nation's strategic forces funded by the administration during the previous twelve months at an added cost of $4 billion, McNamara continued:

> It is not enough . . . for us to have weapons that can survive an enemy attack and that can penetrate enemy defenses. In a world in which both sides may be capable of inflicting severe damage on each other, we must have machinery for the command and control of our forces, which is itself able to survive an attack and to apply the surviving forces in consonance with national security objectives. To this end we are providing alternate command posts at sea and in the air, with communications links to all elements of our strategic force.[15]

What was the main purpose of these measures? The Secretary explained:

> With this protected command and control system, our forces can be used in several different ways. We may have to retaliate with a single massive attack. Or we may be able to use our retaliatory forces to limit damage done to ourselves, and our allies, by knocking out the enemy's bases before he has had time to launch his second salvos. We may seek to terminate a war on favorable terms by using our forces as a bargaining weapon—by threatening further attack. In any case, our large reserve of protected firepower would give an enemy an incentive to avoid our cities and to stop a war. Our new policy gives us the flexibility to choose among several operational plans, but does not require that we make any advance commitment with respect to doctrine or targets. We shall be committed only to a system that gives us the ability to use our forces in a controlled and deliberate way, so as best to pursue the interests of the United States, our allies, and the rest of the free world.[16]

The remainder of the Secretary's address was devoted to a discussion of the need for a wider range of capabilities than just nuclear deterrent power to meet the kind of military challenges posed by the Soviet Union. Essentially, he argued for a greater balance between nuclear and non-nuclear forces which would put the United States in a position of being able to choose, coolly and deliberately, the level and kind of response most appropriate to any given situation. Of particular importance to a consideration of general nuclear war capabilities was the Secretary's insistence on greater flexibility in the choice of plans, options in the use of force, controlled and deliberate responses under any eventuality, and above all, discreet use of force and emphasis on early termination of conflict when and if an enemy was prepared to negotiate on terms satisfactory to the United States and its allies. Quite clearly the administration had embraced many of the theoretical and logical principles to underpin its general war strategy that had long been espoused by civilian defense intellectuals outside the government.

In early May 1962, Deputy Secretary of Defense Roswell Gilpatric publicly summarized the key implications of the administration's budgetary requests in terms of relative American–Soviet strategic postures predictable for 1965. "As a result of our Strategic Force Study," he said, "we now have in our planning, at least as far as 1965, a pretty definite force structure." The force structure would include nearly 950 bombers—a few remaining B-47s, but mostly B-52s and B-58s—carrying, hopefully, 800 air-to-surface missiles, including Skybolts as well as Hound Dogs. Some 1,500 ICBMs would be operational, including Atlases, Titans, Minuteman, and Polarises. Thus, said the Deputy Secretary, "We will have more than double the number of alert weapons that we have today by the end of 1965.... Those warheads will be carrying a yield, a megatonnage, of more than twice the striking power by 1965 that we have at the end of fiscal year 1962." Then Gilpatric concluded importantly, "That is why we feel that no matter what the Soviets can do, based on the intelligence we have today, that we will maintain the margin of superiority that we possess today."[17]

In effect, then, the Kennedy administration decided, with the full knowledge that the nation already possessed a large lead over the Soviet Union in strategic delivery vehicles, to push ahead with a large share of the missile construction planned by the Eisenhower administration—at a time when an apparent missile gap existed—and also to add several hundred more missiles to those previously requested of Congress.

The Policy of Controlled Response

In a keynote address to a conference on arms control at the University of Michigan on December 19, 1962, John T. McNaughton, a high Defense Department official, spoke of the contributions of current military planning to national security and stressed the compatibility of such planning for arms control objectives. Citing the reciprocal fear of surprise attack as one of the serious issues of the age of quick-response missile systems, he went on to discuss in some detail the essential elements of the administration's strategy of controlled and flexible response. The United States, said McNaughton, was emphasizing the survivability or invulnerability of its strategic forces and, as a consequence, was shifting reliance for the nation's security away from relatively vulnerable bombers toward widely dispersed and hardened missiles such as the land-based Minuteman. He announced that the first twenty Minuteman missiles had become operational just a week before. To complement the Minuteman and to assist in reducing effectively the advantage of an enemy first strike, McNaughton stated that nine Polaris submarines were in service, each carrying sixteen missiles. Five additional submarines were launched but not yet commissioned. As a result, he announced, the President had reported early in the week, "that at present and in the foreseeable future the United States can be confident that its forces will ride out any attack. The attacker could be sure that the response of the United States would be swift, but not so swift that the President would lack time to evaluate the attack and match the United States response to the factual situation."[18]

Another key aspect of assuring deliberate and controlled response under conflict conditions was, continued McNaughton, the preservation of the chain of command which would insure continuous and virtually instantaneous communication between the President, as Commander in Chief, and the military commands and from commanders to forces. The increased dangers of the nuclear age, he stressed, made it essential that the nation's command and control system fulfill two purposes: (a) to assure that the United States was capable of reacting instantly and selectively when necessary; (b) to guarantee that combat forces would not be used when they were not supposed to be used. Only a command and control system capable of great flexibility and one able to assemble, evaluate, and utilize accurate and complex information would, said McNaughton, properly meet the challenge of general nuclear war.[19]

The Command and Control System

Not long after the Kennedy administration assumed responsibility for the nation's security, it began to stress the urgency of attaining a command and control system capable of withstanding even the worst exigencies of general nuclear war. During 1961 a special study was conducted to ascertain the requirements for both the civilian and military command and control networks. It was perfectly clear without much surveying that a large number of the major command and control and communications centers of this nation were extremely vulnerable to massive ICBM attacks. The practical alternatives appeared to be hardening, concealment, and mobility.[20]

The first step toward improving the nation's command and control capabilities was taken in 1961 with the establishment of SAC's airborne command and control system. Specially modified KC-135 aircraft kept aloft continuously were able to maintain constant contact with the National Military Command Center, the Air Force Command Post in Washington, and the Strategic Air Command's underground and alternate command and control network.[21]

Testifying before the Senate Armed Services Committee in 1963, Secretary McNamara reviewed the efforts made since 1961 to make the military forces fully responsive to civilian control. The command and control system of the Strategic Air Command, he stressed, was adequate to fulfill the mission in peacetime and during the prestrike phase of nuclear war. He warned, however, that "because this system is only partially hardened and thus vulnerable to enemy ICBMs we cannot count on it functioning after an initial nuclear attack. Therefore, alternative systems must be provided for the postattack phase."[22]

During 1962 the Department of Defense had initiated the development and procurement of an airborne element of the Post-Attack Command and Control System (PACCS). Explained Secretary McNamara, "This airborne element consists of specially equipped KC-135 command post aircraft, and B-47's modified and equipped as communications relay aircraft."[23] By early 1963, most of the command post aircraft and all of the communications relay aircraft were in operation. All command post aircraft were scheduled to be in operation by June 1963.

In mid-February 1963, Secretary McNamara reported the following progress toward a secure command and control network:

> We now have a world-wide military command and control system (WWMCCS) in-being or in the process of implementation, both on the national level and within our military forces. The national military command system, provides intelligence and communications for the high level command, including widely separated and protected landsites, dispersed command ships, and aircraft that can remain airborne for extended periods of time.[24]

Damage Limitation and City Avoidance Strategies

Another fundamental principle of the Kennedy defense policy was to seek to limit damage to the United States in the event deterrence failed and nuclear war occurred. As pointed out by John McNaughton, the measures being taken

> . . . are designed to assure that the United States forces can be used or not used, as the case may be, in a controlled and deliberate way, subject at all times to the direction of the highest civilian authority. Such flexibility means that the United States will not be faced with "all or nothing" decisions. Though it will be capable of all-out attack, the nation will have a much wider choice, so that it can pick the strategy which is best for the United States and not just worst for the enemy. And, perhaps most important, command and control flexibility means there will be a way to stop a war before all the destruction of which both sides are capable has been wrought.[25]

An important corollary to a damage-limiting strategy and one on which McNaughton placed great stress during his Iowa address was the tactic of city avoidance. One of the objectives of a controlled response strategy was to limit the impact of nuclear war on civilian populations. As the Defense official explained it, "It is almost inevitable that military forces will be objects of attack during war; it is not inevitable that *civilian* populations will be targets—at least, not if some efforts are made to provide for the possibility of separating anti-military and anti-civilian attacks."[26]

McNaughton emphasized that the administration was taking two basic steps to prevent wanton destruction of civilian population. First, a major effort was underway to separate geographically the nation's major deterrent weapons systems from its cities. Second, the President was giving his support to a civil defense program capable of saving tens of millions of lives from the hazards of fallout if there should be a war. There was no guarantee that an enemy would refrain from striking American cities, McNaughton conceded, but measures to provide for a city avoidance targeting option—with a reserve of firepower and targeting flexibility—would give an enemy a strong incentive to confine his attacks primarily to military targets.

From the time of the announcement by the administration that it intended to pursue a city avoidance doctrine, critics had challenged it on several grounds. First, the critics asserted that city avoidance must equal a disarming first strike. McNaughton rejoined, "This is wrong. The United States does not think in terms of hitting first." The United States, he said, was merely affirming that whatever other targets may be available and whoever initiates the use of nuclear weapons, this nation will be in a position to refrain from attacking cities. A second criticism raised was even more basic: a city avoidance strategy makes nuclear war more likely by reducing the expected damage and so is contrary to the objectives of both arms control and deterrence. To this, McNaughton replied; "But is this so? Who really knows? Uncertainties probably dominate the calculations. The resulting damage under any strategy would be so great that nuclear war would be elected only in the case of the most extreme provocation."[27]

McNaughton cautioned against attributing too much to the city avoidance doctrine. Nothing, he said, could guarantee that the Soviets would reason as we do. Reason might not prevail in times of extreme crisis. Nevertheless, he concluded:

> The main point is that the United States must have a strategy of one kind or another with respect to targeting cities, and the city avoidance strategy appears to be a move in the right direction—a move which could reduce the damage should war occur. It is an arms restraint the success of which does not depend upon negotiation in the normal sense and one which incidentally stands to benefit both sides.[28]

United States Policy and NATO

In May 1962, Secretary McNamara participated in a regular annual meeting of the North Atlantic Council held in Athens. His remarks to the Council were classified, but it is known that he delivered to the NATO allies a very clear and forthright statement of the Kennedy administration's general war policy and strategy. According to a source close to the Pentagon, the pretext for the Secretary's address was the prevailing feeling in Europe that nuclear weapons offered a panacea. McNamara held that the nuclear deterrent was a highly specialized and therefore limited instrument of policy. Overdependence on nuclear weapons should deterrence fail would guarantee casualties running into millions. At Athens the Secretary sought to persuade the allies that balanced conventional and nuclear capabilities offered the greatest hope of avoiding war or at least of holding damage to lower levels.[29]

In mid-June Secretary McNamara returned home to Ann Arbor to deliver the main address at the University of Michigan commencement exercises. It is widely accepted that the Secretary's speech was essentially the same speech, but devoid of its classified aspects, that he had given at Athens a month before. In his opening remarks, McNamara said he wanted to talk about some of the problems of maintaining a free community in the world today. Of special importance, he said, were the forces and traditions that bound together the United States and the countries of Western Europe. Europe, continued McNamara, had made in a brief ten years a remarkable recovery from the ashes of destruction at the end of World War II and now possessed a new sense of confidence. And yet, the challenge of forces unleashed in the postwar years, such as the population explosion, the accelerated pace of science and technology, the proliferation of new nation-states, and the Sino-Soviet drive for world domination, made difficult at best the achievement by Europeans and Americans of a system of peaceful world order. Movement toward the common objective could not be realized, said the Secretary, unless we moved from strength, part of which must be military strength. He emphasized that military strength was not the principal means of achieving the kind of world we seek, but was "a shield to prevent any other nation from using its military strength."[30]

The United States alone, said McNamara, cannot provide the military power base required to meet the full spectrum of challenges confronting the free world. And since this nation's security is inseparable from the rest of the free world, reliance on a system of alliances becomes necessary, the most important of which is the North Atlantic Treaty Organization. Soon after its establishment, Western statesmen recognized that the effective defense of Western Europe would not be possible over the long term without a major commitment by the United States to that defense. As the alliance grew the task of defending the treaty area concomitantly increased in scope, size, and complexity.

Today, Secretary McNamara stressed, divisive forces are at work within NATO which are potentially corrosive of the strength and unity of the alliance. For example, he said, it is often argued that the very success of Western European economic progress has reduced the need to rely on the United States' share in its defense. Others contend that the increasing vulnerability of the United States to nuclear attack reduces confidence everywhere that the United States will come to Europe's assistance if attacked. Finally, said the Secretary, it is sometimes argued that nuclear capabilities alone are effective in meeting a growing enemy nuclear threat and that independent national nuclear forces are sufficient to protect the nations of Europe.

Rejecting all of these arguments as mistaken, McNamara said he thought it was worthwhile to expose the views of the United States on key defense issues as they had recently been presented to the allies. Clearly, he stressed, a central military issue facing NATO is the role of nuclear strategy. Considering the current balance of nuclear power existing between the Western allies and the Soviet bloc forces, which the Secretary believed the United States could confidently expect to maintain in the years ahead, a surprise nuclear attack was simply not a rational act for an enemy, nor would it be rational for an enemy to initiate the use of nuclear weapons as an outgrowth of a limited engagement in Europe or elsewhere. Nevertheless, the fact that no nation could rationally take steps leading to nuclear war does not guarantee that a nuclear war cannot take place as a result of misjudgment of each other's intentions. Thus, McNamara said, "For our part, we feel we and our NATO allies must frame our strategy with this terrible contingency, however remote, in mind. Simply ignoring the problem is not going to make it go away."[31]

Since the possibility of nuclear war could not be ruled out, Secretary McNamara, in a now-famous statement, summarized United States military objectives as follows:

> The United States has come to the conclusion that to the extent feasible, basic military strategy in a possible general nuclear war should be approached in much the same way that more conventional military operations have been regarded in the past. That is to say, principal military objectives, in the event of a nuclear war stemming from a major attack on the Alliance, should be the destruction of the enemy's military forces, not of his civilian population.[32]

Given the strength and purpose of the alliance forces it would be possible, the Secretary said, to retain, even in the face of a massive surprise attack, sufficient reserve striking power to destroy an enemy society if driven to it. In essence, he said, "we are giving a possible opponent the strongest imaginable incentive to refrain from striking our own cities."[33]

Contributions to deterrence and to the hope of deterring attack on civil societies do not come cheap, the Secretary continued. The United States, he said, planned to spend during fiscal year 1963 some $15 billion on its nuclear weapons to insure their adequacy. In the Secretary's judgment there was no substitute for this investment and he stressed that "relatively weak national nuclear forces with enemy cities as their targets are not likely to be sufficient to perform even the function of deterrence." Such forces if they are small tend to be vulnerable, inaccurate, and thus easily overcome by a major adversary, possibly in a preemptive first strike. In the event of war, the Secretary continued, "the use of such a force against the cities of a major nuclear power would be tantamount to suicide, whereas its employment against significant military targets would have a negligible effect on the outcome of the conflict." In short, he emphasized, "limited nuclear capabilities, operating independently, are dangerous, expensive, prone to obsolesence, and lacking in credibility as a deterrent."[34]

In his concluding remarks, McNamara made clear that the strategy he was proposing magnified the importance of unity of planning, concentration of executive authority, and central direction. Competing and conflicting strategies to meet the contingency of nuclear war should be avoided, he said, and "We are convinced that a general nuclear war target system is indivisible . . . if, despite all our efforts, nuclear war should occur, our best hope lies in conducting a centrally controlled campaign against all of the enemy's vital nuclear capabilities, while retaining reserve forces, all centrally controlled." After reassuring the NATO allies that the United States fully intended to carry out its treaty commitments if Western Europe were attacked, he stressed; "In short, we have undertaken the nuclear defense of NATO on a global basis."[35]

The Ann Arbor speech was, among other things, a declaration by the Kennedy administration in favor of a strategy of controlled counterforce general war, and a rejection of a nuclear strategy for this nation and its allies based on "minimum" or "finite" deterrence.[36] Some defense analysts—primarily civilian—in this country apparently concluded from the President's early speeches and statements that the United States was progressively shifting away from a strategy based on a major counterforce capability—one strongly preferred by the Air Force professionals and most lay strategists—to one oriented toward minimum deterrence.[37] In fact, however, President Kennedy inherited a counterforce doctrine from the Eisenhower administration, albeit without the city avoidance option which Secretary McNamara stressed at Athens and Ann Arbor. It was difficult for the administration to adopt any other strategy. During the campaign of 1960, President Kennedy stressed the inadequacy of the nation's missile forces. By late 1961, the administration was confident it had inherited a large superiority in nuclear long-range bombers and was steadily increasing its lead in intercontinental ballistics missiles. In addition, strong domestic pressures militated against the President's dropping the counterforce doctrine.[38]

Policy of City Avoidance Attacked

The support given by the Kennedy administration to the no cities option of a strategy of controlled general nuclear war quickly evoked criticism by defense analysts on a number of grounds. At the same time vigorous efforts were made by supporters of the no cities option to explain why the United States, given its preponderance of nuclear strength over the Soviet Union, should logically embrace the tactic of conducting strategic nuclear operations without bombing cities.

Writing in the July 30, 1962, issue of *New Republic,* Michael Brower, a professor at M.I.T., attacked the no cities option, characterizing it as the no cities "panacea." He compared the no cities option to the theory of limited nuclear warfare in which the likelihood of keeping the war limited to the immediate battlefield was highly problematical. In a no cities war, said Brower, the Soviet Union and the United States would have to be able to distinguish with their missiles between the bases and the cities of the opponent. Because such military targets as airfields, defensive weapon emplacements, and command, control, and communications systems often are located in close proximity to cities, it seemed inconceivable to Brower that unintended attacks on civilians and nonmilitary targets could be avoided. As a result, the nation attacked would not be able to distinguish the intent of the attacker.

Another complex problem, Brower argued, in addition to assuring firm and continuous command and control over strategic forces in nuclear war, was that of attempting to maintain timely and unbroken communications between the antagonists under the chaotic conditions of a nuclear exchange. To Brower it was more likely, as Jerome Weisner had suggested, that, "in conflict situations . . . statements of the antagonists are evaluated not in terms of the intended meanings, but rather in terms of the most threatening alternatives."[39] For example, in the age of long-range jet bombers and missiles, is it imaginable that either side could accept a pause in the conflict for negotiation without assuming that the other side would use the time to gain maximum advantage?

Also, said Brower, even if the United States refrained from striking Soviet cities, would the Soviets in turn avoid striking our cities? In his judgment the no cities option would be attractive only to a nation which had a well-developed counterforce weapon system. Such a system, for example, requires several missiles for every enemy missile. It is clearly impossible for both the United States and the Soviet Union to possess such superiority simultaneously. Thus, Brower contended, "so long as the U.S.S.R. remains weaker than the U.S., it is unlikely to adopt a no cities strategy." Finally, Brower asked: suppose that nuclear war does occur and American cities are spared, how many people would die nevertheless? Drawing on statistics developed ostensibly by the Department of Defense, Brower stated that casualties would range between 30 and possibly 150 million people, assuming that no civil defense program existed. Assuming even that adequate shelter spaces existed for 235 million people, the Defense Department predicted that a no cities war would result in between 4 and 27 million fatalities.[40]

Brower and others insisted that the no cities doctrine was inextricably linked to a counterforce first-strike strategy, despite denials by administration officials. All talk about a no cities second strike is realistic, Brower argued, only if the Soviets are able to launch a no cities first strike. As long as they remain weaker than the United States they are highly unlikely to contemplate such a strike. No matter what margin of superiority the United States may hold over the Soviet Union in the future, Brower pointed out that the Soviet Union would almost certainly deploy hardened, concealed, and dispersed weapons systems, an increasing number of which would predictably survive an attack by American forces. Then, he asked, would a threat by the United States to strike first remain credible? According to Brower:

> The fact is that our first-strike capability can remain effective for only a very few years more (assuming that it is still today)—unless, of course, you assume that the Soviets, having absorbed a no cities strike that leaves millions of Russians dead, will be more interested in saving what is left of Russia than in destroying America, and will therefore hit a few U.S. bases and negotiate a peace treaty.[41]

Although the Kennedy administration refrained from a vigorous defense of the no cities doctrine and apparently decided to abandon further initiatives on its behalf following much negative and critical reaction to Secretary McNamara's Ann Arbor speech, efforts were made by partisans of the doctrine outside the government to defend its logic and reasonableness. A good example of such defense was made by Morton Halperin, a research associate at the Harvard Center for International Affairs and consultant to the Department of Defense, who rebutted in detail the attack on the no cities doctrine by Michael Brower in the October 8, 1962, issue of the *New Republic*. Inasmuch as the McNamara speech had apparently been widely misunderstood, wrote Halperin, and had thus been the object of unfair criticism, he proposed to outline what it seemed to him the Secretary was saying.

In his Ann Arbor speech Secretary McNamara implied, said Halperin, that "whether the U.S. went first or second in a strategic nuclear war, it would not attack Soviet cities unless the Soviets had previously destroyed American cities." No good military reason existed to target civilian population centers in the event of strategic nuclear war. In fact, Halperin stated, "It is very difficult to argue that one prefers a strategy whereby the U.S. would attempt to kill a large number of Soviet citizens even though this did not reduce the expected damage to the United States."[42] Mr. McNamara, he said, had come to the conclusion

> that no matter who struck first the U.S. was, by avoiding Soviet cities and holding forces in reserve which could devastate almost all of the Soviet Union in the event that Western cities came under attack, giving the strongest possible incentive to the Soviets to avoid attacking Western cities.[43]

Such a strategy would offer the greatest hope of preserving the fabric of Western society in the event of nuclear war, and yet the Secretary recognized that nuclear war would be an unprecedented catastrophe whether or not cities were attacked.

The most fundamental misunderstanding of the no cities doctrine enunciated by Secretary McNamara appeared to be, said Halperin, that it was viable only in a situation where the United States has vastly superior strategic forces and strikes first. In 1962, administration officials conceded that the United States had massive strategic superiority over the Soviet strategic force and was able to hold forces in reserve with which to threaten city destruction. Under such circumstances, Halperin declared, the Soviets were unlikely publicly to accept a no cities doctrine. However, he continued, "even assuming that the United States struck first in a well coordinated attack and the Soviets responded with a no-cities counterforce second strike, the collateral damage to the U.S. and its NATO allies would be great—so great that the Soviets could be confident that the U.S. would not attack out of the blue." Thus, Halperin reasoned, the Soviets ought to fear that the West might launch a strategic nuclear attack if heavy pressure were put on Berlin or the central European front. Especially, he said, "If the alternatives were conventional defeat or else a massive use of tactical nuclear weapons which would destroy Western Europe, the U.S. might prefer to attempt a no cities strategic war." Logically, therefore, the Soviets ought to have a strong incentive to avoid maximum pressure on the West. In the absence of such pressure the Soviets ought to be confident that the United States would be deterred from a first strike. And, finally, the Soviets should have no reason to preempt unless they plan a major provocation which seems almost certain to trigger American retaliation.[44]

It was possible nevertheless, Halperin conceded, that nuclear war might occur by accident or miscalculation. Even in such a bizarre event, he stressed, the Soviets would share with the United States an interest in avoiding destruction and bringing the war to an end as quickly as possible. The reason for this was, Halperin conjectured:

> The extension of the war to city targets would involve much greater destruction in the Soviet Union than in the U.S. and Western Europe, whereas confining the war to strategic targets would probably result in greater civil damage in Western Europe and the U.S. than in the Soviet Union. Thus, even if a war should come with the present strategic imbalance, the Soviets would have a massive incentive to fight a no cities war, although they may not acknowledge this in advance.[45]

In the event that the Soviets decided for one reason or another that they should build better protected and larger strategic forces, the policy of avoiding cities would continue to be in the interests of both sides. Under circumstances where both sides had substantial numbers of invulnerable forces, neither the United States nor the Soviet Union, whether it struck first or second, could hope to destroy most of its opponent's forces and thereby escape serious damage. According to Halperin, the point Secretary McNamara tried to make at Ann Arbor was that it was preferable to hold a large part of our strategic forces in reserve rather than to attack cities simply because there were no other targets to hit. Thus, observed Halperin, the possession of invulnerable forces by both sides could slow the pace of a nuclear war if it happened, in contrast to the widely prevailing view that the outcome of a thermonuclear war would be decided during a decisive phase of very short duration.[46]

Perhaps the most incisive criticism leveled against the no cities doctrine was that there would be no suitable counterforce targets remaining for a force which had to strike second. While admitting that a counterforce first strike would unquestionably be more effective, Halperin pointed out that numerous critical second-strike counterforce targets, such as airfields, staging bases, missile sites having a re-fire capability, defenses, communications, or even tactical military targets, would remain following a Soviet first strike. Halperin did not explain how American bombers and missiles were to distinguish between empty missile holes and abandoned bomber bases and those still active.

As for the argument that a counterforce doctrine placed such importance on striking first that it increased the likelihood of a preemptive war, Halperin stressed that "it is not the particular strategy of one side or the other which is a major determinant of the danger of preemption, but rather the vulnerability of strategic forces." The fact, continued Halperin, that the United States has moved steadily into a position of having a large part of its forces relatively invulnerable to a surprise attack has substantially reduced the need for preemption on its part. Under present conditions the Soviets would have little incentive to preempt because "even a well-executed preemptive counterforce attack would use up their arsenal and leave them disarmed." The United States, argued Halperin, enjoying a relatively superior position, is hardly motivated to preempt but has every reason to use its superiority to force the Soviets to withdraw and seek peace in lesser conflict situations.[47]

It was frequently asked by critics of the no cities doctrine, Halperin said, why one side would waste its missiles even in a first strike against the invulnerable forces of the other side? He suggested a relevant question in return, why either side would waste its missile forces in an attack on cities which would only lead to great devastation in its own country. In Halperin's judgment, "the Administration is saying that the avoidance of city destruction will reduce the catastrophic nature of nuclear war and increase the likelihood of it being ended before all the weapons on both sides are used."[48]

The Strategic Implications of the Cuban Missile Crisis

The Bay of Pigs fiasco in April 1961 had virtually no strategic implications, in the sense that events during this incident in no way threatened to engulf the United States and the Soviet Union in general nuclear war. The Cuban missile crisis in the fall of 1962, however, had important strategic implications, and, during a period of great tension and uncertainty, it seemed to Americans and people everywhere that the world might experience its first general nuclear war. In retrospect, it seems clear that the decisive nuclear superiority possessed by this nation combined with overwhelming conventional superiority in the immediate conflict area converged to forestall the boldest and most reckless gambit of Premier Khrushchev's career.

It appears that the Cuban missile gamble was concocted in July of 1962 during a visit to Moscow by Raul Castro, Minister of the Cuban Armed Forces. Whose idea it was to place Soviet offensive nuclear missiles on foreign soil for the first time and in the hands of a leader of somewhat less than total reliability is not entirely clear.[49] After the crisis had passed, the leaders of both nations involved sought to place the responsibility for taking the initiative on the other. Curiously enough, had the Soviets succeeded in installing and maintaining the planned medium- and intermediate-range missiles in Cuba, the United States would nevertheless have retained at least a two-to-one superiority in nuclear weapons targeted against the Soviet Union. The principal gain to the Soviets would have been political and psychological, and the probe was obviously designed as a supreme test of United States resolve and intentions.

Testifying before a House Subcommittee of the Committee on Appropriations in February 1963, Secretary McNamara told the members, "Up to the spring of 1962, the Soviet Union had supplied the Cuban Army with great quantities of conventional weapons and supplies ranging from pistols and rifles to heavy artillery and medium tanks. Mig-15 aircraft, Mig-17, -19, and -21 aircraft and helicopters had been provided to the Cuban Air Force. Motor torpedo boats and coastal patrol vessels of the Kronstadt class had been delivered to the Cuban Navy."[50] During the period from July 29 to August 5, an unusually large number of Soviet ships unloaded cargo and passengers at the Cuban ports of Havana and Mariel. By mid-August suspicion began to mount within the intelligence community that the Soviet Union was introducing and deploying surface-to-air missile systems in Cuba.

On August 29 a reconnaissance mission was flown over Cuba which resulted in positive identification being established of a surface-to-air missile site (SAM-2 site). According to Secretary McNamara, "Two of these were specifically located and six others tentatively located in western Cuba. A short-range coastal defense missile was identified in the third suspect area."[51] Each subsequent flight between August 29 and October 7 revealed new surface-to-air missile sites and three additional cruise missile sites. Still, as McNamara testified, up to that time, there had been no evidence to prove an offensive capability. All of the missile systems that were located up to that point were defensive in nature.

Meanwhile more and more reports were being received in Washington from refugees about nuclear installations in Cuba, although no one could be sure whether the sources in Cuba could tell a surface-to-air missile from a surface-to-surface missile. Lacking photographic verification, the intelligence community on October 4 recommended a reconnaissance flight over western Cuba. On October 14 a Strategic Air Command U-2 was directed to fly a photographic mission over the suspect San Cristobal missile site. The results of this flight established positive evidence of Soviet ballistic missiles on the island. After October 14 the Strategic Air Command, the Navy, and the Tactical Air Command flew numerous and continuous sorties at high and low levels over every part of the island that might be suspect.

At an extraordinary meeting in strictest secrecy at 11:45 A.M. on October 16th, a group, later to become known as the Executive Committee of the National Security Council, assembled in the Cabinet Room. During the next several days the Executive Committee debated possible courses of action ranging from doing nothing immediately to sending an emissary to Khrushchev to demand that he remove the offending missiles, arraigning the Soviet Union and Cuba before the United Nations Security Council, placing an embargo on all military shipments to Cuba and enforcing it by a naval blockade, delivering a surprise attack to eliminate the missile sites by pinpoint bombing, and finally, but not seriously considered, mounting an invasion of Cuba to destroy the sites and possibly overthrow Castro.[52]

A series of Executive Committee meetings was held during the week of October 15 through 19, the debate among members being both vigorous and searching. For a time the decision seemed to hang on whether the United States would institute a blockade or execute a surgical air strike to destroy the offending medium-range ballistic missiles. Because a blockade was technically an act of war, it was decided that a quarantine was a better way of imposing sanctions. On Saturday, October 20, in an afternoon session, the President presided over the Executive Committee meeting, which, as it turned out, proved to be the final debate. According to Schlesinger's account: "McNamara impressively presented the case for the blockade. The military, with some civilian support, argued for the strike. Stevenson spoke with force about the importance of a political program, the President agreeing in principle but disagreeing with his specific proposals. A straw vote indicated eleven for the quarantine, six for the strike.[53]

At seven o'clock on Monday evening, October 22, President Kennedy told a nationwide television and radio audience:

> The government, as promised, has maintained the closest surveillance of the Soviet military build-up on the island of Cuba. Within the past week, unmistakable evidence has established the fact that a series of offensive missile sites is now in preparation on that imprisoned island. The purpose of these bases can be none other than to provide a nuclear strike capability against the Western hemisphere. . . .

> Several of them include medium-range ballistic missiles, capable of carrying a nuclear warhead for a distance of more than 1,000 nautical miles. Each of these missiles, in short, is capable of striking Washington, D.C., the Panama Canal, Cape Canaveral, Mexico City, or any other city in the Southeastern part of the United States, in Central America or in the Caribbean area.
>
> Additional sites, not yet completed, appear to be designed for intermediate-range ballistic missiles—capable of travelling more than twice as far—and thus, capable of striking most of the major cities in the western hemisphere, ranging as far north as Hudson's Bay, Canada, and as far south as Lima, Peru. In addition jet bombers, capable of carrying nuclear weapons, are now being uncrated and assembled in Cuba, while the necessary air bases are being prepared.[54]

The President's voice was calm and firm and his expression sober as he set forth the evidence without emotion. He warned the Soviet Union that, "It shall be the policy of this nation to regard any nuclear missile launched from Cuba against any nation in the Western Hemisphere as an attack by the Soviet Union on the United States, requiring a full retaliatory response upon the Soviet Union." President Kennedy called upon Chairman Khrushchev "to halt and eliminate this clandestine, reckless and provocative threat to world peace and to stable relations between our two nations."[55]

The morning of the day the President addressed the nation, the Joint Chiefs of Staff issued a quarantine-planning directive to the Atlantic fleet. Air Force missile crews stationed at bases in this country and overseas received maximum alert orders. As of October 22, 156 ICBMs were operationally ready for firing, and all crews went on a seventy-hour work week. At noon on Monday, General Thomas S. Power, Commander of the Strategic Air Command, issued the order from his underground headquarters at Offutt Air Force Base to begin the dispersal of SAC's B-47 bombers to forty civilian airports scattered around the nation. No chances were taken with a possible Soviet missile attack against the permanent strategic bases. The same day the SAC Commander ordered his B-52 bomber alert force to initiate an airborne alert. Said one commentator, "It was the biggest airborne alert in SAC's history. As one B-52 landed, another would take its place in the sky. Every plane on the ground carried its full load of fuel and bombs, ready to take off on fifteen minutes' warning.[56]

Following the President's message, the world entered a period of tension such as it had never experienced in the nuclear age. Tension continued to mount during the next several days as Soviet ships moved closer to the quarantine area; there was no evidence that the Soviets intended to halt the preparation of the missile sites. At one point, they seemed to be increasing the terms for a settlement by suggesting that they would remove their missiles from Cuba and offer a non-aggression pledge in return for the removal of American missiles from Turkey. For a time it appeared that direct force would have to be employed against the Cuban missile sites to remove the threat that Premier Khrushchev appeared reluctant to eliminate. Finally, just as the world appeared to be entering its darkest hour, Radio Moscow announced on the morning of October 28 that an important message would be broadcast to the United States within the hour. On schedule the announcer in Moscow began reading a letter from Premier Khrushchev—the tenth letter to have passed between the White House and the Kremlin in seven days—the key paragraph of which said:

> In order to eliminate as rapidly as possible the conflict which endangers the cause of peace, to give an assurance to all people who crave peace, and to reassure the American people who, I am certain, also want peace, as do the people of the Soviet Union, the Soviet government in addition to earlier instructions on the discontinuation of further work on weapons construction sites, has given a new order to dismantle the arms which you described as offensive, and to crate and return them to the Soviet Union.[57]

Following a meeting with the Executive Committee before noon, President Kennedy drafted a quick acceptance statement to Premier Khrushchev, and the major crisis was passed.

Secretary of Defense McNamara testified before the House Subcommittee on Department of Defense Appropriations during the first week of February 1963 that "there were nine offensive missile sites completed or under construction in Cuba by October 22, with a projected total of 36 launching positions—24 MRBM and 12

IRBM."[58] In all, the Secretary told the subcommittee, the Soviet Union introduced into Cuba eight categories of modern offensive and defensive weapon systems, which he was confident had been maintained under the direct control of Soviet forces in Cuba. The number of Soviet soldiers and technicians estimated to have been deployed in support of these systems was about 22,000.[59]

The IL-28 bombers delivered to Cuba proved to be a stumbling block to the final settlement of the Cuban crisis until mid-November. Although none of the forty-two unassembled bombers delivered to Cuba ever reached full operational status, seven did reach final assembly and were classified as flyable. These medium-range bombers were capable of striking targets in Southeastern United States and Central America. Under sustained pressure from President Kennedy, Premier Khrushchev finally agreed to disassemble the bombers and remove them from Cuban soil.

In the aftermath of the Cuban missile crisis a number of theories were advanced as possible explanations for the bizarre decision by Khrushchev to risk placing offensive missiles in Cuba. According to Sorensen the theory accepted by the President was that Khrushchev believed that the American people were too timid to risk nuclear war and too legalistically inclined to make distinctions between our overseas missile bases and bases in Cuba. Thus, the United States was likely to do nothing but protest and would therefore appear weak and irresolute to the world, causing our allies to doubt our word and seek accommodations with the Soviets. "This was a probe," said Sorensen, "a test of America's will to resist. If it succeeded, he would move in a more important place—in West Berlin or with new pressure on our overseas bases—with missiles staring down our throats from Cuba."[60]

Another plausible theory was that the Soviets realized they could no longer benefit from the fictional missile gap, which by now had been exposed by United States defense officials. As Castro clamored more and more insistently for military protection—magnifying the threat of an American invasion—the Soviets rationalized that by placing some of their older, more plentiful medium- and intermediate-range missiles in Cuba, they would be provided with a cheap and immediate substitute for the newer, more expensive ICBMs. At the same time, this tactic would permit the Soviet Union to stretch out its ICBM program and so ease the pressure on its own resources.[61] The number of missiles targeted on the United States capable of bypassing our missile warning system would pose a threat in particular to the nuclear bomber bases requiring fifteen minutes ground warning in order to launch successfully. Thus, concludes Roger Hilsman, "The motive for the decision was strategic in the broad sense that a general improvement in the Soviet military position would affect the entire political context, strengthening their hand for dealing with the whole range of problems facing them—and unanticipated problems as well.[62]

Other less plausible motives included the notion that if the United States did respond by an attack on Cuba, the allies would be divided, the UN outraged, the Latin Americans more anti-American than ever, and our forces and energies diverted while Khrushchev moved swiftly in on Berlin. Another theory was that Khrushchev regarded a Soviet satellite in the Western Hemisphere of great importance in order to advance his drive for expansion and win another round in his contest with Mainland China. Thus, Cuba could not be allowed to fall. It appeared that the United States was preparing to attack Cuba, and Khrushchev was determined that the internal collapse of Cuba must be prevented at all costs. Finally, some observers felt that Khrushchev was aware of Cuba's sensitive role in domestic American politics; thus, the Premier intended to use these bases in a summit or UN confrontation with the President to bargain for a Soviet settlement of Berlin or the removal of American overseas bases.[63]

The day after Premier Khrushchev announced that the missiles would be dismantled and removed from Cuba, the President in a reflective mood told Arthur Schlesinger that the crisis had three distinctive features: "It took place in a area where we enjoyed local conventional superiority, where Soviet national security was not directly engaged and where the Russians lacked a case which they could plausibly sustain before the world."[64] All in all, the Cuban confrontation gave the administration some basis for believing that the controlled use of force and a strategy based on multiple options had many merits. According to Kaufmann:

If the Cuban experience is any guide, it would appear to strengthen deterrence by putting [a] readily usable force at the President's disposal and forcing the opponent to share more equitably the responsibility for nuclear war. And if deterrence should fail, it offers the hope that force can still be used in a controlled and deliberate way. In an era of transition and danger, it is doubtful that any alternative defense strategy can offer much more than that.[65]

Administration Policy after the Cuban Missile Crisis

Partly because of the adverse public reaction to his Ann Arbor speech and in the wake of the Cuban crisis, Secretary McNamara granted an exclusive interview in December of 1962 to Stewart Alsop. This was the same interview, mentioned in Chapter 2, in which McNamara officially laid the "missile gap" to rest. Alsop opened the interview with a direct reference to the Ann Arbor speech and asked Secretary McNamara whether in his judgment ". . . the price of any kind of nuclear war is so high that the nuclear weapon is not a rational instrument of national policy?" The Secretary replied that to base one's answer on the premise that nuclear war is unthinkable is in fact to have no military foundation at all for national policy. Of course, Secretary McNamara continued, "no sane man wants nuclear war, or any kind of war. But war *has* to be conceivable in support of vital national interests. Otherwise you have no real national power." The Secretary reiterated his conviction that the United States possessed sufficient nuclear power to be able to withstand a full surprise attack and yet respond so effectively as to destroy totally an aggressor. He stressed the point also that this nation had sufficient nuclear power to be able to respond by hitting only military targets.[66]

Alsop asked Secretary McNamara whether the no cities or counterforce response was an important aspect of the administration's new strategy. The Secretary stressed that the no cities doctrine was solely an option in a series of alternatives and said he felt the press had overplayed this part of his Ann Arbor speech. McNamara assured Alsop that he wanted to be absolutely certain that he had other options as well.

The questioning by Alsop then turned to what in retrospect was the most important and controversial part of the interview. "Surely," said Alsop, "we must assume that the time will come when the other side will have a sure second-strike capability—solid-fuel missiles, hardened bases, and all the rest of it." Secretary McNamara's reply bears repeating *in extenso:*

> Yes, and that raises an interesting point. I believe myself that a counterforce strategy is most likely to apply in circumstances in which both sides have the capability of surviving a first strike and retaliating selectively. This is a highly unpredictable business, of course. But today, following a surprise attack on us, we would still have the power to respond with overwhelming force, and they would not then have the capability of a further strike. In this situation, given the highly irrational act of an attempted first strike against us, such a strike seems most likely to take the form of an all-out attack on both military targets and population centers. This is why a nuclear exchange confined to military targets seems more possible, not less, when both sides have a sure second-strike capability. Then you might have a more stable "balance of terror." This may seem a rather subtle point, but from where I'm sitting it seems a point worth thinking about.[67]

This commentary was seized upon by the McNamara critics as an open invitation by the administration to the Soviet Union to concentrate on developing second-strike or invulnerable forces the effect of which would be to diminish any real meaning of American nuclear superiority. Some critics felt that the Secretary was perhaps willing to accept some form of parity or equality with the Soviet Union in strategic nuclear capability, and others, as was revealed in congressional testimony during 1963, felt that Secretary McNamara was willing to settle for a nuclear stalemate.

Secretary McNamara's Ann Arbor speech had confirmed the belief of many defense analysts that under certain precise circumstances the United States might initiate a general war with nuclear weapons—a contingency which President Kennedy apparently sought to disavow in his March 28, 1961 speech. Alsop asked Secretary McNamara during the interview whether there was a possibility of the United States adopting a first-strike strategy. The Secretary was firm in his insistence that, "what I said meant exactly the opposite. Because we have a sure second-strike capability, there is no pressure on us whatsoever to preempt." A bit later in the interview, however, the Secretary did make clear that "there are certain circumstances in which the other side is dead sure we will use the nuclear weapon—an attack on the United States or on our NATO allies, for example." He also went one step further and said that in defense of Berlin, should it be required, the United States would use all weapons necessary for that purpose.[68]

Alsop then asked McNamara whether the no cities doctrine made any sense unless it was coupled with a major fallout shelter program. Secretary McNamara referred to those who simply refused to think about fatalities resulting from a nuclear war on grounds of immorality. He went on to say that fatality levels have to be thought about because there were imaginable situations in which nuclear weapons would be used. The Secretary commented: " . . . you have to recognize that there is a tremendous difference, a vital difference, between, say, thirty percent fatalities and sixty percent. A serious national fallout shelter program could make that sort of difference."[69]

At the end of 1962, a considerable discrepancy existed between the administration's professed need for a major fallout shelter program and the programs to carry out that objective. A major fallout shelter program seemed inseparably linked to a no cities or counterforce option, since if general war should occur and an enemy attack avoided striking American cities, the resulting fallout could be dramatically mitigated by the presence of adequate fallout shelters in large urban centers. This important fact was acknowledged by the major advocates of a counterforce strategy, but for somewhat inexplicable reasons the administration by the end of 1962 had not brought its case cogently enough before Congress in an effort to obtain the necessary funds.

In December 1962, *U.S. News and World Report* concluded that it was now the Soviet Union's turn to worry about a missile gap. Summing up the respective strategic nuclear missile capabilities of the United States and the Soviet Union, *U.S. News* stated: (a) the United States was credited with having 144 Polaris, 103 Atlas, 105 Thor and Jupiter, and 54 Titan missiles for a total of 406, all capable of hitting the Soviet Union; (b) the Soviet Union, on the other hand, was believed to have 75 ICBMs and possibly 50 submarine-launched missiles, for a total of 125. Comparisons of American and Soviet long-range bomber strengths added even further to the disparity of strategic power between the two nations.[70]

Another generally reliable source, the Institute for Strategic Studies in London, gave this comparison of United States and Soviet strategic nuclear capabilities as of late fall 1962: (a) *Soviet Union:* had the ICBM program been accorded sufficient priority, the Soviets would have been capable of deploying a force of several hundred strategic missiles by late 1962. For reasons not entirely clear they appear to have deployed approximately 75 ICBMs during this time period, each having more powerful boosters than its American equivalent and capable of carrying larger warheads. In long- and medium-range bombers the Soviets were credited with having 70 turbo-prop Bears (TU-20), 120 4-jet Bisons, and 1,000 twin-jet medium bomber Badgers. (b)*United States:* about 90 Atlas missiles were operational as were 36 Titan Is with another 18 expected by the end of the year. It was also anticipated that 150 Minuteman solid-fuel missiles would be deployed in hardened silos by the end of 1962. Nine Polaris submarines were deployed carrying 144 missiles. In manned bombers the B-52 force was rapidly approaching its planned ceiling of 14 wings for a total of 630 aircraft. Since the phased reduction of B-47 aircraft had been resumed during the year, the remaining force was something less than 850 aircraft. Two wings of B-58 supersonic medium bombers were scheduled for operation by December 1962.[71]

Quite clearly the comparison of strategic power between this nation and the Soviet Union late in 1962 strongly favored the United States, both in quantity and diversity of weapons systems and their invulnerability.

NOTES

1. John F. Kennedy, State of the Union Message, *Omaha World Herald,* January 11, 1962, p. 9.

2. U.S., Congress, House, Subcommittee of the Committee on Appropriations, *Hearings on Department of Defense Appropriations for 1963,* 87th Cong., 2d sess., 1962, p. 3.

3. Ibid., p. 8.

4. Ibid.

5. Ibid., p. 14.

6. Ibid., pp. 13–14.

7. Ibid., p. 13.

8. Ibid., p. 28. These statements by the Secretary are early admissions that uncertainties in estimating both Soviet capabilities and intentions induced the administration to continue a policy followed by the Eisenhower defense planners called "worst condition" planning which resulted in padding all United States strategic force requirements as a hedge against possible—but not predicted—over-achievement by the Soviets in the strategic offensive and defensive weapon field.

9. Ibid., p. 15.

10. Ibid., p. 17.

11. Robert S. McNamara, Speech before the Fellows of the American Bar Foundation, Chicago, Illinois, February 17, 1962 (DOD, Office of Public Affairs, Release No. 239–62), p. 6.

12. Ibid., p. 4.

13. Ibid., p. 5.

14. Ibid.

15. Ibid., p. 6.

16. Ibid., pp. 6–7.

17. Michael Brower, "Nuclear Strategy of the Kennedy Administration," *Bulletin of the Atomic Scientists* (October 1962), p. 2.

18. John T. McNaughton, "Arms Restraint in Military Decisions." speech prepared for delivery at Ann Arbor, Michigan, December 19, 1962 at the International Arms Control Symposium, University of Michigan, p. 10.

19. Ibid., p.11.

20. U.S., Congress, House, Subcommittee of the Committee on Appropriations, *Defense Department Appropriations for 1962,* 87th Cong., 1st sess., 1961, p. 102.

21. Ibid.

22. U.S., Congress, Senate, Committee on Armed Services, *Military Procurement Authorization, FY 1964*, 88th Cong., 1st sess., 1963, p. 54.

23. Ibid.

24. Ibid.

25. McNaughton, Speech, pp. 12–13.

26. Ibid., p. 13.

27. Ibid., p. 15.

28. Ibid., p. 16.

29. William Kaufmann, *The McNamara Strategy* (New York: Harper and Row, 1964), pp. 113–114.

30. Robert S. McNamara, Address at the Commencement Exercises, University of Michigan, Ann Arbor, Michigan, June 16, 1962 (DOD, Office of Public Affairs, Release No. 980–62), p. 5.

31. Ibid., p. 9.

32. Ibid.

33. Ibid., p. 10.

34. Ibid.

35. Ibid., p.11.

36. A "finite" or "minimum" deterrent is assumed to be a relatively small force of missiles and bombers designed primarily to be able to inflict on an enemy attacker a predetermined number of fatalities and a certain level of industrial damage whether the enemy be a single nation or in league with other nations.

37. Michael Brower, "Controlled Thermonuclear War," *The New Republic,* July 30, 1962, p. 10; Brower, "Nuclear Strategy," pp. 3–8; Ralph E. Lapp, *The Weapons Culture* (New York: W. W. Norton & Co., 1968), p. 65.

38. Brower, "Controlled Thermonuclear War," p. 10.

39. Ibid., p. 12.

40. Ibid., pp. 13–14.

41. Ibid., p. 15.

42. Morton H. Halperin, "The 'No-Cities' Doctrine," *New Republic,* October 8, 1962, p. 17.

43. Ibid.

44. Ibid., p. 18.

45. Ibid.

46. Ibid.

47. Ibid., p. 19.

48. Ibid.

49. See Arthur M. Schlesinger, Jr., *A Thousand Days* (Boston: Houghton Mifflin Co., 1965), p. 795.

50. U.S., Congress, House, Subcommittee of the Committee on Appropriations, *Hearings on Department of Defense Appropriations for 1964,* 88th Cong., 1st sess., 1963, Part I, p. 2.

51. Ibid., p. 3.

52. Elie Abel, *The Missile Crisis* (New York: Bantam Books, 1966), pp. 32–33, 48–50.

53. Schlesinger, *A Thousand Days,* p. 808.

54. Abel, *Missile Crisis,* pp. 104–105.

55. Ibid., p. 106.

56. For the material relating to military emergency procedures, see ibid., pp. 97–98.

57. Ibid., p. 181.

58. House, Subcommittee, *DOD Appropriations for 1964,* Part I, p. 7.

59. Ibid., p. 21.

60. Theodore Sorensen, *Kennedy* (New York: Harper and Row, 1965), pp. 666–667.

61. Roger Hilsman, *To Move a Nation* (New York: Doubleday and Co., 1967), p. 164.

62. Ibid.

63. Sorensen, *Kennedy,* p. 677.

64. Schlesinger, *A Thousand Days,* p. 831.

65. Kaufmann, *McNamara Strategy,* p. 274.

66. Stewart Alsop, "McNamara Thinks about the Unthinkable," *Saturday Evening Post,* December 1, 1962, p. 18.

67. Ibid.

68. Ibid.

69. Ibid.

70. "Why It's Russia's Turn to Worry About a 'Missile Gap'," *U.S. News and World Report,* December 3, 1962, pp. 47–48. The article credited the United States with having 600 intercontinental bombers with about 200 for Russia. The West also held the edge according to *U.S. News and World Report* in medium-range bombers, something on the order of 1,630 to 1,400. Finally, the margin of Western nuclear strength was even further enhanced when taking into consideration the tactical fighter-bomber forces located in Western Europe.

71. *The Communist Bloc and the Western Alliances—The Military Balance 1962–1963* (London: The Institute for Strategic Studies, 1962), pp. 3–10.

CHAPTER 4

Nuclear Superiority, Mutual Deterrence, and Limited Test Ban

By the beginning of 1963, the furtive attempt by the Soviet Union to install nuclear-tipped offensive missiles in Cuba, ostensibly to offset partially a growing strategic disadvantage, was liquidated as a military threat. Uneasiness persisted in Berlin because of uncertainty over Soviet intentions toward the allied forces remaining there. Overt aggression by the Chinese Communists against the northern frontiers of India had ceased, but prospects for peace and stability in the Far East were unpredictable. Undeçlared war continued in Vietnam against the government of South Vietnam, bringing the United States another step closer to a major decision regarding the extent of its commitment. Obvious Communist probes in the Near East and Africa appeared to be increasing; these were viewed as manifestations of the Communist drive toward their basic objective of world domination. Thus, the world remained in a state of tension and hostility (although free momentarily from widespread armed conflict), when Secretary McNamara made his annual appearances before the Armed Services and Appropriations committees of Congress to review the status of the nation's military posture and to recommend defense programs for the next five years.

The International Situation in Early 1963

Appearing before the House Subcommittee on Defense Department Appropriations in February 1963, McNamara began his lengthy prepared statement with an assessment of the international situation as it related to military policies and programs. He told the committee that the defense program being recommended by the administration was designed to meet the nation's global requirements over the long term and not simply the immediate situation as it then existed. Speaking broadly of the worldwide communist threat, the Secretary observed that there was increasing evidence that the apparent monolithic structure of world communism had been fractured, perhaps irreparably. There is, he said, "emerging a bipolarization of power in the Communist camp, the Chinese Communists trying to capture control of the Communist revolution and the Soviet Communists seeking to retain their present leadership."[1] The Secretary characterized the Soviet Union as a nation emerging after forty-five years of unrelenting sacrifice and deprivation from its status as a "have-not" nation. China, on the other hand, had barely, if at all, made a start toward self-sufficiency. Yet, despite obvious handicaps, McNamara could foresee no abandonment by the Soviet Union of its support for wars of national liberation. He predicted that the Communists would intensify their efforts in this sphere and declared that the free world must be prepared to meet the challenge.

In Latin America the Cuban crisis, said the Secretary, had greatly solidified the unity and cohesion of the American states, but he warned of a shift of Communist effort to other areas, taking advantage of fundamental instability engendered by the widespread lack of adequate economic progress. Africa, McNamara felt, was similar to Latin America in that the Communists would seek to exploit political and economic instability as a means of gaining a foothold from which to expand their influence. In the Near East the United States faced a somewhat different situation. Nations, such as Greece, Turkey, and Iran, with whom we had firm military commitments were directly exposed to Communist military power. Consequently, the United States was pledged to continue substantial military assistance to those nations most vulnerable to Soviet encroachment, and the Secretary pointed out, for example, that the defense of Iran against an attack could not be separated from the larger problem of the collective defense of the free world.[2]

Turning to South Asia, Secretary McNamara declared that events there affecting the security of India appeared to be reaching a critical point. He spoke of the recent Chinese attack on Indian territory and conjectured that the drain on the Chinese economy coupled with Indian determination to defend herself against future attack and Western determination to assist her offered a strong deterrent to Chinese expansionist designs. In Southeast Asia the Communist threat to take complete political control of Laos was not averted. In Vietnam the United States was continuing to support the government in its undeclared war against the Communist guerrillas, and, said the Secretary, "including the military assitance advisory group, there is now a total of more than 11,000 U.S. military personnel in Vietnam, providing training, airlift, communications, and advice to Vietnamese forces, and administering the military assistance program."[3] Because of a 1,000-mile common frontier with Laos, the United States was now engaged in a major effort to assist the government of Thailand in improving the capability of its military forces to meet the threat of Communist infiltration and subversion. In his judgment all of Southeast Asia was highly vulnerable to Communist aggression, posing for the United States and the free world a major threat which could not be left unchallenged.

In the Far East the major threat to peace and stability was unquestionably posed by Communist China. In the Secretary's judgment, "Although the situation in the Far East has remained fairly stable during the last year, the threat of aggression from Communist China has not abated."[4] On the other hand, he believed that the logistic effort required during the attack on India might detract from China's ability to undertake military adventures elsewhere. The largest recipient of American military assistance was still Korea, where two divisions were maintained in support of the large Korean military establishment. In addition, firm defense commitments existed with the Philippines, Nationalist China, and Japan.

In the European theater, Secretary McNamara portrayed a picture of growing economic, technical, scientific, and military strength. He suggested that the time had come for NATO to bear a greater proportion of its own defenses, particularly strategic nuclear defenses. The Secretary proposed no changes in the principle of collective defense under which an attack upon one member of the alliance would be regarded as an attack against all. Thus, he stressed that an attack on NATO would evoke a global nuclear war. Clearly, said the Secretary, "a partial and uncoordinated response could be fatal to the interests of all the members of NATO. That is why we have consistently stressed the importance of a single integrated strategic nuclear force responsive to a single chain of command, to be employed in a fully integrated manner against what is truly an indivisible target system." It was not essential, he stated, for such a force to be under exclusive American control as long as efforts were successful to avoid the fragmentation and compartmentalization of NATO's nuclear power. In fact, Mr. McNamara explained, "if our European NATO partners wish to create a European strategic nuclear force, we certainly should have no objections."[5]

Reviewing the recent series of agreements entered into at Nassau with the British, he stated that agreement was reached for the sale of Polaris missiles to the United Kingdom on the basis that it would furnish its own submarines and warheads. As a consequence, said the Secretary, "Both the Prime Minister and the President recognized that such an arrangement could not only meet the needs of the United Kingdom but could also open up entirely new opportunities for enhancing the unity and cohesion of the NATO alliance by making possible the creation of a truly multilateral NATO nuclear force." McNamara envisaged that under such an arrangement the ballistic missile submarines constructed under the agreement would be assigned as part of a NATO nuclear force and targeted in accordance with NATO plans. For its part, the United States would assign at least equal forces to the NATO command, and, except where supreme national interests were at stake, these forces would be used solely for purposes of international defense of the Western alliance. In order to make a start in the development of a multilateral NATO nuclear force, the United States and the United Kingdom had agreed to assign to NATO nuclear forces already in existence and to target them in accordance with NATO plans.[6]

The creation of a multilateral NATO force would not, the Secretary said, obviate the need for sizable conventional forces in Europe capable of meeting less than massive attacks from enemy forces.

He could imagine situations arising in Europe where it would not be advantageous initially to use even tactical nuclear weapons—provided conventional forces were available in sufficient numbers. NATO should be in a position, McNamara said, to confront an aggressor at any level of provocation with an appropriate military response. And he concluded, "The NATO powers have all the resources, the talents, and the skills needed to match our opponent at any level of effort in Europe.[7]

McNamara turned next to an assessment of the strengths and weaknesses of the Soviet Union and Communist China. As for the Soviet Union, he said:

> There is no gainsaying that Soviet resources, industry, and technology have given that country the potential to challenge the primacy of U.S. military power in the world. While the size, variety, and power of our strategic retaliatory forces still greatly exceed those of the Soviets, the Kremlin leaders have at their command the resources, production capacity, and technology to produce strong forces of their own. We believe they will continue to make great efforts to do so. The Soviet Union can also be expected to maintain large and well-equipped conventional forces to insure the internal security of the Soviet Union, to control its European satellites, to secure its eastern frontiers, and to threaten Western Europe.[8]

On the debit side, the Secretary noted there had been a pronounced decline in the growth rate of Soviet industry coupled with sharp increases in defense and space expenditures. This had been accompanied by a sharp decline in the rate of new investment. Clearly, then, increased defense costs could be supported only at the expense of increases in other sectors of the economy. McNamara adduced evidence that the increasing military burden on the economy had led to debate within the Soviet leadership during the past two years.[9]

As for Communist China, despite the attack on India, economic prospects were believed by Secretary McNamara to be extremely bleak and would, at least during the next few years, serve to limit the size and character of any military adventures. More specifically, he noted:

> The calamitous collapse of Chinese agriculture has forced a sharp curtailment of industrial production; first, because China's industrial

production is heavily dependent on agriculture for raw materials and, second, because additional workers have had to be transferred from industry to help revive the faltering farm program.[10]

Furthermore:

Communist China's economic difficulties and the strain of the recent campaign against India should tend to limit her ability to engage in large-scale aggression against other of her neighbors, particularly where such aggression might involve a direct confrontation with U.S. military forces. A large-scale overt attack elsewhere in southeast Asia, or against Taiwan or South Korea, is not very likely under present circumstances.[11]

Following the tour d'horizon of the international situation, Secretary McNamara moved on in his formal statement to a detailed consideration of the nation's strategic retaliatory forces. He began with the following statement:

Last year I told this Committee "there is no question but that, today, our Strategic Retaliatory Forces are fully capable of destroying the Soviet target system, even after absorbing an initial surprise attack." This statement is still true. We have a total of about 650 manned bombers on 15 minute ground alert and over 200 operational ATLAS, TITAN, and MINUTEMAN missiles on launchers and about 144 POLARIS missiles in submarines. And this force is rapidly expanding as additional MINUTEMAN and POLARIS enter our operational inventory.

Allowing for losses from an initial enemy attack and attrition enroute to target, we calculate that our forces today could still destroy the Soviet Union without any help from the deployed tactical air units or carrier task forces or THOR or JUPITER IRBM's.[12]

Having given the committee his estimate of the prevailing balance of nuclear power, the Secretary turned to a discussion of a complicated strategic problem of the future, arising, as he saw it, from observed trends in Soviet military preparations. The Secretary spoke of increasing evidence that the Soviet Union was hardening and dispersing its ICBM forces and making efforts to acquire a number of missile launching submarines. From this evidence the Secretary concluded: ". . . it is even more important today than it was last year that we concentrate our efforts on the kind of strategic offensive forces which will be able to ride out an all-out attack by nuclear-armed ICBMs or submarine-launched missiles in sufficient strength to strike back decisively."[13]

What significant meaning did Secretary McNamara see in these apparent Soviet military trends? Clearly, said the Secretary:

> A very large increase in the number of fully hard Soviet ICBMs and nuclear-powered ballistic missile-launching submarines would considerably detract from our ability to destroy completely the Soviet strategic nuclear forces. It would become increasingly difficult, regardless of the form of the attack to destroy a sufficiently large proportion of the Soviet's strategic nuclear forces to preclude major damage to the United States, regardless of how large or what kind of strategic forces we build.[14]

It would not be enough, continued McNamara, if we were to double and triple our forces in an effort to ensure the destruction of all or almost all of the Soviet Union's hardened ICBM sites. And even if that were possible, no way is known at present to destroy an enemy's missile-launching submarines at the same time. What is more, the Secretary stressed; "We do not anticipate that either the United States or the Soviet Union will acquire that capability in the foreseeable future." In addition, he said, in order to minimize the damage to the United States, a projected force would have to include extensive missile defensive systems and a far more elaborate civil defense program than is now contemplated. "Even then," McNamara concluded, "we could not preclude casualties counted in the tens of millions."[15]

Secretary McNamara reemphasized the administration's decision to base the nation's strategy for general war on a second-strike capability, stressing that the United States should have the capability to strike back decisively at the entire Soviet target system simultaneously or to strike back first exclusively against such military targets as bomber bases and missile sites. Then, if necessary, remaining forces could attack the Soviet urban and industrial complex in a controlled and deliberate way. He conceded that Soviet leaders have always threatened to strike our entire target complex at the outset of general war, but if they did so, the United States would have no choice but to retaliate in kind. It seemed possible to McNamara, as a consideration in our defense planning, that the Soviet Union might realistically prefer to limit the awful consequences of all-out nuclear exchange and decide to avoid initial attacks on American cities. Thus, the Secretary reasoned, "By building into our forces a flexible capability, we at least eliminate the prospect that we could strike back in only one way, namely, against the entire Soviet target system including their cities. Such a prospect would give the Soviet Union no incentive to withhold attack against our cities in the first place."[16]

Taking into account estimates of force capabilities projected for the next five years, McNamara declared:

> In planning our second-strike force, we have provided throughout the period under consideration, a capability to destroy virtually all of the "soft" and "semi-hard" military targets in the Soviet Union and a large number of their fully hardened missile sites, with an additional capability in the form of a protected force to be employed or held in reserve for use against urban and industrial areas.[17]

Nonetheless, the Secretary cautioned, "We have not found it feasible, at this time, to provide a capability for ensuring the destruction of any very large portion of the fully hard ICBM sites, if the Soviets build them in quantities, or of missile-launching submarines. Fully hard ICBM sites can be destroyed but only at a great cost in terms of the numbers of offensive weapons required to dig them out. Furthermore, in a second-strike situation we would be attacking, for the most part, empty sites from which the missiles had already been fired."[18]

On the assumption that the Soviet Union would continue to make an even larger proportion of its strategic nuclear forces relatively invulnerable to attack, Secretary McNamara questioned the value of trying to provide in the future a capability to destroy a very high proportion of the Soviet hard ICBM sites or its expected missile-launching submarine forces. In partial substantiation of this, the Secretary stressed, "Although we are investing very large sums in research and development in the anti-submarine warfare and anti-ballistic missile areas, it is not very likely that our efforts will produce enough of an increase in our capabilities during the period under consideration [1963–1968] to change the prospects significantly."[19]

Nuclear Deterrence or Nuclear Stalemate?

The year 1962 had witnessed repeated proclamations by the Kennedy administration of the overwhelming superiority of United States strategic nuclear strength, thus laying to rest for all time the myth of the missile gap. In 1963, Secretary McNamara took his case before Congress and the attentive public for a thorough airing of the future implications of a large, relatively invulnerable Soviet strategic missile force. Was the world entering inexorably into an era of mutual deterrence despite all efforts on the part of the United States to maintain meaningful superiority? Was it conceivable that this nation would in the future reach a point of diminishing returns in the procurement of additional increments of strategic missiles because of the excessive cost entailed in achieving a high "kill" probability against relatively invulnerable Soviet missile forces? Under such imaginable circumstances what did the future appear to mean for effective American nuclear superiority? Was some approach to parity or equality with the Soviet Union inevitable? And, finally, was the United States really prepared to accept a nuclear stalemate as an inescapable fate? The answers to many of these questions were attempted by Secretary McNamara during the cross-questioning by the House and Senate Armed Services and Appropriations committees.

The most controversial issue with which Secretary McNamara had to deal during his testimony before Congress in early 1963 was whether in a sense the United States was unilaterally opting out of the quantitative arms race with the Soviet Union and was therefore disposed to accept the fact of a nuclear stalemate. As will be recalled from his earlier statements, the Secretary expressed some doubt about the value of trying to provide a capability to destroy the essentially invulnerable elements of the Soviet strategic forces, which suggested that the United States was already approaching the point of diminishing returns. Secretary McNamara's views were almost immediately challenged by critics, who proclaimed that the administration was abandoning the doctrine of nuclear deterrence for a doctrine of nuclear stalemate. In the opinion of one critical observer, "The strategic umbrella, under shelter of which major Soviet aggression has been deterred or repulsed at many times and in many places since the end of World War II, is being replaced by a strategic ceiling—rigid, immovable, and possibly brittle."[20] Another critic argued that "the Administration now obviously believes that superiority is not necessary, that it is undesirable because it is provocative and that it is meaningless because nuclear war is unthinkable."[21] He went on to say that to eliminate the requirement for strategic superiority the United States was abandoning the doctrine of counterforce which the Secretary of Defense had enunciated in a speech at Ann Arbor the previous June. It is not surprising, therefore, that congressional leaders were quick to demand a full explanation of the issues from McNamara when he appeared before the Armed Services and Appropriations committees to present the Defense Department annual posture statement.

During cross-examination by the House Subcommittee on Appropriations, the Secretary was asked by Chairman Mahon whether he meant to imply at all in his statement before the committee that he recognized the existence now of a nuclear stalemate between the United States and the Soviet Union. Secretary McNamara replied, "No, I at no place used the word 'stalemate.' I have said, and I believe it is true, that the Soviet nuclear forces, particularly their strategic forces, are increasing in size, that as they increase they will become increasingly capable of achieving severe damage by an attack on the United States."[22] In the course of his testimony before the Senate Armed Services Committee, McNamara was asked by Senator Margaret Chase Smith to answer a number of prepared questions in writing. Among them he was asked, if a point of nuclear stalemate should be reached, would the United States in any way have a "decisive margin of superiority" and should this be the case, in what form would it be—and of what significance? Secretary McNamara responded, "I do not consider that a point of 'nuclear stalemate' will be reached but rather that both sides will continue to improve their capabilities to damage one another." He envisaged that in the absence of an effectively verified arms control agreement, both sides would constantly strive to exploit their respective weapons technologies. In the Secretary's judgment, however, "the prospect that remarkable new weapons can provide a sudden change in the margin of superiority is not... likely."[23] Finally, in response to another question from Senator Smith on the possibility of a nuclear stalemate, Secretary McNamara again emphasized that the issue of a nuclear stalemate was not genuine, and that in reality a dynamic relationship existed between the communist bloc and the free world.

Somewhat later in McNamara's testimony before the Mahon Subcommittee, Congressman Gerald Ford called the Secretary's attention to a passage from his prepared statement in which he purportedly alluded to the grim prospect of mutual deterrence. Mr. Ford asked the Secretary, "As I read that statement I come to the inevitable conclusion that you are saying that at some point we, the United States, will reach a point of mutual deterrence, a nuclear standoff, or a nuclear stalemate with the Soviet Union. Is that correct?" Secretary McNamara replied, "No, that is not what I have said.... Particularly, I think the terms 'nuclear standoff,' 'nuclear stalemate' may mislead individuals into believing that our military program does not provide for the maintenance of our nuclear superiority measured in terms of quantity of nuclear power... ." What he had said, McNamara stated, was that the nation was approaching an era when it would become increasingly improbable that either side could destroy a sufficiently large portion of the other's strategic nuclear force, by surprise or otherwise, to preclude a devastating retaliatory blow.[24]

Congressman Ford pressed his argument further, stating that the Secretary had left an impression with many people that the nation will be reaching a period of nuclear standoff or nuclear stalemate under the programs the administration was submitting to Congress. Then he asked the Secretary, "Can you differentiate between mutual deterrence and the other two phrases?" McNamara, however, turned aside the issue of definitions and replied to Congressman Ford: "I am trying to be very precise in stating the situation as I visualize it developing, particularly I wish to be precise in making clear that the military program we are presenting to the Congress for fiscal year 1964 will in my mind maintain a superior nuclear force in the United States compared to the strategic force of the Soviet Union . . . .''[25]

Openly expressing his dismay and disagreement with the Secretary over the likely course of events, Congressman Ford asked McNamara, ''When do we reach this period of mutual deterrence which is a 'grim prospect'?'' The Secretary rejoined that it was impossible to specify a date with any accuracy partly because deterrence was ''a frame of mind.'' Why, Mr. Ford continued, must we assume that this situation (nuclear stalemate) is going to come to pass? To this McNamara replied: ''Well, I have not assumed it. I have said, 'I do not assume it is coming to pass.' I believe we are approaching that era.'' Congressman Ford retorted, Is it conceivable that this nation so lacks imagination, skill, and diligence to permit this to be upon us relatively soon? To this line of questioning Secretary McNamara replied:

> I do not believe we are either unimaginative, or lacking in skill, but I believe that a careful assessment of the probable increases in the Soviet nuclear power as estimated by the experienced intelligence evaluators in our Government indicate that power will increase in such ways, particularly in such types, that there will not be a possibility for us to build a force that can destroy that power to such a degree that there will not remain elements so large as to cause severe damage to our nation in retaliation for our destructive effort directed against that power.[26]

McNamara's reply did not wholly satisfy Mr. Ford. He reiterated again his refusal to accept the idea that the competence, the quality, and the technical skill of the American people as a whole was insufficient to prevent the grim prospect from happening which the Secretary had described. Again Secretary McNamara's reply is cogent:

> If by that you mean you refuse to believe that with the ability and imagination which we possess we cannot develop a sure means to destroy the missile-launching submarines, then I can only disagree with you, because I have carefully considered this problem with the best of minds and the best brains in the Defense Department, with the best minds and the best brains in the scientific community, on which

the Defense Department draws for technical assistance and counsel, and I have found no one who states that they anticipate it will be possible in the next several years.[27]

Still unconvinced that the United States had no choice but to anticipate the approach of an era of mutual deterrence, Congressman Ford told Secretary McNamara he was surprised that the ingenuity and the industry of some 180 million American people cannot be channeled to preclude this grim prospect from being on the doorstep of the United States. To this McNamara replied forthrightly:

> Mr. Ford, yesterday, you quite properly pointed out the danger of underestimating one's opponent. I would simply emphasize today that I share your sentiments. I think you seriously underestimate our opponent if you believe that between now and the period we are talking about the ingenuity of the American people can develop certain techniques and systems such as to destroy the Soviet nuclear forces to such an extent as to leave surviving such a small force that it could not accomplish severe damage when directed against this nation. I know of no responsible person, including our leading military advisors, and including our leading scientific and engineering consultants, who would share your conclusion.[28]

Somewhat later, Congressman Laird of Wisconsin, also a member of the Mahon Subcommittee, returned to the issue of a nuclear stalemate, citing the recent interview between the Secretary and Stewart Alsop in the *Saturday Evening Post*. The Congressman asked McNamara, "You do not believe we have anything near a nuclear stalemate at the present time, do you?" The Secretary replied: "I am wary of tagging a word like 'stalemate,' or 'non-stalemate' onto our present condition. . . . I do not personally believe the word 'stalemate' is the proper word to apply. 'Stalemate' implies lack of action and I visualize our military program leading to quite the contrary. I visualize it leading to action in the foreign policy field." Emphasizing what he estimated to be the present power balance, the Secretary said: "I believe we have sufficient power to absorb the first strike of the Soviet Union and, even then, destroy the Soviet Union. I also believe they have today, and will have increasingly in the future, the power to cause severe damage to the Western World, including the United States, in the event of a nuclear exchange." Such a situation, McNamara concluded, could not be described by the term "stalemate," and particularly not so in the area of foreign policy.[29]

Congressman Laird also raised questions about the broad objectives of United States national defense policy. He praised Secretary McNamara's statement and responsiveness before the Mahon Subcommittee, but said he was still not sure in his own mind what the objectives of our defense policy actually were. Was it, he asked, to deter war, avoid war, destroy communism, or to coexist peacefully? Secretary McNamara replied that he believed the basic objective of our policy was the protection of our national security and our vital interests. McNamara did not think that the long-range objective was a negative one of containment but rather that of promoting the spread of freedom throughout the world. He was confident, he said, that we were achieving that objective, but he did not feel it could be achieved primarily through the development and application of military force. However, the Secretary cautioned, we are not prepared to accept the destruction of this nation in the process of attempting to advance freedom elsewhere in the world.[30]

Somewhat later Congressman Laird shifted to a discussion of the controversial issue of parity, superiority, and the damage levels the United States and the Soviet Union were currently capable of inflicting on each other. Mr. Laird asked Secretary McNamara what level of casualties the United States would have to accept if an assumed number of Soviet warheads impacted on targets in this country. On the basis of assumed capabilities McNamara replied that at absolute minimum the fatalities in this country would be ten million, and in all probability the figure would be several times that.[31] Next the Congressman asked Secretary McNamara whether it was true that both the Soviet Union and the United States were capable of inflicting "unacceptable" damage on each other, and if in the Secretary's judgment this did not mean some kind of damage parity? McNamara rejected the notion of damage parity, saying, "Our force today can create far greater damage in the Soviet Union than their force can in the United States."[32] Mr. Laird then asked whether the damage the Soviets could inflict on the United States would indeed be unacceptable. The Secretary hedged somewhat in his reply, "I think that is for you to decide. I can only give you the level of damage I think they can inflict upon us. Whether that is acceptable or not, I think, depends upon the circumstances and your own judgment."[33]

In response to a question put to him in writing by Senator Margaret Smith of the Senate Armed Services Committee relative to the issue of unacceptable damage, the Secretary's reply clarified to a greater extent how he regarded such damage prospects. He said:

> The term "unacceptable damage" is a relative one. The extent of damage which the United States would be willing to accept must, in my judgment, always be related to the degree to which her security interests are involved in any given issue. For example, we have made it quite clear that the defense of Western Europe is as vital to us as the defense of our own continent and that we are prepared to back up our commitments there with our strategic nuclear power no matter what degree of damage might result should the deterrent aspect of this policy fail. . . . The fact that the United States is maintaining a superior strategic nuclear power should not blind us to the growing destructive power of Soviet nuclear forces. This fact makes it increasingly important for us to make clear to the Soviet Union, in advance, those vital U.S. interests which we must support with our total power. The increasing capability of Soviet nuclear forces must not be permitted to lull our allies, our own citizens, or our enemies into the belief that we would be less willing to defend these vital interests.[34]

The last major issue aired during the testimony by Secretary McNamara was the hardy question of whether existing United States policy included the objective of eventual defeat of communism. Congressman Laird asked the Secretary whether the United States was pursuing a "win" philosophy. Secretary McNamara emphatically rejected the notion that our objective did not include the defeat of communism. Stressing again his feelings that the United States could not defeat communism by engaging in nuclear war, Secretary McNamara reiterated: "I do not believe we can achieve the defeat of communism by engaging in strategic nuclear war. There are some who do believe that. I do not. I think it is very dangerous, as a matter of fact, for any significant number of our people to believe we can achieve defeat of communism by engaging in strategic nuclear war."[35] Congressman Laird then asked the Secretary, Accepting the fact of our nuclear superiority, and forced to engage in nuclear war by circumstances beyond our control, would our superior position allow this nation to win? The McNamara reply is historically noteworthy:

> No, sir; I do not believe we can, not in the normal sense of the word "win," because in my opinion there would be so much severe damage done to this country that our way of life would change, and change in an undesirable direction. Therefore, I would say we had not won. In another sense of the word "win" we would win. We would win in the sense that their way of life would change more than ours because we would destroy a greater percentage of their industrial potential and probably destroy a greater percentage of their population than they destroyed of ours.[36]

The Secretary clarified that he was talking solely about the United States. He suspected that in terms of facilities the amount of industrial destruction in the West would exceed that of the Soviet Union especially when adding the probable destruction of Western Europe. General Taylor, accompanying Secretary McNamara, was also asked for his views on the matter of winning a nuclear war. He replied: "I quite agree with the Secretary, that when you talk about 'winning' a general nuclear war it is usually in a sense I do not understand. The losses on both sides would reduce these two world powers to secondary or tertiary powers."[37]

As an important footnote to the discussion of this nation's capability of winning a nuclear war, both Secretary McNamara and General Taylor were asked whether they felt it was necessary to go forward to maintain our superior force in order to deter the use of military force by the communist powers. Secretary McNamara's reply was a terse, "Always." And to do this, the Secretary said, we would never be satisfied with an impasse. Technical change is inevitable and, "We must watch pretty carefully and pursue all the research and development programs you are concerned with. We do not have a balance. We have a dynamic offsetting situation which may change, not overnight, but in the course of a few years."[38] It was, however, in response to a question from Senator Smith that the Secretary most clearly specified what he believed to be the real meaning of our present nuclear superiority, "It does give us a war-fighting and war-winning nuclear capability, in the sense that we are confident that we can completely crush the Soviet Union if forced to do so."[39]

One of the criticisms levelled at the Kennedy administration strategy for general nuclear war, which particularly seemed to perturb Secretary McNamara, was the accusation that the Defense Department was leading the nation in the direction of nuclear stalemate by placing undue reliance on an all-missile strategy.[40] In an exclusive interview early in February 1963, McNamara replied to his critics, "There is no justification for such claims. . . . The existence of the manned bomber is not a determining factor in the relative effectiveness in strategic strength of the United States and the Soviet Union."[41] In response to charges that failure to provide a sizable manned bomber force in the future would make United States defenses inflexible, the Secretary rejoined:

> To the contrary, the manned bomber itself introduces inflexibility in the 1970s when the Soviet Union will have more missiles which it could use against the United States. This is because you can't leave a bomber on the ground if an attack is imminent. You must have it in the air.
>
> On the other hand, mobile or hardened missiles can be held in their silos indefinitely and fired at the discretion of the proper authority.
>
> Missiles provide more flexibility than the bomber.[42]

Continuing to state the case for missiles, McNamara pointed out that whereas missiles could reach their targets in a matter of minutes, a bomber would take up to twelve hours. Also, missiles were considered by the Secretary to be more effective against most major fixed targets—missile and bomber bases, cities and air defenses—whereas bombers in the missile age were best suited to "mopping up" strategic targets. In other words, he contended, the crux of planning an optimum mix of weapon systems for given target complexes was related to the capability of a given weapon to hit a specific target, and this capability was not necessarily inherent solely in the manned bomber to the exclusion of the missile.

The Strategy of Controlled Response

Late in February 1963, one of Secretary McNamara's top planners, Deputy Assistant Secretary Alain Enthoven, spoke to audiences in the states of Washington and California, during which he explained in detail the rationale which had come to underlie the administration's strategy for controlled counterforce general war. In his prepared remarks Enthoven highlighted certain points which he particularly felt underpinned Department of Defense thinking. He believed, he said, that, "The theory and practice of strategic bombing in World War II, the use of the atomic bombs, and the unconditional surrender policy left in their aftermath a widespread belief that war could only be total." Increasingly, Enthoven declared, as the size and destructiveness of nuclear arsenals increases, total war between nuclear powers will come to mean total destruction. "Thus," he said, "it is my own opinion that with the widespread realization of this fact will come the general belief that all wars should be limited. At no time should we deliberately choose to fight an unlimited uncontrolled war."[43]

"What this means," Enthoven said, "is that we are working to acquire a flexible, balanced defense posture giving us capabilities for the selective use of force for all kinds of conflict, from counterinsurgency and antiguerilla warfare through large scale conventional (non-nuclear) warfare, through major thermonuclear war." What we should aim to do, he said, borrowing a phrase from the Mikado, is "to make the punishment fit the crime."[44]

Enthoven emphasized that when force is used "the military action must not be allowed to control events and compel the President's decisions; rather it should be the other way around." Referring to the hard lessons of the Korean War, he stated that the United States had to relearn the lesson of fighting for limited objectives in order to avoid the risks of touching off another world war, which would likely leave both South Korea and the United States much worse off than the final outcome actually achieved. The same principle of control was applied during the recent Cuban crisis, said Enthoven. "Each military move was, in effect, a carefully formulated message from the President to Khrushchev, intended to convince him that the United States would use military force to the extent necessary to achieve removal of the offensive weapons." "But," he pointed out, "each move was also intended to convince him that he could withdraw without armed conflict."[45]

The Deputy Secretary analyzed in some detail what he considered to be the very great difference between nuclear weapons and non-nuclear weapons. Nuclear weapons, he said, "are not simply high explosives writ large." Their destructive power makes them a completely new kind of military force which must be understood and related to our national security objectives in new ways. Despite the progress in recent years in developing small nuclear weapons having yields measured in a few thousands of tons of TNT or less, Enthoven argued against the notion that soon no distinction would exist between nuclear and non-nuclear war; there was a recognizable qualitative distinction that both combatants could recognize and agree upon, if they wanted to agree upon one. And in the nuclear age they would have a very powerful incentive to agree upon this distinction and limitation, because if they did not, there did not appear to be another easily recognizable limitation on weapons.[46]

There were many situations, Enthoven continued, wherein the use of nuclear weapons would be inappropriate. "For the same reasons that a sledge hammer does not make a good substitute for a fly swatter, nuclear weapons are not a good substitute for non-nuclear forces against a wide range of military threats."[47] The use of nuclear weapons would automatically risk the possibility of escalation to a more and unnecessarily destructive level of conflict. Nuclear weapons, he argued, must be reserved for only the most desperate circumstances. And by agreeing to do so, the side with the strong conventional forces would be likely to be able to have its way on all issues less than vital. The President, stressed Enthoven, should not be put in the position of choosing between suicide or surrender, holocaust or humiliation.

The Deputy Secretary rejected the notion that a buildup of conventional forces would be a signal to an enemy that this nation no longer had the necessary resolve to use nuclear weapons in its own defense. The important thing, he argued, is not to convince an aggressor that we will use nuclear weapons but to convince him that we will use whatever force that is necessary to preserve our freedom. He also rejected the criticism levelled at the buildup of conventional forces "that it will be fruitless, extremely costly, and unable to achieve the objective of adequacy because we are so badly outnumbered by the Communist hordes."[48] He exposed as fiction the idea that NATO was incapable of matching Soviet bloc forces at all levels of conventional strength, people, technology, and industrial production. Finally, he rejected the argument that non-nuclear weapons put the Western nations at a disadvantage because of the numerical superiority enjoyed by the communists. Enthoven contended that the wealth and technology of the West conferred on it the necessary advantages to overcome enemy numerical superiority in a number of imaginable situations. Summarizing his argument for a clear distinction between nuclear and conventional weapons, he said:

> . . . conventional military force is usable force. In Korea and in the Cuban crisis, we found that the non-nuclear forces were the cutting edge of our military power. We can use conventional force with a minimal risk of self-destruction. Therefore, it provides a more credible deterrent to non-nuclear aggression. As the destructiveness of nuclear war increases, and as nuclear weapons systems become less vulnerable to sudden attack, the effectiveness of the threatened use of nuclear weapons as a substitute for conventional forces will diminish, and we will have no sensible alternative to building up our conventional forces to the point at which they can safely resist all forms of non-nuclear aggression. Our forces will be adequate if we can never be forced because of weakness to be the first to have to resort to nuclear weapons.[49]

Turning next to a discussion of the United States posture for thermonuclear war, Deputy Assistant Secretary Enthoven argued that the relationship between nuclear and conventional forces is one of complementarity. Now that the communist bloc was equipped with nuclear weapons, conventional war could not be fought successfully except under the umbrella of nuclear strength. Thus, the most important objective of the nation's nuclear posture was to make thermonuclear war unlikely by deterring deliberate calculated nuclear aggression. In addition, said Enthoven, "if war does occur, we want to be able to bring it to a speedy termination on military terms favorable to ourselves, and we want to do what we can to limit the damage caused to ourselves and our allies."[50]

Our first task, said Enthoven, is to deter deliberate premeditated attack by maintaining secure second-strike retaliatory capabilities immune to surprise attack. To do this task the United States was depending on relatively invulnerable weapons systems such as Minuteman, Titan, and Polaris, and secure, protected, survivable command and control facilities able to survive an attack and direct the use of force against an aggressor. Enthoven rejected strategies which would compel attacks against enemy cities or guarantee a spasm of massive retaliation. Our approach, he said, "is based on options, deliberation, flexibility and control. Rather than decide ahead of time which targets must be hit by which weapons, and then commit ourselves to it, our approach is to give the President a range of choices so that he can select the plan whose targets and timing of attacks are most appropriate to the circumstances at hand."[51]

Despite our best efforts, Enthoven continued, a nuclear war may still occur. It would be foolish, he said, to base our planning on an assumption that a thermonuclear war could never happen. Almost any kind of nuclear war would be an unprecedented disaster, but if such a war is forced on us, there are worthwhile things that could be done to mitigate its consequences. For example, he stated, "We are making preparations whose purpose is, in the event of war, to enable us to maintain a favorable military position, to bring the war to an end quickly, and to hold to a minimum the damage to ourselves and our allies."[52]

One of the major preparations Secretary Enthoven had in mind as a hedge against the possibility of nuclear war was the provision of fallout shelters for the entire American population. In the event of a thermonuclear attack on this country many millions of people would die, even though they were far from the blast and thermal effects. Even though various studies were not in complete agreement, he said, "most . . . suggest that whereas several tens of millions might die from the blast and thermal effects of a nuclear attack on the United States, because of fallout the total deaths could swell to over a hundred million in the United States alone." Thus, said the Secretary, civil defense preparations were a vital aspect of overall defense planning and were inseparable from active defense and other preparations. If, he said, "we defended our cities with impenetrable anti-missile defenses, but had no fallout protection for the inhabitants, an attacker could still destroy all the people in those cities simply by surface bursting thermonuclear weapons upwind and killing the people with fallout." Therefore, he concluded, civil defense was essential if this nation was to have any hopes of limiting the effects of a major thermonuclear war and making meaningful a strategy of controlled use of nuclear weapons.[53]

In his closing remarks Enthoven asked his audience whether current United States defense policy, which emphasized deterrence, control, and the use of appropriately limited amounts of force, represented a good reconciliation of the traditional doctrine with the facts of life in the nuclear age. He said that in his opinion we had indeed achieved some success with the controlled use of force. Specifically, he concluded, "We are still alive and free today, and the missiles are out of Cuba.[54]

The Limited Test Ban Treaty

By the beginning of summer 1963, President Kennedy's hopes for achieving a comprehensive test ban were fading fast. Not only had Premier Khrushchev hardened his position in a letter to the President in early May, but domestic opposition to a test ban reached serious proportions, seemingly placing a test ban treaty in jeopardy with the Senate even if some accommodation proved possible with the Soviet Union. Late in May the President told McGeorge Bundy in strict confidence that he had decided the time had come to deliver a major address on peace. The forum he chose was the commencement address at American University on the pleasant Monday morning of June 10.

In his opening words the President said he had chosen this time and this place "to discuss a topic on which ignorance too often abounds and the truth is too rarely perceived—yet, it is the most important topic on earth: world peace." He was not, he said, seeking the kind of peace, such as a *Pax Americana,* to be enforced on the world by American weapons of war. The President continued,

"Total war makes no sense in an age when great powers can maintain large and relatively invulnerable nuclear forces and refuse to surrender without resort to those forces. It makes no sense in an age when a single nuclear weapon contains almost ten times the explosive force delivered by all the Allied air forces in the Second World War."[55]

Insisting that the United States and the Soviet Union had important common interests, the President said, "no nation in the history of battle ever suffered more than the Soviet Union suffered in the course of the Second World War. At least 20 million lost their lives." And, he stressed: "Today, should total war ever break out again—no matter how—our two countries would become the primary targets. It is an ironical but accurate fact that the two strongest powers are the two in the most danger of devastation. All we have built, all we have worked for, would be destroyed in the first twenty-four hours."[56] Above all, he said, "while defending our own vital interests, nuclear powers must avert those confrontations which bring an adversary to a choice of either a humiliating retreat or a nuclear war. To adopt that kind of course in the nuclear age would be evidence only of the bankruptcy of our policy—or of a collective death wish for the world."[57]

Arguing for the need to achieve world law and to limit the intensity of the arms race through negotiated arms control, President Kennedy stressed that one area of negotiations where the end was in sight, and where a fresh start was necessary, was in a treaty to outlaw nuclear tests. He declared, "The conclusion of such a treaty—so near and yet so far—would check the spiraling arms race in one of its most dangerous areas."[58] Toward the achievement of this goal the President announced his agreement to the holding of high-level discussions in the near future in Moscow looking to an early conclusion of a comprehensive test ban treaty.

Several weeks passed which afforded the Russians an opportunity to study the American University speech. Apparently, the speech made a deep impression on Premier Khrushchev, for on July 2, 1963, during a visit to East Berlin, he praised the speech for its "sober appraisal of the international situation" and countered with an offer for a limited ban which would outlaw tests in the atmosphere, in outer space, and under water. He asserted that if the Western powers would accept his proposal, there would no longer remain the question of inspection.[59] Although Khrushchev did not insist this time on a concurrent and unpoliced moratorium on underground tests, he said that once a test ban agreement had been reached, it would be necessary to conclude a non-aggression treaty between the NATO and the Warsaw Pact states.

On July 15, a small but highly able American delegation under the leadership of Averell Harriman arrived in Moscow to begin negotiations. According to Sorensen, "Once it appeared that a reasonable treaty was possible, the President was determined that no quibbling over language or sniping from his subordinates would prevent it. The force of his leadership in the daily sessions overrode all the nit-picking the skeptics could devise."[60] Following resolution of a last obstacle the negotiators in Moscow phoned the President who gave his final approval on July 25, just six weeks after the American University address. There remained, however, a formidable hurdle—Senate approval.

Of all those testifying for the treaty on behalf of the administration none was abler or more persuasive than Secretary of Defense McNamara, who appeared before the Senate Committee on Foreign Relations on August 13, 1963. In his introductory remarks, Secretary McNamara told the committee: "I should like to begin by putting this treaty in the context of our present military posture."[61] The Secretary reminded the committee of his earlier statements to the effect that the United States possessed a secure second-strike strategic capability to destroy the Soviet target system, even after absorbing a surprise attack. Furthermore, he said, this job could be done by strategic forces alone without dependence on the deployed tactical air units, carrier task forces, or overseas Thor or Jupiter IRBMs. It is clear from these statements, the Secretary stated, that the United States enjoys nuclear superiority. And, he continued, "We are determined to maintain that superiority. In order to achieve it, we maintain a total number of nuclear warheads, tactical as well as strategic, in the tens of thousands."[62]

McNamara reaffirmed the substantial increases made in the United States' nuclear forces during the previous five years, and stated that during the past twenty-four months alone, there had been:

A 100 percent increase in the number of nuclear warheads in the strategic alert forces.

A 60 percent increase in the tactical nuclear forces deployed in Western Europe.

And, significantly, "During that period the megatonnage of our strategic alert forces has been more than doubled and during the next twenty-four months it will be further increased."[63] The primary purpose for mentioning these strengths was, the Secretary emphasized, that his assessment of the limited test ban treaty was made from the point of view of what is best for the security of the United States.

Since Secretary Rusk had already testified on the political aspects of the proposed treaty, McNamara said he would deal with the military benefits and risks. To put the question of the military balance in its proper perspective the Secretary began by comparing the capabilities of the United States and the U.S.S.R. in the field of nuclear technology. One of the standards used for comparing technological capabilities is yield-to-weight ratios. In this respect the Secretary said, "The Soviet Union appears to be technologically more advanced than we are in the high-yield range, that is to say, in the tens of megatons; below that yield, the relative capability shifts progressively in favor of the United States. The apparent advantage of the Soviets in the upper end of the yield spectrum was more than anything else the result of this nation's refusal to concentrate effort in this field." And, McNamara continued:

The U.S. advantage in the low and intermediate part of the yield spectrum is in my judgment a very important advantage. Our high yield-to-weight ratio in relevant range has facilitated the development of more powerful warheads for Minuteman and Polaris without concomitant increase in vehicle size or decrease in range. It is because of this that the United States has had the advantage over the Soviets of being able to deploy large numbers of hardened and dispersed Minuteman missiles and a large number of long-range sublaunched Polaris missiles. And U.S. superiority in the lower ranges facilitates further development of relatively small warheads which would be used to assure

> penetration by saturation of sophisticated and very elaborate ballistic missile defenses.[64]

Of course, McNamara acknowledged, the purely military aspects of the strategic balance included other important factors, such as numbers of weapons and their accuracy; the variety of systems, their dispersal, mobility, and hardening; decoy and salvo techniques; and the possible deployment, in the future, of an anti-ballistic missile system. On this basis, he concluded, "The net of the relevant factors is that the U.S. nuclear force is manifestly superior to the Soviet Union's."[65]

To reinforce his case the Secretary made a numerical comparison of the United States and U.S.S.R. weapons system strengths:

> The U.S. force today now contains more than 500 missiles—Atlas, Titan, Minuteman, Polaris—and is planned to increase to over 1,700 by 1966. In addition, the United States has SAC bombers on quick reaction alert.
>
> By comparison, the consensus is that today the Soviets could place less than half as many bombers over North America on a first-strike mission; the Soviets are estimated to have today only a fraction as many ICBM missiles, and their sub launched ballistic missiles are short range, require surface launch, and generally are not comparable to our Polaris force. Between now and 1966, it is estimated that our ballistic missile numerical superiority will increase both absolutely and relatively.
>
> Further, the United States at present has in stockpile or planned for stockpile a large number of nuclear explosives for tactical purposes. These weapons are planned for employment on the battlefield, in anti-submarine warfare, and against aircraft; they consist of warheads for artillery, battlefield missiles, demolition munitions, bombs, depth charges, air-to-air missiles, and surface-to-air missiles. The yield spectrum associated with these weapons extends from the subkiloton range to hundreds of kilotons.

Thus, McNamara concluded, "The consensus is that the United States is presently superior in design, diversity, and numbers in this class of weapons."[66]

The Secretary then turned his attention to a discussion of four important defense areas: (a) very large yield weapons, (b) missile site survivability, (c) antiballistic missile defense, and (d) missile penetrability. With respect to the first area he asked the question whether there was a military advantage to the United States in deployment of very high-yield weapons. Extensive analysis of this issue led to the Secretary's conclusion that two or three smaller weapons were more efficient for most military missions than one large weapon. In addition, McNamara concluded that very high-yield warheads were relatively inferior as second-strike, retaliation weapons; it was much more difficult and costly to make them survivable.

The second area evaluated by Secretary McNamara was missile site vulnerability, which he described as a special aspect of the military balance. He launched into a discussion of Minuteman silos, which were, he said, designed to withstand thermal and pressure effects and ground motion effects of typical Soviet weapons detonated at relatively close quarters. Although the Secretary admitted that the United States had not tested large-yield weapons against Minuteman silos to observe effects, it was possible, he felt, to eliminate some uncertainties by underground tests of substantial yields. On balance he felt that remaining uncertainties were a problem for the Soviets of at least equal proportion. Taking even the most pessimistic view of these uncertainties, McNamara pointed out,

> suggests a vulnerability ratio for our hardened, dispersed Minuteman sites of less than two sites killed on the average by a single very large-yield Soviet missile. It is clear that the Soviets do not have anything like the number of missiles necessary to knock out our Minuteman force, nor do they appear to have any present plans to acquire such a capacity. If they were to undertake the construction and deployment of a large number of very high-yield missiles, we would probably have knowledge of this and would have ample time to expand our Minuteman force, or to disperse it more widely.
>
> We know, and the Soviets know, that in the event of a surprise Soviet first strike, at least a substantial proportion of our Minuteman missiles will survive. Also, we and they know that the Polaris submarines at sea and many strategic aircraft will survive. We can say with assurance, therefore, that, even after a Soviet strike, the total surviving U.S. strategic nuclear force will be large enough to destroy the enemy.[67]

The Secretary next assessed the capability of United States ballistic missiles to penetrate an enemy ABM system. Describing the elements of the ABM system to detect, distinguish, and track incoming enemy warheads, he stressed that in designing an anti-ballistic missile system, the major factors are reaction speed, missile performance, traffic handling capacity, capacity for decoy discrimination, resistance to blackout effects, and warhead technology. He admitted that resistance to blackout effect and warhead technology were dependent on nuclear testing, but asserted that the United States already had the capability, without further testing, to weaponize a variety of possible ABM warheads, including those needed for the Nike-X system. Then he stated:

> The ABM system which we are now designing will provide us with a high confidence of achieving a low miss distance, a short distance between the intercepting missile and the incoming warhead. At such miss distances, the ABM warhead designs which we now have or can develop through underground testing will provide a high probability of killing Soviet warheads even if they incorporate advanced technology far beyond what now exists.[68]

The Secretary concluded that with or without a test ban, this nation could proceed with the development of an ABM system.

The final area discussed by the Secretary and relating to the military balance was the penetration capability of United States missiles. Penetration of an enemy anti-ballistic missile system, he said, depended on the capability to destroy, disrupt, or saturate the system. Current United States philosophy employed saturation which McNamara described as related to problems of decoy design and salvo techniques. A key technological problem was related to the vulnerability of the ballistic missile warhead to kill by blast or by radiation. Whereas radiation effects could be tested underground, atmospheric testing was necessary to confirm the enhanced resistance of new, hard-warhead designs to blast. Then the Secretary explained:

> But, regardless of the design of any Soviet ABM system, in view of the warhead improvements we can make under the treaty, of the massive U.S. force available to saturate their defenses, and of the array of

penetration aids which are being developed and will continue to be developed and improved, by underground testing where necessary, the United States will continue to have the capability, and most importantly, the Soviets will know that we will continue to have the capability—to penetrate and to devastate the Soviet Union if a retaliatory blow is required.[69]

McNamara pointed out that the indefinite continuation of testing on an unrestrained basis would very likely result ultimately in technical parity and perhaps technological parity between the United States and the U.S.S.R., except for weapons of very high yield where the United States had no particular interest. It was essential to consider, said the Secretary, that by limiting Soviet testing to the underground environment, where testing is more difficult and more expensive and where the United States has substantially more experience, we can at least retard Soviet progress and thereby prolong the duration of our technological superiority.

Having assessed the risk of successful Soviet clandestine testing, McNamara said that a thorough examination had convinced him that the Soviet Union could obtain no major results by testing in the atmosphere and deep space or underwater without incurring a high risk of detection and a high risk of identification.[70] Finally, the Secretary told the committee that the military consequences of a surprise Soviet abrogation of the treaty had been weighed and overall:

The consensus is that the Soviets could not, in a single series of tests, however, carefully planned those might be, achieve a significant or permanent lead in the strategic field, much less a superweapon capable of neutralizing our deterrent force.[71]

In his concluding remarks, Secretary McNamara reiterated, "We have created an enormous military force, powerful and flexible enough to guarantee our ability to deal with aggression under all contingencies. And in Cuba, in Vietnam, in Berlin, and elsewhere around the globe, we have demonstrated that our will matches our might."[72] Speaking of the growing capability of the Soviet Union to inflict damage on the United States, despite the gain by this nation in absolute numbers of weapons, the Secretary conceded that such a situation "has narrowed the range of contingencies in which our nuclear deterrent is credible. Thus, his judgment was that "the risks under the treaty are either small or under our control, and the values of the treaty are substantial even if we consider only the military area. The scales are clearly tipped in favor of the treaty, Mr. Chairman. It has my unequivocal support."[73]

In the ensuing cross-examination of Secretary McNamara by members of the Senate Foreign Relations Committee a number of important issues bearing on national security were raised. For example, Senator Bourke Hickenlooper of Iowa asked McNamara whether today the Soviet Union and the United States were in a condition of substantial relative parity so far as the ability to inflict damage on each other was concerned. The Secretary replied that he did not think so and went on to indicate that the strategic retaliatory forces of the nation were substantially larger in terms of numbers and capability for inflicting damage. As for whether the Soviets were capable of inflicting substantial damage on the United States, McNamara admitted that the damage would run into the tens of millions of people if the Soviets struck the United States, despite the certainty of retaliation. Senator Hickenlooper than asked the Secretary whether there was any difference in the comparative strength of the two nations today as compared with 1959 when the Soviets refused to discuss an environmental test ban. The Senator made it clear he meant whether the Secretary felt the Soviet Union today was much nearer in military parity than it was in 1959. McNamara replied, "No, sir; quite to the contrary. I believe the difference lies in favor of the United States and I believe that one of the reasons they are willing to consider it [a test ban] today when they were not willing to consider it in 1959 is just exactly that." The Secretary went even further; he stated that the United States was comparatively stronger than the Soviet Union in 1963 than it was in 1959.[74]

Another issue rather throroughly aired during the question period was the adequacy of and the requirement for an ABM system. Senator John Pastore, of Rhode Island, asked Secretary McNamara whether he agreed with a statement made by the President at an August 1 press conference when he purportedly said, "The question of developing a defense against a missile is beyond the Soviets technically and I think many who work on it feel that perhaps it can never be successfully accomplished because the whole problem, as you know, is to have 100 objects flying through the air at thousands of miles an hour to be able to pick them out.''[75] The Secretary said he did agree with the President's statement, and went on to declare that in his judgment the Soviets did not then have an operational anti-ballistic missile system, despite progress they had undoubtedly made during the 1961 series of tests.

McNamara was questioned by Senator John Stennis and others as to whether the United States was capable of deploying an operational ABM without atmospheric testing. The Secretary's reply was an unequivocal, "yes"; he asserted that other technical problems associated with ABM, such as radars, detection and tracking problems, and missiles, posed much more difficult problems. Largely for these reasons, he said, the administration was opposed to a decision to deploy ABM at this time.[76] It was later pointed out to McNamara that research and development expenditures to date on ABM had amounted to some $4.85 billion. Asked by Senator Frank Lausche whether he considered the development of an anti-ballistic missile as a vital project, the Secretary said: "I believe we should try to develop an effective anti-ballistic missile system.''[77]

During that congressional session the junior Senator from South Dakota, George McGovern, speaking on the floor of the Senate, had stated that the United States possessed an overkill capacity in armaments which it could not afford economically, politically, or morally. Senator Stuart Symington during the test ban hearings asked Secretary McNamara to comment on the statement. The latter's reply was: "I don't believe that we have excessive armaments today. I don't believe we have excessive strategic forces, which I believe were those portions of our armaments that Senator McGovern was speaking about. As I tried to outline in my statement this morning, there are a number of uncertainties which we must recognize in evaluating the relative positions of the U.S.S.R. and the United States.''[78] In response to Senator McGovern's urging that $4 billion be eliminated from the defense budget, McNamara said he would not recommend that one dollar be taken out of it.

The limited test ban treaty was undoubtedly one of the most thoroughly investigated and debated proposals ever to be considered by the United States government. Throughout the summer of 1963, proponents and opponents of the treaty were given ample opportunity by the Senate Foreign Relations Committee and the Joint Atomic Energy Committee to make their views known publicly. Feelings ran deep as to whether the security of the United States would be seriously compromised if the treaty were entered into or whether on balance the United States stood to gain more than it could possibly lose from adhering to the treaty. Finally, on August 5, 1963, the issue was resolved in favor of the treaty when it was initialed in Moscow by the United Kingdom, the Soviet Union, and the United States. Subsequently, on September 24, ratification was advised by the Senate. President Kennedy signed the instruments of ratification of the limited test ban on October 7, 1963, and the treaty took effect three days later.

On November 18, 1963, just four days before the assassination of President Kennedy, Secretary McNamara spoke to the Economic Club of New York. His speech was intended as a hard look at the events since the end of World War II that had a significant impact on the power relationships between the two major military alliances. In doing so the Secretary could more effectively explain how specific changes did—and were continuing to—affect choices of strategy for nuclear and conventional forces, deployment of specific weapons systems to carry out preferred strategy, and the meaning of the present balance of power between the United States and the Soviet Union for the national security of the nation. Problems of this magnitude and complexity, McNamara said, were dealt with annually by the administration in power in developing the details of a proposed national budget for consideration by the Congress and the public.[79]

McNamara admitted that any attempt to plan for or resolve issues of national security inevitably raised differences of opinion but said that, nevertheless, an airing of these differences was desirable and essential. However, he continued, "some controversies reveal underlying differences in perspective that scarcely suggest the participants are living in the same world." For example, he said, within the past few weeks, some critics have suggested that we have literally hundreds of times more strength than we need; others have accused us of risking the whole future of the nation by engaging in unilateral disarmament. Such a discrepancy in the consensus of our national military posture and objectives, the Secretary said, he found less than reassuring. Unfortunately, "it indicates that we have failed to convey to some part of our audience even the broadest outlines as we see them, of the problems that our military strategy and force structure are meant to address."[80] McNamara said that he hoped his remarks would permit movement away from controversy toward consensus in military affairs at least on the broad issues of national security policy confronting the nation, the major alternative paths to their solution, and the "dominant goals, obstacles, costs and risks affecting choice."

As an indication of the growing strength of the Western alliance, McNamara summarized the current status of the balance of strategic nuclear forces. The strategic equation, expressed in purely numerical terms is, said the Secretary, a familiar one. Specifically:

> The U.S. force now contains more than 500 operational long-range ballistic missiles—ATLAS, TITAN, MINUTEMAN, POLARIS —and is planned to increase to over 1,700 by 1966. There is no doubt in our minds and none in the minds of the Soviets that these missiles can penetrate to their targets. In addition, the U.S. has Strategic Air Command bombers on air alert and over 500 bombers on quick reaction ground alert. By comparison, the consensus is that today the Soviets could place about half as many bombers over North America on a first strike. The Soviets are estimated to have today only a fraction as many intercontinental missiles as we do. Furthermore, their submarine-launched ballistic missiles are short range, and generally are not comparable to our POLARIS force. The Soviets pose a very large threat against Europe, including hundreds of intermediate and medium-range ballistic missiles. This threat is today and will continue to be covered by the clear superiority of our strategic forces.[81]

The full implications of United States strategic nuclear superiority, the Secretary continued, should act as a powerful deterrent to a planned Soviet surprise attack, and should even this contingency arise, remaining forces of this nation could retaliate against all the urgent Soviet military targets and destroy its society. Thus, the Secretary concluded, "Deterrence of deliberate, calculated attack seems as well assured as it can be, and the damage-limiting capability of our numerically superior forces is, I believe, well worth its incremental cost." Since he did not feel that the much smaller forces of the Soviet Union could rival this capability, Secretary McNamara stressed this comparison as one reason "why I would not trade our strategic posture for that of the Soviets at any point during the coming decade."[82]

Despite his confident mood, McNamara cautioned that the facts of life since the mid-1950s indicated a substantial growth in Soviet strategic delivery capabilities, progressively hardened and concealed, so there was at long last the need to recognize "that strategic nuclear war would under all forseeable circumstances be bilateral—and highly destructive to both sides." What were the primary implications of this situation for the United States and the Soviet Union? According to the Secretary, "Larger budgets for U.S. strategic forces would not change that fact. They could have only a decreasing incremental effect in limiting somewhat the damage that the U.S. and its allies would suffer in a general nuclear war. In short, he said, we cannot buy the capability to make a strategic bombing campaign once again a unilateral prospect." Essentially, the same situation confronts the Soviets as well. In fact, he explained, "enormous increases in Soviet budgets would be required for them to achieve any significant degree of damage-limiting capability."[83]

The Secretary dwelt at some length on the tactical nuclear superiority possessed by the West in Central Europe. He emphasized, however, that NATO did not have a monopoly at the tactical nuclear levels either and would not be able to buy such a monopoly back, or have any assurance of unilateral use. Continuing, McNamara recounted the substantial growth of American general purpose (conventional) forces during the past two years, stressing particularly the improvements in combat readiness and mobility. He rejected the prevailing impression that NATO conventional forces in Europe were inferior to the so-called Communist hordes. Specifically, he said, "In Central Europe, NATO has more men, and more combat troops on the ground than does the Communist bloc. It has more men on the ground in West Germany than the bloc does in East Germany. It has more and better tactical aircraft, and these planes on the average can carry twice the payload twice as far as the Soviet counterparts." The Secretary put the Soviet Union on notice that large-scale aggression in Central Europe would mean war about the future of Europe and consequently, the future of the United States and the Soviet Union.[84] He hinted that a nuclear response by superior American strategic forces to such aggression would likely result.

At the close of his address, McNamara made the following key observation:

> Let us not delude ourselves with obsolete images into believing that our nuclear strength, great as it is, solves all of our problems of national security, or that we lack the strengths to meet those problems that it does not solve.... Let us be fully aware of the wide range of our military resources, and the freedom they can give us to pursue the peaceful objectives of the free world without fear of military aggression.[85]

On November 20, President Kennedy began his hoped-for political healing visit to Texas. Upon his arrival the President was soon aware that the prevailing mood among Texans was strongly tinged with hostility punctuated only now and then by warm and enthusiastic feeling. While in Texas President Kennedy took up the theme of America's military strength along similar lines to those expressed by the Secretary of Defense to the Economic Club of New York. His speech before a friendly audience in Fort Worth dealt particularly with the contributions by the United States to the preservation of the security of the free world.

The speech the President proposed to give before the Dallas Citizens Council was to have been a major foreign policy address. The speech's theme was that there are many kinds of strengths and no one kind will suffice. Overwhelming nuclear strength, for example, was incapable of stopping guerrilla war. Arguing for national strength ranging from the most massive deterrents to the most subtle influences, the address reviewed the nation's progress in the major areas of strength. Of the nation's power at the level of general nuclear war, the President would have said,

> ... as Secretary McNamara made clear in his address last Monday, the strategic nuclear power of the United States has been so greatly modernized and expanded in the last 1,000 days, by the rapid production

> and deployment of the most modern missile systems, that any and all potential aggressors are clearly confronted now with the impossibility of strategic victory—and the certainty of total destruction—if by reckless attack they should ever force upon us the necessity of a strategic reply.[86]

The President's speech closed loftily:

> We in this country, in this generation, are by destiny—rather than choice—the watchmen on the walls of world freedom. We ask, therefore, that we may be worthy of our power and responsibility—that we may exercise our strength with wisdom and restraint—and that we may achieve in our time and for all time the ancient vision of peace on earth, good will toward men. That must always be our goal—and the righteousness of our cause must always underlie our strength. For as was written long ago: "Except the Lord keep the city, the watchman waketh but in vain."[87]

It would have been entirely unexpected—and in fact did not happen—if significant changes had been proposed by newly designated President Lyndon Johnson in the immediate aftermath of President Kennedy's assassination on November 22, 1963. In less than a month after being sworn in as President, Mr. Johnson assured the nation that he would continue to maintain the preeminent military striking force already in-being and planned for the remainder of the 1960s. A small testimony to this fact was given by the Department of Defense on the last day of 1963 when it announced in a brief bulletin that the last Titan II intercontinental missiles had become operational, thus giving the nation 534 ICBMs ready to fire.[88]

Arrayed against the formidable strategic bomber and missile forces enunciated by the President and Secretary McNamara, one reliable source estimated that by the end of 1963 the Soviet Union possessed on the order of 100 ICBMs fully operational and partially hardened, a total of 750 IRBMs aimed at targets in Western Europe, and a bomber force consisting of approximately 200 heavy intercontinental bombers and 1,000 medium bombers.[89]

NOTES

1. U.S., Congress, House, Subcommittee of the Committee on Appropriations, *Hearings on Department of Defense Appropriations for 1964,* 88th Cong., 1st sess., 1963, Part I, pp. 90, 91.

2. Ibid., p. 95.

3. Ibid., p. 96.

4. Ibid., p. 97.

5. Ibid., p. 99.

6. Ibid., pp. 100–101.

7. Ibid., p. 102.

8. Ibid., p. 103.

9. Ibid., p. 105.

10. Ibid.

11. Ibid., p. 106.

12. Ibid., p. 110.

13. Ibid., p. 111.

14. Ibid.

15. Ibid.

16. Ibid.

17. Ibid., p. 112.

18. Ibid.

19. Ibid.

20. John F. Loosbrock, "Strategic Retreat from Reality," *Air Force and Space Digest,* January 1963, p. 1 (reprint).

21. Claude Witze, "Farewell to Counterforce," *Air Force and Space Digest,* February 1963, p. 27.

22. House, *DOD Appropriations, 1964,* p. 224.

23. Senate, Armed Services Committee, *DOD Appropriations for FY 1964,* p. 89.

24. House, Subcommittee, *DOD Appropriations for FY 1964,* p. 311.

25. Ibid., pp. 311–312.

26. Ibid., p. 312.

27. Ibid., p. 313.

28. Ibid.

29. Ibid., pp. 339–340.

30. Ibid., p. 330.

31. Ibid., p. 333.

32. Ibid., p. 334.

33. Ibid.

34. Senate, Armed Services Committee, *DOD Appropriations for FY 1964*, p. 89.

35. Ibid., p. 340.

36. Ibid.

37. Ibid., p. 341.

38. Ibid.

39. Ibid., p. 90.

40. "McNamara Denies Skybolt Loss Threatens Strategic Strength," *Washington Post–Times Herald*, February 4, 1963. See also Witze, "Farewell to Counterforce," pp. 27–29; Loosbrock, "Strategic Retreat from Reality," pp. 28–31.

41. *Washington Post–Times Herald*, February 4, 1963.

42. Ibid.

43. Alain Enthoven, Address before the Loyola University Forum for National Affairs, "United States Defense Policy for the 1960s," at Los Angeles, California, February 10, 1963, p. 3. The same address was presented at Seattle University on February 11, 1963.

44. Ibid., p. 4.

45. Ibid., pp. 4–5.

46. Ibid., p. 7.

47. Ibid.

48. Ibid., p. 11.

49. Ibid., p. 12.

50. Ibid., p. 13.

51. Ibid., p. 14.

52. Ibid., p. 16.

53. Ibid., p. 17.

54. Ibid., p. 23.

55. U.S., Arms Control and Disarmament Agency, *Documents on Disarmament 1963*, (Washington, D.C.: Government Printing Office, 1964), p. 215.

56. Ibid., pp. 217–218.

57. Ibid., pp. 218–219.

58. Ibid., p. 220.

59. Arthur M. Schlesinger, *A Thousand Days* (Boston: Houghton Mifflin Co., 1965), p. 904.

60. Theodore Sorensen, *Kennedy* (New York: Harper and Row, 1965), p. 736.

61. U.S., Congress, Senate, Committee on Foreign Relations, *Hearings on the Nuclear Test Ban Treaty*, 88th Cong., 1st sess., 1963, p. 97.

62. Ibid., p. 98.

63. Ibid.

64. Ibid., p. 99.

65. Ibid., p. 100.

66. Ibid.

67. Ibid., pp. 102–103.

68. Ibid., p. 103.

69. Ibid., p. 104.

70. Ibid., p. 105.

71. Ibid., p. 107.

72. Ibid., p. 108.

73. Ibid., p. 109.

74. Ibid., pp. 120–121.

75. Quoted in Ibid., p. 114.

76. Ibid., p. 137.

77. Ibid., p. 194.

78. Ibid., p. 146.

79. Robert S. McNamara, Address before the Economic Club of New York, November 18, 1963 (Department of Defense, Office of Public Affairs, Release No. 1486–63).

80. Ibid., p. 1.

81. Ibid., p. 6.

82. Ibid., p. 7.

83. Ibid., p. 8.

84. Ibid., pp. 12, 14.

85. Ibid., p. 21.

86. Quoted in William W. Kaufmann, *The McNamara Strategy* (New York: Harper and Row, 1964), p. 315.

87. Ibid., p. 319.

88. *Washington Post–Times Herald*, December 11, 1963, p. A-1, and December 31, 1963, p. A-1.

89. *The Military Balance, 1963–1964* (London; The Institute for Strategic Studies, 1963), pp. 3–4.

CHAPTER 5

Missiles Versus Manned Bombers: Is There a Choice?

Whereas the United States was just emerging from the gravest crisis in its postwar history in early 1963, at the beginning of 1964 the nation had passed through an entire year without having to face either a crisis provoked by the Soviet Union or armed aggression by Communist China. More and more, the Cuban crisis was beginning to appear as a watershed in American-Soviet relations; there seemed to be a moving away from recurring crises which had punctuated the postwar world. The relaxation of tensions fostered by the Limited Test Ban Treaty, the Hot Line, and the United Nations General Assembly resolution of October 17, 1963, expressing the intention of the United States and the Soviet Union not to station any weapons of mass destruction in outer space showed few signs of early abatement. All remaining Soviet combat forces had been removed from Cuba during the previous year, and in December 1963 Premier Khrushchev announced a modest reduction in the Soviet defense budget and hinted at impending reductions in military personnel. Thus, an observer could legitimately ask: Was a basic change taking place in Soviet policy toward the United States and the free world, or were there constraints operating on the Soviet leaders, forcing them temporarily to shift their tactics, hoping for greater long-run gains?

Although it was conceded that the Communist Chinese had trained and equipped armed forces capable of mounting a renewed attack on India, for a number of reasons it seemed improbable that such an attack was likely to occur. Mainland China was just beginning to emerge from the near collapse of its economy in 1961–1962, which had been precipitated by a succession of agricultural disasters. Many of its ambitious industrial plans were abandoned in an effort to achieve agricultural self-sufficiency. Intensification of the Sino-Soviet split seemed to insure that Soviet industrial and military assistance would be withheld. Further, much of the equipment used by the Chinese armed forces was Soviet in origin and was becoming old and obsolete. China's industrial base appeared to be inadequate to supply the aircraft, equipment, and weapons to modernize the armed forces needed to enable it to engage in possible military adventures dictated by a militant leadership. At most it seemed likely that China might well intensify its efforts during 1964 to further isolate India by seeking a broader position of influence in Nepal and Pakistan.

The situation in Vietnam following the overthrow of the Diem government in the fall of 1963 appeared to be worsening, thus forcing the United States ever closer to a major decision about whether to commit the necessary military force to ensure the survival of an independent government in South Vietnam as an essential step toward preserving the security of all Southeast Asia. Considerable support seemed to be growing for a challenge to the Communist assertion that aggression could succeed through subversion. Instability and unrest continued to characterize the situation in Laos, Indonesia, Thailand, Cambodia and the Arab nations and Israel in the Middle East.

The aftermath of the Chinese attack on India left the latter in need of broad economic and military assistance. Commitments by the United States and its allies to assist India in the rebuilding of its defenses had sharp repercussions in Pakistan, which viewed any Indian buildup as a primary threat to its own security. In addition, the United States was engaged in a serious effort to encourage NATO to undertake a comprehensive and systematic study designed to relate strategy to force requirements and force requirements to resources, so that realistic force goals might be developed which all members of the alliance would consider attainable within the resources they were willing to commit to the common effort. While reassuring the NATO allies that the United States would keep its forces in Western Europe as long as a threat to its security existed, defense officials in this country undertook to demonstrate that the NATO forces already deployed in Europe were more evenly matched with Soviet bloc forces than was generally accepted by the allies themselves. Thus, in January 1964, estimates of the overall power balance strongly favored the United States and its free world allies, and it seemed doubtful that the Communist nations would become involved in situations that might risk war with this nation.

The Johnson Foreign and Defense Policies

In his first annual message to Congress on the State of the Union delivered on January 8, 1964, President Johnson clearly stated his intention to carry on the basic foreign policy enunciated by the Kennedy administration. He told Congress:

> Our ultimate goal is a world without war, a world made safe for diversity, in which all men, goods, and ideas can freely move across every border and every boundary.
>
> We must maintain—and our reduced defense budget will maintain—that margin of military safety and superiority obtained through three years of steadily increasing both the quality and the quantity of our strategic, our conventional, and our antiguerrilla forces.[1]

With respect to arms control and disarmament he stated:

> We must take new steps—and we shall make new proposals at Geneva—toward the control and the abolition of arms. Even in the absence of agreement, we must not stockpile arms beyond our needs or seek an excess of military power that could be provocative as well as wasteful.[2]

Concluding his remarks on foreign and defense policy, the President said:

I would say to the Congress that we must be constantly prepared for the worst, and constantly acting for the best. We must be strong enough to win any war, and we must be wise enough to prevent one.

We shall neither act as aggressors nor tolerate acts of aggression. We intend to bury no one, and we do not intend to be buried.

We can fight, if we must, as we have fought before, but we pray that we will never have to fight again.[3]

As promised in his State of the Union address, President Johnson, in a message to the Eighteen-Nation Disarmament Conference which was resuming its negotiations in Geneva, told that body on January 21, 1964:

While we continue our efforts to achieve general and complete disarmament under effective international control, we must first endeavor to halt further increases in strategic armaments now. The United States, the Soviet Union and their respective allies should agree to explore a verified freeze of the number and characteristics of strategic nuclear offensive and defensive vehicles. For our part, we are convinced that the security of all nations can be safeguarded within the scope of such an agreement and that this initial measure preventing the further expansion of the deadly and costly arms race will open the path to reductions in all types of forces from present levels.[4]

On the same day that his arms control message was delivered to the Eighteen-Nation Conference, President Johnson presented his annual budget message to the Congress for fiscal year 1965. In the portion of the budget relating to defense, the President reaffirmed his intention to preserve freedom and protect our vital national interests in these years of uneasy peace. The nation, he said, had invested heavily in the improvement of its defenses and would not concede to our opponents supremacy in any type of potential conflict, whether nuclear war, conventional warfare, or guerrilla conflict. He then called attention to the increases in military preparedness achieved during the past three years:

—A 100 percent increase in the number of nuclear weapons available in the strategic alert forces.

—A 60 percent increase in the tactical nuclear forces deployed in Western Europe.

—A 45 percent increase in the number of combat-ready Army divisions.
—A 35 percent increase in the number of tactical fighter squadrons.
—A 75 percent increase in airlift capability to improve mobility.[5]

Although the administration was proposing an $800 million reduction in cash outlays for fiscal 1965, the President's message declared that defense expenditures would nevertheless remain high —estimated to be $55.2 billion. Substantial improvements in present and planned military capabilities would be realized, including additional Minuteman missiles, further improvements in our air, land, and sea tactical forces, procurement of additional airlift aircraft, and continued research and development to ensure America's ability to counter new threats.[6] And once again, the President recommended that in order to reinforce the total defense effort, Congress should authorize funds for fallout shelters in public buildings, schools, hospitals, and other institutions.

"Overkill" or "First Strike"?

Defense Secretary McNamara appeared before the House Armed Services Committee on January 27, 1964 to present his third defense program and budget since 1961. Speaking of the requirement for strategic retaliatory forces, the Secretary pointed out that the size and character of these forces was influenced importantly by the basic strategy they were designed to support. America's basic strategy had been the topic of a great deal of discussion during the past year, McNamara explained, which was only proper considering its critical importance. However, he continued, "the wide differences in perspective that this discussion has revealed would seem to indicate that we have failed to convey, at least to certain important sections of the American public, the fundamentals of the strategic problem confronting our nation in this nuclear age."[7] At one extreme, said McNamara, were the advocates of the "overkill" theory who "argue that the United States already has enough nuclear weapons to destroy all of the major cities of the Soviet Union several times over, even after absorbing the first blow and that, therefore, no further investments in the strategic retaliatory forces are required or can be justified."[8] At the other extreme, he said, were the proponents of the "full first-strike" theory who believed that this nation should build a strategic force large enough so that if we struck first the damage which a Soviet retaliatory strike could do to United States population and industry could be held to "acceptable" limits.

The overkill advocates, McNamara explained, wanted to restrict American strategic forces to those optimumly required against cities only. This was not a new concept, he stated, but one that had been debated within the Department of Defense before he came to the Pentagon. The Secretary asserted that he did not know a single responsible official in the department who would support such a theory. In his judgment American strategic retaliatory forces, in order to serve as a maximum deterrent to nuclear war, must be clearly capable of totally destroying the Soviet society under all conditions of retaliation. Also, in the event that war was forced upon the nation, such forces ought to have the power to limit the destruction to our cities and population "to the maximum extent practicable."

Secretary McNamara developed a scenario in which the Soviet Union attacked the United States and Western Europe but did not fire all of its strategic nuclear weapons in a salvo launch. Regardless of whether the Soviets attacked American cities and military installations singly or together, the Secretary believed it was likely that a Soviet attack would extend over a sufficient period of time to permit United States forces to strike back not only at cities, but also at elements of the enemy's forces that had not already been launched. Thus, to achieve such a capability, McNamara contended that the nation required a strategic force considerably larger than one needed solely to destroy cities.

Advocates of the overkill theory argued "that the United States would have already been gravely damaged by the initial attack, that it would be very difficult to destroy the enemy's residual force, and that in any event we could not know which of their missiles had not been fired and which were the 'empty holes.' " Why, then, the overkill advocates argued should the United States even try to destroy an enemy's residual nuclear threat forces? Secretary McNamara readily agreed that the nation would be seriously damaged by an initial Soviet attack. And he conceded that as time went on and the Soviet Union continued to harden its missile sites and deploy missile-firing submarines, it would become increasingly difficult to destroy any substantial part of its residual forces. But, the Secretary added, "it is one thing to recognize the facts of life; it is quite another to throw up one's hands and not even make the attempt to save what we can of our nation and our society."[9]

McNamara revealed that during the past several years many comprehensive studies had been made of alternative United States strategic retaliatory forces engaged in a nuclear exchange against a wide range of possible Soviet forces and under a wide variety of assumed situations in which war broke out. Based on the results he concluded: "In every pertinent case, we found that forces in excess of those needed simply to destroy Soviet cities would significantly reduce damage to the United States and Western Europe. And the extent to which damage to ourselves can be reduced depends importantly on the size and character of our own forces, particularly the surface-to-surface missiles, such as MINUTEMAN that can reach their targets quickly."[10] In addition, said the Secretary, even an assured and persuasive cities only strategy would require forces much larger than those apparently advocated by the overkill supporters. Such factors as numbers of targets and their defenses, weapons required to saturate defenses and assure penetration, damage to one's own forces by enemy attack, and the readiness and reliability of our own weapons demanded, McNamara stressed, that such uncertainties be compensated for by extra insurance—deliberate overprogramming of American forces against any predictable Soviet threat.

If a cities only strategy would be dangerously inadequate, the Secretary continued, a full first-strike force is, "on the basis of our estimates of the Soviet nuclear strike forces in the fiscal year 1967–1969 period, simply unattainable." And, he emphasized, "I know of no responsible Pentagon official, certainly none of the Joint Chiefs of Staff, who proposes such a force." McNamara reminded the committee members that the Soviets were hardening some ICBM sites and were building missile-launching submarines. Although he acknowledged the ability of our forces to sink a large number of enemy submarines in a protracted war of attrition at sea, there was virtually no prospect of being able to destroy most of the Soviet ballistic missile fleet with one quick first strike. Neither could we count, he said, "with any reasonable degree of assurance, on destroying all or almost all of the Soviet's hardened missile sites, even if we were to double or triple our forces." Thus, in the Secretary's estimation, a full first-strike capability would have to be supported by large programs of anti-missile, anti-bomber, and civil defenses. Even then, in Mr. McNamara's opinion, fatalities would almost certainly run into tens of millions.[11]

On the basis of the foregoing analysis, the Secretary said, he had come to the conclusion that a damage-limiting strategy appeared to be the most practical and effective course for the United States to follow. Such a strategy would require forces considerably larger than those needed for a cities only strategy. And he concluded:

> While there are still some differences of judgment on just how large such a force should be, there is general agreement that it should be large enough to ensure the destruction, singly or in combination, of the Soviet Union, Communist China, and the Communist satellites as national societies, under the worst possible circumstances of war outbreak that can reasonably be postulated, and, in addition, to destroy their war-making capability so as to limit, to the extent practicable, damage to this country and to our allies.[12]

Secretary McNamara turned next to a more detailed discussion of present and planned strategic bomber and missile forces. He noted that in June 1964 the number of ICBM and Polaris missiles would, for the first time, just about equal the number of manned bombers in the strategic force. Also, he said, "during the three-year period from end fiscal year 1961 through end fiscal year 1964, the number of weapons in the alert forces will have been increased about two and one-half times and the megatonnage of these weapons almost three times, even though a large number of B-47s will have been phased out of the force during the same period." Therefore, the Secretary concluded that on the basis of the latest estimates of Soviet strategic forces he was prepared to say, "There is no question but that today our strategic retaliatory forces are fully capable of destroying the Soviet target system, even after absorbing an initial surprise attack."[13]

Role of Manned Bombers in the Strategic Force

In planning the strategic retaliatory forces through fiscal year 1969, Secretary McNamara told the committee that, "We plan to continue a mixed force of missiles and manned bombers throughout the entire planning period. . . ."[14] In his judgment most of the aiming points in the Soviet target system could best be hit by missiles; thus, long-range bombers would continue to be used in follow-up attacks, i.e., against hard missile sites and targets, such as weapon storage sites not requiring urgent attack. On this basis the Secretary said he planned to continue the B-52 and B-58 forces through the five-year planning period, with only a slight reduction in B-58s due to expected attrition. Existing B-47 forces would continue to phase out on schedule. McNamara recommended no new additions in the B-52 fleet, but he said $1.6 billion would have been invested by the end of the coming fiscal year to strengthen structurally and provide new equipment for the B-52s to enable them to overcome enemy defensive improvements and reach their assigned targets. The Secretary announced his intention to maintain half of the strategic bombers on fifteen-minute ground alert and a small number on airborne alert. McNamara also announced that $5 million had been included in the FY 1965 budget "to examine the technical feasibility and military value of possible new advanced strategic aircraft which would serve as airborne missile platforms."[15] As a result, the major issues affecting the future choice among strategic weapons systems, and thoroughly aired during the 1964 congressional hearings, related to the future of the manned strategic bomber in the anticipated 1970s weapons environment.

During the hearings before the House Armed Services Committee in late January, Secretary McNamara was asked by Representative Mendel Rivers, "Do we take it that the day of the manned bomber is over—I mean is the bomber on its way out? This is the first time in our lifetime we haven't had some kind of plans for a manned bomber. . . . does this mean that we won't have any manned aircraft other than the fighter-bomber in the future after these present inventories are phased out?" McNamara replied that the manned bomber, especially as the intercontinental ballistic missiles come into our inventories and the inventories of our opponents in ever-increasing numbers, "becomes less useful as an offensive weapon against the time-sensitive targets, and when I say time-sensitive targets, I mean targets that if they are to be destroyed, must be destroyed in a very short period of time." He went on to explain that for other types of targets, particularly those that are thought of as the normal interdiction or tactical type of targets—troop concentrations, transportation centers, battlefield targets—the manned bombers would continue to be a useful weapon. For that reason, the Secretary said, "we have under development new aircraft such as the TFX, which, while it carries the label 'fighter-bomber,' is much more of a fighter-bomber than anything we have every had before in terms of range." Congressman Rivers asked the Secretary whether it was true that the Department of Defense was not seriously looking for a successor to the B-52—especially in view of the five-year lead time. McNamara answered, "We are continuing studies, but we have no plan at the present time to produce a successor to the B-52."[16]

Early in February 1964, during his appearance before the combined Senate Committee on Armed Services and the Subcommittee on Department of Defense Appropriations, Secretary McNamara was reminded by Senator Leverett Saltonstall that the main emphasis of his statement had been more on missiles than on bombers. McNamara replied:

> That is correct. However, we still continue to explore possible bombers for use in our strategic forces. I asked the Air Force many months ago to examine all possible types of bombers—long endurance bombers, stand-off bombers, high altitude—low altitude missile-carrying bombers—and to determine whether any of these would add so significantly to our strategic strength, as to warrant developing and procuring the bomber.
>
> These studies are continuing, and we have provided in the fiscal 1965 budget $5 million for program definition of such aircraft.
>
> I haven't seen or heard of anything yet that warrants development and production.
>
> The Air Force, particularly the Chief of Staff of the Air Force, feels otherwise. But the matter has not yet been fully considered by the Chiefs. There are still a number of questions to be answered in

relation to it, but in any case we have $5 million in the fiscal 1965 budget.[17]

Somewhat later during the same sequence of questions, Senator Stennis remarked that the $5 million recommended by the Department of Defense for bomber-concept definition seemed very small. He asked the Secretary to be a bit more explicit about the recommended amount of money. McNamara said it had been recommended in order to allow the Air Force to define clearly the characteristics and specifications of a manned bomber to supplement the missile force if and when it reached a point where it could conceive a definite mission, which as yet it had not. The Secretary agreed to a further question by Senator Stennis that the concept for a long-range bomber was new and in no way was just an improvement over the B-52 concept. But, McNamara emphasized, he did not think the Air Force should spend substantial funds until it had developed "a formal justification for the requirement of such a bomber, setting forth the concept of employment and estimate of survivability and penetrability in relation to other weapons systems. . . ."[18] He went on to explain that the future role of a bomber was necessarily uncertain after something on the order of 1,000 to 2,000 missiles had been placed on the Soviet Union. What, the Secretary asked, would be left to mop up? If no mop-up operation exists, then what is the role of a manned bomber?

The future of the strategic bomber was also carefully examined during Secretary McNamara's appearance before the House Subcommittee of the Committee on Appropriations. The matter first arose in the course of a discussion of funds for research and development. Congressman Mahon told the Secretary it seemed to him that a very minor amount was being requested by the Air Force for the exploration of new types of bombers. McNamara told the committee that of a total of $5.5 billion being requested for research and development of new weapons systems, a total of $2.6 billion of that sum would go toward insuring

that our offensive and defensive strategic systems of the future are superior to any other systems developed any place else in the world, and this matter of a few tens of millions of dollars that tends to lie between my recommendations and those you may have heard that the Air Force proposed to the authorizing committee in the House is negligible in size in relation to the total development effort that we are directing to improve our strategic offensive and defensive systems.[19]

Mahon asked the Secretary to comment specifically on aircraft, meaning the funds at issue in the hearings. McNamara stated that not even the Air Force was proposing an increase in the total research and development funds for strategic systems. At most, he said, "they have proposed that roughly $90 million—$50 million for a manned bomber and $40 million as I recall for an interceptor—be authorized for expenditure, the funds to be obtained from other programs already recommended in the budget for the Air Force."[20] The Secretary reiterated that to the best of his knowledge no proposal had been made to him by the Secretary of the Air Force or the Air Force Chief of Staff that any money be added to the budget for the Air Force.

Secretary McNamara acknowledged that the Air Force would like to see the amount—$5 million—being recommended by the Defense Department augmented by some $50 million, but added that he believed the request represented only the view of the Chief of Staff, General Curtis LeMay. He stated, however, that "the purpose for the additional funds is not clear... and I would not at this time support that recommendation." Moreover, the Secretary continued, not even the Chief of Staff of the Air Force was asking for the addition of $50 million to the budget; "he has simply said he would like to reallocate funds within the total budget which I am proposing for the Air Force in such a way as to make available, should he later decide to spend them, an additional $50 million for the work on manned bombers." Mahon asked the Secretary pointedly, "Well, would you recommend that we appropriate funds in excess of your budget?" And, McNamara replied: "I would strongly recommend against it, (a) because I do not believe it is necessary to spend the funds, and (b) even if it is necessary to spend the funds, the Chief of Staff of the Air Force has said he does not need any extra funds. He would simply wish to reallocate funds included in the budget that I am recommending to you." Representative Ford then asked McNamara if he would oppose the reallocation of this money. The Secretary answered: "I would unless, (a) I knew and approved what he was going to spend it for and why, and (b) unless I knew what he was going to take it from."[21]

The manned bomber of the future emerged as an issue again later in the hearings. General Maxwell Taylor was asked by Congressman Daniel Flood at what period he thought the nation would no longer depend on a manned bomber. General Taylor's reply is noteworthy:

> One of the toughest problems we are faced with in the weapon field is the rate at which we should replace manned bombers by missiles. I think the present trend is about right. When we should retire the B-52 itself is not entirely certain. There are the questions of fatigue to the metal of the aircraft and so forth. These matters are being studied very closely now so we can form some reasonably good estimate of their useful life.[22]

Following a discussion off the record, General Taylor continued, "The emotionally charged decision is one which is going to be faced by the Department of Defense very shortly, that is, whether or not to accept the recommendations of the Air Force with regard to a follow-on bomber. As the Secretary had indicated, no completed conceptual proposal has been made yet, nor have the Joint Chiefs of Staff passed on the follow-on bomber as a military requirement."[23]

Representative Robert Sikes later asked the Secretary of Defense whether it would be possible to spend more than $5 million effectively in the coming fiscal year on the development of a future manned bomber. McNamara repeated that the characteristics of such a bomber, its operational concept and purpose, had not been presented to him in detail, and thus he was satisfied that $5 million was sufficient. Pressed further by Congressman Sikes, McNamara said he had no basis for a judgment whether another manned bomber was essential or not. But he agreed to retain an open mind on the issues until the Joint Chiefs had an opportunity to review the Air Force's proposal and had forwarded their recommendations to him.[24]

Representative Harold Ostertag asked Secretary McNamara what action he would take if his studies of the Joint Chiefs of Staff proposal on the manned bomber indicated support for it. The Secretary said he would either recommend a supplemental request or reallocate funds on a priority basis. Sikes then asked, "Would it be your purpose if a need should clearly be demonstrated for a more rapid development of a new bomber to seek funds by one of the other methods?" The Secretary answered, "Without question." As the questioning continued, McNamara was asked why the Air Force had not yet presented its conceptual bomber study for his justification. He replied, "They are having difficulty because of the complexity of the problem in developing strategic concepts and operational plans which justify such an expenditure." An interesting exchange followed:

> *Mr. Minshall:* They have presented it to the Congress, but not to the Secretary of Defense?
>
> *Secretary McNamara:* I am not aware they have presented any strategic concept and operational plan and detailed design objectives to the Congress.
>
> *Mr. Minshall:* They must have something in their hip pocket, or they would not have presented it to the Armed Services Committee.
>
> *Mr. Ostertag:* Why would you resist the authorization of these funds when there is a possibility you might ask Congress for them?
>
> *Secretary McNamara:* As a matter of principle, I do not believe Congress should authorize funds simply because there exists a "possibility." There should be a clear justification as a basis for the authorization.[25]

The Chief of Staff of the Air Force, General Curtis LeMay, was called to testify by the House and Senate Appropriations and Armed Services Committees. Appearing before the combined Senate Committee on Armed Forces and the Subcommittee on Department of Defense Appropriations of the Committee on Appropriations on February 19, 1964, General LeMay stated:

> I consider that our present strategic posture provides us with an adequate deterrent. However, in looking into the future, I am extremely concerned over the lack of a follow-on manned strategic system to replace our aging bomber fleet.[26]

Several weeks later, on February 25, in an appearance before the

House Appropriations Subcommittee, General LeMay was asked by Representative Jamie Whitten to describe the difference between his view and that of the Secretary of Defense on the issue of a follow-on manned bomber. The Chief of Staff stated that he preferred to let the Defense Secretary speak for himself, but he agreed to give his own views as to what was needed for the defense of the nation. Specifically, General LeMay explained:

> I firmly believe that the best defense lies in a mixture of weapons, what we call a mix of manned and unmanned systems. All of our war gaming and all our experience indicates that you get a more efficient campaign if you fight with a mixture of unmanned systems and manned systems. You then can use the unmanned systems to do the things they can do better and you use the manned systems to do the things they do better. Therefore, your overall results are much more efficient than if you only had one system that would do one thing well.[27]

He contended that the greatest value of the bomber was its deterrent value. A manned system, he believed, possessed greater flexibility for use in preventing war, whereas with a missile system only two operations were possible, "you either fire it or you do not fire it." General LeMay elaborated this point further, saying, "There is no way of showing force with a missile. With a manned system, you can maneuver and change bases. You can fly them out so they can be seen on the radar screen, or actually conduct some limited attacks if you want to. There are many options you have with a manned system you do not have with a missile system."[28]

During further extensive discussion of future manned bomber issues before the Appropriations Subcommittee, General LeMay testified that it was estimated that the total cost for the research and development program would be approximately $1.8 billion. In this context, Representative William Minshall asked General LeMay whether the planned TFX might be used against strategic targets. The General replied: "I do not think the TFX could be used as a strategic weapon system. We need a bigger airplane."[29] Later on Representative Flood asked General LeMay why the TFX with refueling would not serve adequately as a strategic weapon system? The Chief of Staff stated:

The Air Force has conducted extensive analysis of many alternative aircraft for the strategic role. The TFX was designed for the tactical mission, and in this role the Air Force is confident that it will provide an important contribution to overall United States military power. In terms of the strategic role, however, the TFX has serious limitations in range, payload, capability for military subsystems, and crew size.[30]

Chairman Mahon asked Secretary of the Air Force Eugene Zuckert and General LeMay to provide the committee with as much background information as possible on the requirement for a follow-on bomber. General LeMay pointed out that it had been apparent to the Air Force for some time that the administration would not accept the B-70 as a weapon system. Thus, he continued, "feeling as strong as we do about the need for a manned system, we set about to come up with another manned system that perhaps they would approve. We have had a great number of studies going on, not only in the Air Force, but in the nonprofit research organizations and our scientific advisory boards on the various phases of this subject."[31] General LeMay testified that the Air Force had actually been engaged in studies over the past eighteen months to two years. Personnel from the Office of the Secretary of Defense had been represented in the studies throughout the period. Thus, he said, to some extent the Secretary of Defense was aware of what was going on.[32]

In an apparent effort to clarify some of General LeMay's remarks, Secretary Zuckert told the committee that he had asked for answers to a number of questions involving the proposed manned bomber. He explained that the Air Staff prepared a great deal of documentation in answer to the questions and some in response to the Joint Chief's request. Then he acknowledged, "At the moment I have not reviewed the material which the Air Staff has presented. So at the moment there is nothing that has gone out of the Air Force to the Secretary of Defense on any specific program." Representative Flood pressed Secretary Zuckert very hard on this issue, asking him if it was true that nothing presently existed but a vague, conceptional notion about the controversial bomber? The Secretary said, "Let me try to explain again. In fairness now both to the Air Force and the Secretary of Defense, there is no formal proposal. The proposal is sitting on my desk at this moment, the formal proposal." Flood thought this situation astounding, which prompted the following reply from Secretary Zuckert: "I think what I did was tell the Secretary of Defense that the Air Force had made a choice as to the selection of the airplane and that they would require a substantial amount of money in fiscal 1965. I considered $50 or $52 million a substantial sum of money. The formal proposal had not gone forward."[33]

Representative Flood then asked General LeMay whether his (Flood's) impression was correct that the Air Force could not have completed its studies in time for the current budget cycle? The Chief of Staff admitted that all of the studies were not completed. For example, he said, "The Forecast report is not yet delivered to the Secretary. Part of the study was in the Forecast project."[34] Despite the fact that the data put before Secretary Zuckert by the Air Staff had not been evaluated and a judgment made by the Secretary, General LeMay was insistent that a year could be saved in reaching the initial operating capability of the first squadron of a follow-on manned bomber if $50 million was provided by Congress in the FY 1965 budget.

Secretary Zuckert was again asked about the status of the review he was undertaking of the studies submitted to him by the Air Force. The Secretary told the committee that his Under Secretary and Assistant Secretary had reviewed the studies, but that he had not yet found the time to do a thorough job. He acknowledged, however, that he would be ready to make a recommendation to the Secretary of Defense in a couple of weeks.[35] Representative Harry R. Sheppard asked Secretary Zuckert whether $50 million was involved in the studies he was about to examine. The Secretary said money was not presently at issue, rather the information the Air Force presented was a basis for justifying the request for $52 million.

Representative Flood, a rigorous and incisive cross-examiner, questioned General LeMay about the role of the bomber in the hostile environment of the 1970s. General LeMay welcomed the challenge and began by stating that the perfect missile system, which could be depended upon in the 1970s to hit its target every time it was fired, was inconceivable. Again he attacked the inflexibility of a pure missile force. A missile once fired, he reminded the committee, could not be recalled, nor could it hit imprecisely defined targets. Flood rejoined by asking General LeMay what targets would be left to hit after an exchange of large megatonnages by the United States and the Soviet Union? LeMay replied, "If you are going to assume a war in which both sides fire enough missiles to completely destroy the whole country, then you do not have any other mission." But, the General said, he did not think a war would likely be fought in one massive spasm. In any event, he said, "I want all the flexibility in the world I can think about so that I can do something in case I am surprised, which I am sure I will be."[36]

In an apparent move to permit the Air Force to make the strongest possible case for a follow-on strategic aircraft, Representative Flood asked General LeMay to take advantage of the record to revise and extend his remarks. General LeMay's reply is worthy of comment. He challenged the wisdom of relying solely on ballistic missile forces "that have never reacted to the conditions of actual war or even to conditions which constitute a peacetime simulation to the wartime environment." Furthermore, the General believed that the employment of strategic missiles in a crisis or a lower-level conflict "would be an inappropriate response and would immediately escalate the situation, uncontrollably to an intensity which could be vastly disproportionate to the original aggravation." General LeMay believed, also, that in any future conflict forces would be needed capable of responding quickly under careful national direction to a wide variety of unforeseen and rapidly changing circumstances. Ballistic missiles, he felt, "inherently were designed to be—and remain—a single shot, irrevocably committed weapon system. In this regard, the manned element of the force, with its unique capability to react immediately to redirection, to exploit fleeting advantages, and to execute a broad range of missions, provides an effective complement to the ballistic missile forces."[37]

Another important way in which aircraft and ballistic missiles complemented each other, according to General LeMay, was to compound the offensive and defensive problems of the enemy. Specifically, he said, "since the alert aircraft can be launched under positive control in conditions of ambiguous warning, the enemy is unable to achieve a high confidence that he can attack successfully a major portion of our strategic force. Similarly, so long as he is faced by a mixed strategic force, the enemy cannot concentrate his resources either on ABM or Air Defense; he must dilute and divide his resources between the two."[38] Finally, General LeMay said he considered it important that the nation have a long-range strategic system capable of supporting war operations against the Soviet Union or engage in limited conflicts which were not dependent upon forward basing.

Later discussion of the manned strategic bomber concept before the House Appropriations Subcommittee helped clarify the design characteristics and operational employment plan for the weapon system. Under questioning General LeMay noted that the bomber would possess higher resolution sensors to assess target conditions and determine whether an attack should be made. The bomber could be employed in a post-strike intelligence and damage assessment role and would be particularly effective in assuring the destruction of hard targets. Of major importance, he believed, the bomber would have a low level penetration capability permitting it to nullify the effectiveness of enemy defenses. And, finally, unlike the B-52 which was not designed to operate from a widely dispersed posture, the advanced manned aircraft would possess low footprint pressure and short takeoff characteristics and sacrifice neither range nor payload. In General LeMay's judgment, "this mobile dispersal concept will provide for high survival of the force under any reasonable assumption concerning future Soviet capabilities."[39]

Missile Dependability

In presenting his posture statement to the House Armed Services Committee, Secretary McNamara announced that the nation's strategic missile forces, which had almost tripled in fiscal year 1963 and more than doubled again in fiscal year 1964, would increase more slowly during the next several years. A total of 800 Minuteman I missiles were included in the current program augmented by the first increment of 150 Minuteman IIs which were included in the fiscal 1964 budget.[40] By themselves the Minuteman II missiles were expected to provide increased range or payload; a smaller target error (CEP); a much greater flexibility in the choice of preassigned targets; and the capability of being launched by radio from an airborne command post. By the end of June 1964, some 600 Minuteman I missiles were expected to be operationally ready, and by the end of June 1965, some 800.

Secretary McNamara announced to the House Armed Services Committee a major revision to the planned Minuteman force which, in his judgment, would greatly increase combat effectiveness at the added cost of $500 million through fiscal year 1969. Specifically, he said, "Minuteman I and Minuteman II squadrons will be integrated into a single system through the 'internetting' of their communications and control systems, thus greatly enhancing the targeting flexibility of the force as a whole." In order to get the major revisions in the Minuteman program underway promptly and on an orderly schedule, the Secretary recommended that only 50 new Minuteman silos be started during fiscal year 1965. McNamara left open the question of whether the total Minuteman force would exceed 1,000. He told the committee, "We have tentatively programmed the funding of additional Minuteman II silos after fiscal year 1965, but the actual number to be started will depend upon the situation prevailing a year or two years from now."[41]

A significant milestone was reached in the history of the American strategic missile forces during 1964. Secretary McNamara announced to the Congress a plan to begin phasing out the earlier squadrons of Atlas ICBMs. In stating that the Atlas Ds and Es as well as the Titan Is would phase out over a period of years, he explained that their high cost of operation and maintenance, estimated at about $1 million per missile as compared to about $100,000 per year for a Minuteman, warranted such a decision.

It was perhaps inevitable that at about the time the strategic missile force reached approximate parity in numbers with the strategic bomber force questions would be asked about whether the missile could be depended upon to hit its planned target, and whether missile dependability was nearly so great as that of the manned bomber which had been undergoing perfection for many years. On January 10, 1964, an article appeared in the *New York Times,* under the byline of John H. Fenton, reporting on a statement allegedly made by Senator Barry Goldwater the day before. The following statement appeared in quotation marks, purporting to be the exact words of the Senator: "I do not feel safe at all about our missiles, to tell you the truth. I wish the Defense Department could tell the American people how undependable the missiles in our silos actually were."[42] The same day—January 9—that the alleged statement appeared, Secretary McNamara issued the following statement:

> Senator Goldwater's reported statement that the United States long-range missiles are not dependable is completely misleading, politically irresponsible, and damaging to the national security. There is no information, classified or otherwise, to support the false implication that our long-range missiles cannot be depended on to accomplish their mission.
>
> The importance of the long-range missiles to the defense of this country and the evaluation of their effectiveness to our leading military authorities is indicated by the strong support given by the Joint Chiefs of Staff to the missile program.[43]

As a consequence of Senator Goldwater's apparent public attack on the reliability of the nation's long-range missiles, Secretary McNamara discussed at great length what he termed the dependability of strategic systems in his prepared statement before the House Armed Services Committee on January 27, 1964. He began this portion of his statement by insisting that a sharp distinction needed to be drawn between mechanical reliability, in the sense of the incidence of mechanical malfunction, and the dependability with which a vehicle in the strategic retaliatory forces accomplished its mission—the destruction of assigned enemy targets. Continuing his case, the Secretary stressed:

> Reliability in this sense is only one of the factors determining system dependability. Equally important are the factors of readiness, survivability, and penetration. The readiness rate is the proportion of the force that is ready to launch on schedule; the survivability rate is the proportion of the force which can be expected to survive, in operating condition, an initial enemy attack; and the penetration rate is the proportion of the launched force which can be expected actually to reach and destroy its targets.[44]

To illustrate the many factors taken into account in order to derive system dependability, McNamara explained a series of calculations which applied the four factors of readiness, survivability, reliability, and penetration to the number of B-52s and Minuteman missiles planned to be in the force by mid-1965. In this way an estimate could be made of the number of each weapons system that might be expected to reach and destroy its targets under varying assumed conditions. Considering, for example, that United States forces would total 630 B-52s and 600 Minuteman missiles by the end of June 1964, the Secretary stated that only 50 percent or 315 of the B-52s could be maintained on ground alert and ready to be launched in fifteen minutes, the warning time expected from the Ballistics Missile Early Warning System (BMEWS). In the case of the solid-fuel Minuteman, it also had to be accepted that some of the missiles would not be ready for launch. It was assumed, too, that of the Polaris submarines at sea on patrol, a high percentage of the missiles were ready for launch at all times.

Even more important than the launch readiness of missiles, according to the Secretary, was the fact that Minuteman missiles were dispersed, one to a site, in hardened silos, and were, therefore, less vulnerable to surprise nuclear attack than the aircraft on the ground. This, he said, was one of the greatest concerns with the manned bombers. Thus, a single thermonuclear weapon striking a SAC base would destroy all the bombers on that base. Moving on to reliability rates Secretary McNamara admitted that the B-52s had been with the force for many years and thus a considerable amount of operational experience had been acquired. Therefore, he said, "the reliability rate of the surviving alert force—the probability that a bomber will not abort because of mechanical malfunction—can be established within a relatively narrow range at a rather high level. On the other hand, the Secretary conceded, the Minuteman missile was just coming into the force, and the amount of operational data available was very sparse. Although operational test firings through January of 1964 indicated a fairly high reliability rate, the number of firings had been too small, he said, to serve as a basis for a firm estimate.[45]

On the basis that the missiles were equipped with penetration aids and outnumbered the forces of the Soviet Union, Secretary McNamara was confident "that once our missiles are launched and on their way they would destroy their targets." Bombers, on the other hand, raised greater uncertainties because it was not clear what proportion would get through the extensive Soviet air defenses. From his analysis the Secretary said, "two striking conclusions emerge.... The first is that in both the optimistic and pessimistic cases a higher proportion of the Minuteman force than of the B-52 force can be counted upon to reach targets in a retaliatory strike.... The second striking conclusion is that there is greater uncertainty about the systems dependability of the B-52, although it is an old and experienced aircraft, than about the Minuteman, a brand new missile system."[46]

Coming even more strongly to the defense of the missile, McNamara told the Armed Services Committee, "although we have used a rather wide range of reliability rates for the Minuteman in this calculation, we believe the reliability of the missiles now in place is closer to the upper limit of the range." Illustrating his point, he affirmed, "The Polaris A-2, which is much further along than Minuteman, has had a high percentage of successful shots. The Minuteman at the present stage of operational testing compares favorably with the Polaris A-2 experience." Furthermore, he asserted, as the operational tests of the strategic missiles continued, reliability rates were expected to increase even further.[47]

McNamara argued strongly against even attempting to achieve 100 percent reliability in the strategic missile forces. In his judgment, "the cost of doing so, if it could be done at all, would be prohibitive, and beyond a certain point not worth the cost in view of the other important factors affecting systems dependability." Instead, he said, "we simply buy more missiles and thus provide a combat reserve, just as we do in the case of aircraft, to cover the targets of those vehicles which abort for any reason whatsoever." As a result of his rigorous analysis, the Secretary felt confident of his conclusion that "on the basis of the evidence already in hand and our plans for the future, I have no hesitancy whatsoever in saying that the missile force we have programed can be depended upon to carry out its military mission under all of the conditions we can foresee, and indeed, that we can predict the results of a missile attack with greater confidence than those of a bomber attack."[48]

In his appearance before the Senate Armed Services Committee and the Appropriations Subcommittee in early February 1964, Secretary McNamara was asked by Senator Stennis very early in the question period to explain the basis of his evaluations on the dependability and reliability of strategic missiles. Senator Stennis told the Secretary that Senator Goldwater, Chairman of the Senate Preparedness Subcommittee, was very much interested in obtaining up-to-date information on the overall missile program as a basis for forming his own opinion about it should it become an open issue—presumably in the presidential election campaign. Expressing his willingness to cooperate fully with the committee to provide detailed information on missile dependability and reliability, McNamara told the committee members, "I do feel this: that when we are talking about dependability of our missile systems, we are talking about the fundamental deterrent to a nuclear strike on this country. As long as I am Secretary of Defense and as long as the facts will support me, I cannot allow our public to be misled as to the dependability of our system. It is dependable." The Secretary also told the committee that he had with him statements from the Chief of Naval Operations and the Chief of the Air Staff which corroborated his own testimony that the missiles were dependable.[49]

During these hearings, Secretary McNamara volunteered, in view of Senator Goldwater's press comment, to put in the record statements by General LeMay relating to missile dependability. By agreement with the committee, McNamara introduced the text of a Joint Statement on Missile Reliability by the Secretary of the Air Force and the Chief of Staff.[50] The text began with an admission that considerable discussion had taken place on the issue of the reliability of the nation's long-range missile forces. In carrying out its war planning objective, said the two Air Force officials, "the military plans both for enough weapon systems and enough weapons so that we can expect that an enemy's system will be destroyed with a margin of safety." Both officials concurred that the nation's ICBM systems could be depended upon to perform their assigned part in the war plan, and as added operational experience was gained, their capabilities and role in war plans would be increased.

Secretary Zuckert and General LeMay sought to allay concern over unsuccessful missile shots, since, they said, it was expected that even the Polaris A-2 and Minuteman tests would not all be successful. They then affirmed:

> We think the greatest reassurance concerning the missile system, at least so far as Minuteman is concerned, is to be derived from the experience and assessment of Minuteman by the Commander of the Strategic Air Command, General Power. The first time that he ever had an operational readiness inspection of Minuteman, SAC crews were able to successfully count down [deleted] missiles stationed at our Malmstrom Base. Although this does not mean that all those missiles would have been successfully launched, it does give us a high degree of confidence that our alert readiness requirements would be met.
>
> The test in General Power's planning has to be the number of Minuteman missiles that he feels confident can be targeted in his war plan. That number exceeds not only the planning factor currently in use by the Joint Chiefs of Staff, but also exceeds what we expected would be our position in the Minuteman program today.[51]

Secretary Zuckert reported that the total expenditures on the Minuteman program through fiscal year 1964 would amount to some $7 billion. He said special efforts had been exerted in every step of the missile program to ensure having a dependable weapon system for the strategic forces. In other words, the Secretary said, "we are confident from every measure that we can use that the Minuteman today exceeds the degree of dependability we have expected and is fully capable of carrying out its part of the military mission." The joint statement concluded with this assessment:

> General LeMay concurs in the foregoing statement regarding reliability. In fact, he would consider the missile program a success with a reliability factor less than we are sure to receive. His main concern is that there are other factors more important than reliability in evaluating the overall effectiveness of our strategic capability. He, therefore, believes that our missile force, along with our manned bomber force, will provide adequate security. A missile force alone will not. Therefore, we must continue our development and procurement of adequate manned systems.[52]

On February 19, 1964, Secretary Zuckert and Chief of Staff LeMay testified before a joint session of the Senate Armed Services Committee and Subcommittee on Appropriations on the issue of the reliability of strategic missiles. Chairman Russell informed the Air Force officials that he had been asked by Senator Goldwater to ask a few questions inasmuch as the Senator was unable to be present. Senator Russell began the questioning by asking whether there have been practical alerts in which our strategic missiles have been brought to the point of firing, i.e., simulating the factors of surprise that might be the circumstances under which a decision would be made to fire against an enemy. General LeMay answered that such tests had been held and were conducted under very rigorous performance standards. Asked by the Chairman whether he was satisfied with the tests, General LeMay replied, "Not at the present time. I think we are in fairly good shape. I am not satisfied with it; no." Russell asked General LeMay what percentage of American missiles could have been launched prior to the arrival of an incoming salvo from the Soviet Union. The General told the committee, "I think we could launch the bulk of our missiles within the fifteen-minute warning time that we would allow."[53]

LeMay was asked also by the committee chairman whether he felt that sufficient testing was actually being conducted to permit us to be confident of the reliability of our strategic missiles. The Chief of Staff stated that a very small sampling of missiles were actually fired, and from the data derived a mathematical formula was applied in order to predict reliability of the total system. As a consequence, the General continued, "I don't feel that you are going to ever get to the point where you will have the same confidence in the missile as you have in the manned systems." Furthermore, LeMay stated, it was impossible to do a true operational test with a missile system since the missiles were removed from their operational silos and taken to one of the test ranges for firing. Chairman Russell was prompted to ask, "So we cannot be perfectly confident that the missiles in their silos or in other emplacements would survive a sustained nuclear attack?" General LeMay agreed that a small degree of uncertainty did exist.[54]

In testifying on the issue of missile reliability, Secretary Zuckert told the joint Senate Committees that he thought General LeMay and himself were essentially in agreement. The Secretary said that one of the difficult problems was that of defining reliability. And he went on to explain:

> As long as we have B-52's and missiles in our planning, in the military planning, we contemplate an increasing degree of missile effectiveness, particularly with the Polaris and the Minuteman.
>
> I think that we have confidence today, General LeMay and I, that the missiles would perform their part of the plan, and an increasing confidence that as the missiles continue to come in, particularly the Minuteman, they will turn out to be a highly dependable system.
>
> We will continue to find out things about these missiles, but I would say that a fair assessment of the problem is that the missiles are as dependable today as the Department's war plan demands, that this is, in my opinion, an amazing achievement.[55]

Finally, Secretary Zuckert was asked by Chairman Russell what comparison he would make between the reliability and efficiency of American missiles with those of the Soviets. The Secretary answered, "One thing I would say, and General LeMay would be more competent than I; I would rather have the solid-fueled Polaris and Minuteman than any liquid-fueled missile that I can imagine." When asked, General LeMay affirmed his confidence that the United States was ahead of the Soviet Union in solid-fueled missiles.

Later the same day Chairman Russell brought up the issue of the Joint Statement on Missile Reliability purportedly prepared and agreed to by Secretary Zuckert and General LeMay. He asked General LeMay whether the statement represented the combined views of himself and Secretary Zuckert. General LeMay replied, "No, sir; it is not. The Secretary and I made an attempt to come up with a combined statement, but never quite succeeded, and the last I saw of it, I found two or three errors in it that had to be corrected, and as I left the Secretary, it was my understanding we weren't going to have one." The General said he had not seen the corrected copy of the statement, but was not happy with the attempt at compromise anyway. Thus, in LeMay's opinion no such Joint Statement existed. In an effort to explain what had happened Secretary Zuckert told the committee, "The General did say that he was not happy with the statement because . . . he wouldn't feel happy with it standing by itself without the opportunity to explain it, in answer to the kind of questions brought out here today." It was, he stated, his clear understanding that an agreed statement had been arrived at. Because Secretary McNamara had earlier read the ostensible Joint Statement on Missile Reliability into the record, Secretary Zuckert insisted to the committee that McNamara had been justified in believing it was a Joint Statement. If no Joint Statement actually existed, said the Secretary, it was the result of a misunderstanding between General LeMay and himself.[56]

A week later in an appearance before the House Appropriations Subcommittee, Representative Gerald Ford asked General LeMay to explain the apparent differences of opinion between himself and Secretary McNamara on the issue of missile reliability. The General readily agreed and told the committee, "I think, generally speaking, I would probably not give as optimistic a picture as the Secretary would. But first let me say I am satisfied with our missile programs, particularly the solid propellant programs. They are coming along very well."[57] He explained that as is the case with every new weapons system, the reliability of missiles during their early phases would be low, and it would rise with experience. When new systems were put in the war plan, General LeMay explained, enough weapons were planned to offset the low reliability of particular systems. There were, however, several unknowns or uncertainties which he thought the committee ought to be aware of. Again LeMay questioned the artificiality of the operational testing program and reminded the committee that in the past the Joint Chiefs had recommended testing strategic missiles in an operational configuration with a nuclear warhead on them. General LeMay said that he and General Power of the Strategic Air Command had reservations about the vulnerability of the weapons system and felt that a test program permitting the explosion of a nuclear weapon on a missile site would have been desirable.

The Polaris Fleet

In his posture statement prepared for the House Armed Services Committee, Secretary McNamara affirmed that the Polaris program was nearly on schedule, slowed only by the institution of rigid inspection procedures put into effect after the *Thresher* disaster. The last six of the planned fleet of forty-one submarines had been fully funded in the FY 1964 budget. And he added that nine Polaris submarines carrying 144 missiles were deployed at sea by July of 1963. The Secretary predicted that the entire force of forty-one submarines carrying 656 missiles could be deployed by mid-1966. The first five Polaris submarines were equipped with the 1,200 nautical mile A-1 missile; the sixth through the eighteenth would be equipped with the 1,500 nautical mile A-2 missile; and the nineteenth through the forty-first submarine would be equipped with the 2,500 nautical mile A-3 missile. Although in 1963 the Defense Department was planning to equip all forty-one submarines with the A-3 missile, McNamara recommended during 1964 that the first five submarines be replaced with the A-3, and the submarines equipped with the A-2 missile be left unchanged, at least for several years, since a large fraction of the targets were well in the range of the 1,500 nautical mile missile. Thus, said the Secretary, "a force consisting of twenty-eight submarines equipped with A-3 missiles and thirteen submarines equipped with A-2 missiles should be able to handle effectively the targets assigned to the Polaris force."[58]

Secretary of the Navy Paul Nitze, testifying before the House Subcommittee on Appropriations late in February 1964, said that eleven Polaris submarines were then deployed at sea, increasing to fifteen on July 1. Of the eleven deployed, he stated, "eight are on station and targeted to commence firing within minutes of receiving the executive command; one is at sea in an operating area undergoing prepatrol training and targeted to fire promptly the missiles on board, and two are alongside the tender maintaining a condition of readiness to insure getting underway on short notice."[59] The Navy Secretary stressed that in time of crisis all eleven submarines with supporting tenders would be at sea within twenty-four hours, a capability demonstrated during the recent Cuban crisis.

Nitze told the committee that the essential element of deterrence was the credibility that retaliation would be devastating and inevitable. In his estimation and that of the Chief of Naval Operations, Admiral David McDonald, the Polaris force as then deployed could not be prevented from retaliating. Part of the reason for this conclusion, the Secretary continued, was that the Polaris fleet at sea was practically invulnerable. And, of parallel importance, the Navy regarded the penetration capability of the Polaris missile to be completely adequate to strike any area protected by possible ballistic missile defense systems. Nitze went on to explain the great flexibility inherent in the Polaris system, making it possible to target and retarget both urban and military targets. He cited an example of the damage the Polaris force alone could inflict on an enemy in retaliation for an attack on American cities. "The results," he said, "indicate that the damage to enemy warmaking capability would be of such major proportions as to make the initiation of a nuclear war by an enemy irrational—population fatalities alone would be between 25 and 35 million."[60]

As part of his formal remarks, Secretary Nitze discussed at some length the reliability factors associated with the Polaris missiles, A-1 and A-2, and cited a statement by Admiral Ricketts, Vice Chief of Naval Operations, on January 9, 1964, on total weapons systems reliability:

> The missiles have proved remarkably reliable. The first Polaris submarine went to sea over three years ago. Since that time, no Polaris has been late in development; no patrol has been aborted; no submarine has returned early from its patrol; no communication message has been missed. Over 99 percent of the time at least fifteen of the sixteen missiles have been ready for firing and all sixteen have been ready for firing over 95 percent of the time.[61]

During the appearance of Secretary McNamara and General Taylor before the Appropriations Subcommittee, General Taylor was asked by Mahon whether the Joint Chiefs of Staff had recently examined the desirability of providing for a fleet of more than forty-one Polaris submarines. General Taylor replied, "No, sir, we have not reviewed that particular figure. I personally would feel that the currently planned fleet, coupled with the Minuteman force of hardened missiles, represents about the right balance in this time frame." Mahon asked whether the Navy agreed with General Taylor's assessment. And the Chief of Staff answered, "So far as I know, the Navy has made no proposition to increase the currently planned forty-one submarine fleet, certainly not within the arena of the Joint Chiefs." Secretary McNamara volunteered that the Navy had made no proposals to him for an increase above forty-one Polaris submarines for inclusion in the fiscal year 1965 budget. Mahon then asked the Secretary, "Do you think yourself that we will probably at a later date want to increase the Polaris fleet?'' McNamara stated, ''No, I do not. I don't see any need in the near future to increase the Polaris fleet.'' He did, however, agree that it would be desirable to consider modernization of the existing fleet, particularly in the sense of providing more advanced and versatile missiles.[62]

The Nike Missile Defense System

The nuclear war strategy of the Kennedy administration rested basically on two important postulates. First, in order to serve as a maximum deterrent to nuclear war United States strategic retaliatory forces must be visibly capable of fully destroying the Soviet society under all conditions of retaliation. Second, in the event that war was forced on the United States, its strategic offensive and defensive forces should have the power to limit the destruction to the nation's cities and population to the maximum extent possible. In the course of his appearance before the House Armed Services Committee in late January 1964, Secretary McNamara emphasized that the strategic threat to the nation was steadily shifting from manned bombers to ICBMs and submarine-launched missiles. He added, ''Our present continental air and missile defense forces were, for the most part, built during the 1950s and were designed primarily to defend against the manned bomber threat. As a result, today, they provide only a limited capability to reduce the damage of a nuclear attack in which long-range strategic missiles are used. Clearly, we should be recasting our defensive programs to recognize the change in the nature of the threat.''[63] With the purpose of improving the damage-limiting capability of the nation's defense forces in mind, McNamara recommended the continuation of the development of a new missile system, the Nike-X, and the expansion of a broad program to create a system of shelters, equipped and provisioned to protect the population from the fallout effects of nuclear attack.

McNamara told the House Armed Services Committee that in initiating the Nike-X development program during 1963 he was hoping to gain three important improvements over the Nike-Zeus program which had been reduced to the study of reentry phenomena and defense techniques. First, the Nike-X system would include a high acceleration missile, Sprint, which would be fast enough to provide time for discrimination of reentering objects before it had to be fired. Second, the system would include a Multi-function Array Radar (MAR), which would have the capability to acquire and track a large number of objects simultaneously, thus reducing the probability that the system's rate of fire could be limited by saturating the radar. And, third, the components of the Nike-X system would be susceptible to hardening to make direct attack on the system unprofitable. In addition, the Defense Department planned to include a number of Nike-Zeus missiles with each battery for purposes of providing a capability for extra-range interception. Finally, it was anticipated that several missile sites would be needed around most cities.[64]

According to McNamara, "The continued testing of the Nike-Zeus and preliminary studies of the Nike-X system's characteristics and effectiveness provide grounds for believing that the technical problems of at least a partial defense against a ballistic missile attack may be solved within the next several years."[65] The Secretary acknowledged, however, that a number of major problems needed solving before sufficient data would be available as a basis for a decision whether to produce and deploy the system. Projects already underway would contribute importantly to an eventual decision. For example, McNamara pointed out that a ZEUS discrimination radar had been installed at Kwajalein in the Marshall Islands in September 1963 and over the next year should produce a considerable amount of information concerning discrimination techniques against various types of penetration aids. In addition, a prototype Multi-function Array Radar (MAR) would be installed at White Sands Missile Range in June 1964, and several other phased-array radars would be tested during the next year in order to expand our knowledge of this type of technology. Thus, according to McNamara, "by next year . . . we should have considerably more information upon which to base a judgment on the technical feasibility of the NIKE-X system."[66]

McNamara urged a cautious approach to a final decision on whether to deploy a Nike-X ABM system. He pointed to the many and complex technical, strategic, and economic problems which remained to be solved before any effective ballistic missile defense system could be deployed. And even if all of these difficulties can be surmounted, the Secretary said, "we will still have to determine whether the potential effectiveness of the system would justify the very high cost of its deployment." He explained, for example, that the estimated research and development and investment cost of a hypothetical Nike-X defense program was likely to be some $16 billion, and it would cost a very substantial additional amount each year to operate the system. McNamara also cautioned, "And these estimates may prove to be low."[67]

The Nike-X system alluded to only in general terms by McNamara would, in his estimation, be relatively effective against small to moderate missile attacks, providing that an active ballistic missile defense system were coupled with adequate civil defense shelters. Even then the Secretary believed that fatalities would run into several tens of millions. If a ballistic missile defense were to be deployed against a large Soviet attack, McNamara said that the Nike-X program would have to be considerably expanded to take into account enemy missiles equipped with penetration aids and decoys. And in this connection he told the committee members, "it should be borne in mind that the cost to the Soviets of adding additional missiles to their force or augmenting their missiles with penetration aids would probably be but a fraction of the cost to us of offsetting these additional missiles or increased penetration capability with additional defensive measures." After explaining further the need to carefully plan effective civil defense measures and urging improvements in the nation's defense against manned bomber attack, the Secretary concluded, "Accordingly, we propose to continue the NIKE-X as a high priority research and development program without any commitment at this time to its ultimate production and deployment."[68]

Second only in importance to the defense of the nation against ICBM attack, according to McNamara, was the problem of defending against submarine-launched missiles. McNamara said that the problem was threefold: (1) the detection and tracking of enemy submarines; (2) the destruction of these submarines before they have an opportunity to launch their missiles; (3) the detection, tracking, and destruction of the missiles once they have been launched.[69] As for the capability to detect and track enemy submarine systems, the Secretary said the Navy had significantly augmented its anti-submarine warfare forces during the past several years. Destruction of the submarines was the responsibility of the Navy's ships, aircraft, and hunter-killer submarines. The Defense Secretary pointed out, however, that "we do not now have any significant defense against missiles once they are launched by enemy submarines."[70] To overcome this deficiency the Defense Department was studying and testing the feasibility of modifying certain coastal radars to give them a capability for detecting missiles launched from submarines. Since the tests were successful, McNamara announced that selected air defense radars on the East, West, and Gulf coasts would be modified to provide some warning against an attack by shorter range missiles. If, he said, the Nike-X system were eventually deployed, it would provide the primary capability against submarine-launched missiles.

Secretary McNamara was questioned by members of the House Appropriations Subcommittee on the issue of deploying at some future time the Nike-X system. Representative Ford asked the Secretary whether he would recommend funds for the procurement of Nike-X unless the administration and Congress approved a fallout shelter program. McNamara answered: "I would not recommend the expenditures for the procurement and deployment of Nike-X unless that procurement and deployment were accompanied by authorization for a satisfactory fallout shelter program."[71] Although the Secretary was not sure he would recommend funds for the deployment of Nike-X in any event, without adequate fallout shelters, he stressed, an enemy could negate the Nike-X system by targeting its missiles upwind of the defended areas, thus achieving its objective anyway.

A short time later on March 1, 1964, Dr. Harold Brown, Director of Defense Research and Engineering, also testified before the House Appropriations Subcommittee on the deployment of Nike-X. He was asked by Chairman Mahon whether he felt that the Nike-X offered sufficient promise that, if the technical objectives were met, it would be deployed. Brown replied, "That is the $20 billion question.... I should say from the research and development point of view that NIKE-X appears to be the best active ABM system, from the point of view of cost effectiveness, that we will be able to achieve over the next ten years."[72] It was conceivable, he said, that a better system would not be developed, but in any event he did not think that a decision to deploy Nike-X should be made on the basis that something better would be coming along, which was the basis on which the Defense Department made the adverse Nike-Zeus decision.

Mahon then asked Dr. Brown whether adequate funds were being provided by Congress for the Nike-X program. Brown stressed that the program was moving as fast as a development program should go. Mahon asked whether a decision to deploy could be made now. Dr. Brown again emphasized that such a decision could not be rationally made now, and must, he said, be made in a larger context of an evolving enemy threat. Finally, Representative Sikes asked Dr. Brown whether it would be a more realistic and practical and economical thing just to concentrate on shelters rather than defenses against missiles. Brown's reply was somewhat surprising: "If one is going to spend $5 billion on damage limitation and no more, shelters are the thing to spend it on. If one is going to spend $20 billion on damage limitation, shelters for the first $5 billion, then Nike-X would be the proper thing to spend the next $15 billion on."[73]

Civil Defense

In presenting his posture statement to the House Armed Services Committee, Secretary McNamara characterized civil defense as an integral and essential part of the nation's overall defense posture. He observed that a well-planned and -executed nationwide civil defense program centered around fallout shelters could contribute much more, dollar for dollar, to the saving of lives in the event of a nuclear attack upon the United States than further increases in either offensive or defense forces. Indeed, he said, "our studies indicate that an effective civil defense program could increase the number of persons surviving a determined Soviet nuclear attack in the 1970 period by tens of millions, at a total investment cost to the Federal Government of about $3.5 billion."[74]

An effective civil defense program required, according to McNamara, two major elements: a nationwide system of fallout shelters, properly equipped and provisioned, to protect the nation's population from the fallout effects of a nuclear attack and planning and organization of the capabilities essential to the effective use of this system, including the ability to carry out essential post-attack emergency operations. There were four sources from which fallout shelters for the entire population could be derived. These included: (1) independent private initiative, represented by the efforts of thousands of home owners and business organizations who have developed their own fallout protection; (2) the national shelter survey, marking, and provisioning program; (3) fallout shelter protection in federal buildings; (4) dual-purpose shelter development programs designed to encourage the provision of low-cost shelters in selected public and institutional buildings through federal financial assistance. All in all, the four sources for fallout shelters were expected to yield by the early 1970s some 385 million shelter spaces. And for fiscal year 1965 the Defense Department was recommending a total of $358 million for the civil defense program, a prospective increase of almost $250 million over the previous fiscal year.[75]

China's Nuclear Capability and the Soviet Union's Change of Leadership

On September 29, 1964, Secretary of State Dean Rusk announced to the American public that the United States had known for some time that the Chinese Communists were approaching the point where they might be able to detonate their first nuclear device.[112] It was not a secret, Rusk said, that the Chinese Communists had been working on the development of a nuclear device since the 1950s. And he emphasized that the detonation of a first device would not mean a stockpile of nuclear weapons and the presence of modern delivery systems. Furthermore, Rusk observed, "The United States has fully anticipated the possibility of Peking's entry into the nuclear weapons field and has taken it into full account in determining our military posture and our own nuclear weapons program."[76]

On October 17, 1964, Peking radio broadcast an announcement that during the afternoon of October 16, China had successfully exploded an atom bomb. The rationale given for the development of the atom bomb was that "China is developing nuclear weapons not because we believe in the omnipotence of nuclear weapons and that China plans to use nuclear weapons. The truth is exactly to the contrary. In developing nuclear weapons, China's aim is to break the nuclear monopoly of the nuclear powers and to eliminate nuclear weapons."[77] The Chinese government, continued the broadcast, would never at any time and under any circumstances be the first to use nuclear weapons. It called on all governments of the world to join in convening a summit conference to discuss the complete prohibition and thorough destruction of nuclear weapons.

In a brief statement to the nation on October 16, 1964, President Johnson confirmed the Chinese Communist announcement that it had exploded a nuclear device. He chose to minimize the meaning of the event, saying that its military significance should not be overestimated. Many years and great efforts, he said, separate testing of a first nuclear device from having a stockpile of reliable weapons with effective delivery systems. The President reaffirmed United States defense commitments in Asia, saying, "Even if Communist China should eventually develop an effective nuclear capability, that capability would have no effect upon the readiness of the United States to respond to requests from Asian nations for help in dealing with Communist Chinese aggression." And he pointed out that the Chinese Communist nuclear detonation was a reflection of policies which did not serve the cause of peace. There is, he said, no reason to fear that it will lead to immediate danger of war. "The nations of the free world will recognize its limited significance and will persevere in their determination to preserve their independence."[78]

Just one day before Communist China detonated a nuclear device on an isolated test site in Sinkiang province, the Soviet government announced from the Kremlin a change in its leadership. Three days later on October 18, 1964, President Johnson told the American public:

> We do not know exactly what happened to Nikita Khrushchev last Thursday. We do know that he has been forced out of power by his former friends and colleagues. Five days ago he had only praise in Moscow. Today we learn only of his faults. Yet, the men at the top today are the same men that he picked for leadership. These men carried on the administration of the Soviet government when he was absent from the Soviet capital, and that was nearly half of the time that he was in power.[79]

The President speculated cautiously about the new leadership saying that two men now share top responsibility in the Soviet Union and their exact relation to each other is not very clear. However, he stated, "they are experienced, but younger men and perhaps less rooted in the past. They are said to be realistic. We can hope that they will share with us our great objective—the prevention of nuclear war."[80] In this same vein the President told his audience that Ambassador Anatoli Dobrynin, the day before yesterday, had officially informed him that the new Soviet government planned no change in basic foreign policy.

In its highly regarded assessment of the military balance existing between the Communist powers and the Western alliance, the Institute for Strategic Studies interpreted the change in leadership of the Soviet Union this way:

> The overthrow of Mr. Khrushchev in October 1964 does not appear to have been primarily motivated by dissatisfaction with his military policies. The military establishment seems to have stood aloof from the proceedings, and in spite of the fact that most of the incumbent military leaders were Khrushchev appointees who had been associated with him in the war, there have not been major changes. They are almost all in their middle or late sixties, and of a cautious and conservative cast of mind.[81]

The departure of Premier Khrushchev did raise the question of whether his policy of emphasizing the efficacy of missile deterrence at the expense of the modernization of conventional forces would be continued or undergo significant change. Where the locus of power would rest which would dictate future Soviet military strategy was by no means clear during the final months of 1964.

Late in 1964 the balance of strategic nuclear power between the Soviet Union and the United States appeared to be approximately as follows: the total of Soviet operational ICBMs had reached about 200, a third of which were second generation ICBMs, having storable liquid fuel and therefore somewhat easier to conceal. Soviet missiles were assumed to have powerful boosters, and very high-yield warheads compared to the missiles of the United States. Although it was not fully clear, it was assumed by one source that the Soviets had begun to harden some of their ICBM sites. In addition, the number of MRBMs and IRBMs operationally ready for striking targets in Western Europe and the Far East appeared to be holding steady at between 700 and 750. Compared to the previous year, the long-range strategic bomber strength of the Soviet Union appeared to remain stable during 1964. The Institute for Strategic Studies estimated the Soviets to have about 70 turbo-prop Bear bombers capable of carrying one large winged missile; the operational inventory included 120 four-jet Bisons, also able to carry one winged missile. The Soviet medium bomber force, consisting of about 1,000 twin-jet Badgers, was expected to begin receiving the high performance twin-jet bomber, the Blinder, having a supersonic dash capability, but rather short range for use against targets in the United States. If as expected the Blinder began to replace the Badger, it appeared that the new aircraft would be equipped with a stand-off air-to-surface missile carrying a nuclear warhead.[82]

By comparison—excluding United States tactical aircraft and missile capabilities and NATO capabilities—United States long-range missile forces as of late 1964 included 126 Atlas missiles organized into thirteen squadrons at eleven bases, 108 Titan intercontinental ballistic missiles organized in twelve squadrons, and over 600 solid-fuel Minuteman missiles mounted in hardened silos. Of the total Navy program calling for forty-one Polaris submarines and 656 missiles, twenty-six of the submarines were in operation by the fall of 1964, carrying 416 missiles. (All of the submarines with their missile complements were not, however, on station prepared to execute their wartime mission.) The American Strategic Air Command possessed bomber forces totalling about 1,100 aircraft. Of the total there were 652 B-52s organized into fourteen wings and based in the United States. A large number of the B-52 aircraft carried the Hound Dog air-launched missile having a range up to 600 miles and carrying a thermonuclear warhead. Augmenting the B-52 fleet were two wings of B-58 Hustler supersonic medium bombers, totalling about 90 aircraft. The balance of the strategic bomber forces consisted of obsolescent B-47 bombers, which were scheduled to be phased out during the coming year.[83]

On balance, by the end of 1964 the United States continued to enjoy a substantial lead over the Soviet Union in effective strategic nuclear power. However, it was evident from the more rapid buildup of Soviet strategic missile power, particularly with its greater emphasis on hardening and concealment, that the time was fast approaching when numerical superiority would no longer be exploitable as a credible threat in a future crisis situation. Within several years, the Soviet Union would undoubtedly possess a secure second-strike long-range missile force capable of inflicting unacceptable damage on the United States even after suffering a first strike.

The détente atmosphere, which began in the wake of the Cuban crisis and was materially advanced by United States–Soviet agreement on a partial test ban and the so-called hot line, continued during 1964 as no new crises arose that potentially could involve the world in a nuclear war. Both the Soviet Union and the United States avoided public emphasis on their respective strategic nuclear capabilities, but each continued methodically to increase its strength substantially. It was not clear by year's end what the meaning would likely be for the free world of Premier Khrushchev's fall from power and the explosion of a nuclear device by the Chinese, but it appeared that the consequences of these events were as potentially complex for the Soviet policymakers to deal with as they were for the leadership of the free world. All in all, the logic of the evolving political-strategic situation seemed to suggest that in future years the resort to force by the communist powers and the free world would be confined largely to the direct or indirect use of conventional power, because of a growing realization on both sides that nuclear force could not be used by national leaders except under conditions of extreme threat to vital national security.

NOTES

1. *Public Papers of the Presidents of the United States: Lyndon B. Johnson, 1963–64*. (Washington, D. C.: Government Printing Office, 1965), p. 116.

2. Ibid., pp. 116–117.

3. Ibid., p. 117.

4. Ibid., p. 171.

5. Ibid., p. 184.

6. Ibid.

7. U.S., Department of Defense, *Statement by Secretary of Defense Robert*

S. McNamara before the House Armed Services Committee on the FY 1965–1969 Defense Program and 1965 Defense Budget, January 27, 1964, p. 29.

8. Ibid. It is significant that the Secretary's statement is almost identical word for word with the opening part of a speech made before the Economic Club of New York in November 1963.

9. Ibid., p. 30.

10. Ibid.

11. Ibid., p. 31.

12. Ibid., pp. 31–32.

13. Ibid., p. 32.

14. Ibid., p. 33.

15. Ibid., p. 40.

16. U.S., Congress, House, Committee on Armed Services, *Hearings on Military Posture,* 88th Cong., 2d sess., 1964, pp. 6934–6935.

17. U.S., Congress, Senate, Committee on Armed Services and Subcommittee on Department of Defense Appropriations of the Committee on Appropriations, *Hearings on Military Procurement Authorizations, FY 1965,* 88th Cong., 2d sess., 1964, p. 47.

18. Ibid., p. 57.

19. U.S., Congress, House, Subcommittee of the Committee on Appropriations, *Hearings on Department of Defense Appropriations for 1965,* 88th Cong., 2d sess., 1964, p. 49.

20. Ibid.

21. Ibid., p. 50. The House Armed Services Committee had earlier recommended the addition of approximately $50 million to the administration budget.

22. Ibid., p. 66.

23. Ibid.

24. Ibid., p. 309.

25. Ibid., pp. 309–310.

26. Senate, Committee on Armed Services and Subcommittee on DOD of the Committee on Appropriations, *Military Procurement Authorizations, FY 1965,* p. 708.

27. House, Subcommittee, *DOD Appropriations for 1965,* Part 4, p. 458.

28. Ibid., pp. 459–460.

29. Ibid., p. 484.

30. Ibid., p. 533.

31. Ibid., p. 485.

32. Ibid., p. 493.

33. Ibid.

34. Ibid., p. 494.

35. Ibid., p. 500.

36. Ibid., pp. 495, 496.

37. Ibid., pp. 497–498.

38. Ibid.

39. Ibid., pp. 537, 540.

40. Department of Defense, *FY 1965–1969 Defense Program,* p. 34.

41. Ibid., pp. 34, 35.

42. House, Subcommittee, *DOD Appropriations for 1965,* p. 158.

43. Ibid.

44. Department of Defense, *FY 1965–1969 Defense Program,* p. 36.

45. Ibid., p. 37.

46. Ibid., pp. 37–38.

47. Ibid., p. 38.

48. Ibid.

49. Senate, Committee on Armed Forces and Subcommittee on DOD of the Committee on Appropriations, *Military Procurement Authorizations, FY 1965,* pp. 58–59.

50. Ibid., pp. 307–309.

51. Ibid., p. 309.

52. Ibid.

53. Ibid., p. 721.

54. Ibid., p. 722.

55. Ibid., p. 724.

56. Ibid., p. 753.

57. House, Subcommittee, *DOD Appropriations for 1965,* p. 514.

58. Department of Defense, *FY 1965–1969 Defense Program,* p. 35.

59. House, Subcommittee, *DOD Appropriations for 1965,* p. 658.

60. Ibid., pp. 659, 660.

61. Ibid., p. 659.

62. Ibid., pp. 51–52.

63. Department of Defense, *FY 1965–1969 Defense Program,* p. 44.

64. Ibid., p. 51.

65. Ibid.

66. Ibid., p. 52.

67. Ibid.

68. Ibid., pp. 52–53.

69. Ibid.

70. Ibid., p. 54.

71. House, Appropriations Subcommittee, *DOD Appropriations for 1965*, p. 349.

72. Ibid., Part V, p. 43.

73. Ibid., p. 48.

74. Department of Defense, *FY 1965–1969 Defense Program*, p. 137.

75. Ibid., p. 143.

76. U.S. Arms Control and Disarmament Agency, *Documents on Disarmament 1964* (Washington, D.C: Government Printing Office, 1965), pp. 440–41.

77. Ibid., p. 449.

78. Ibid., pp. 451–52.

79. Ibid., p. 465.

80. Ibid., p. 466.

81. *The Military Balance, 1964–65* (London: The Institute for Strategic Studies, 1965), p. 1.

82. Ibid., pp. 3–4.

83. Ibid., pp. 22–23.

CHAPTER 6

Damage Limitation: Will It Work?

In 1965 the focus of the United States defense problem shifted perceptibly to the Far East. By early summer it was apparent that Communist forces in Vietnam were massing men and equipment with a clear purpose of destroying the South Vietnamese army and bringing its government down. A growing sense of crisis, beginning early in 1965, culminated in February in a decision by the United States to bomb targets in North Vietnam and was followed in April by the doubling of American ground forces in South Vietnam. When in July the North Vietnamese, supported and encouraged by the Chinese Communists, launched an all-out drive to destroy effective resistance in South Vietnam, President Johnson countered swiftly by increasing United States ground forces from 75,000 to 125,000.

With the escalation of the conflict in Vietnam it became less clear whether the Sino-Soviet rift would give way to new unity to confront the United States and its allies with a political and military challenge which, if pursued without caution, might substantially increase the danger of nuclear war. Possibly, however, the persisting internecine competition between the two major communist powers would result in a Soviet challenge to the Chinese bid for leadership in Southeast

Asia, thus creating a triangular situation less likely to lead to all-out nuclear war and enabling the United States to meet the challenge of aggression with whatever forces were necessary to preserve the independence of South Vietnam and frustrate the apparent communist goal of taking over other nations of Southeast Asia.

While the threat of major conflict loomed in Southeast Asia, the countries of Europe continued to sense a relaxation of tensions and a diminishing prospect of conflict between the two alliance systems. European prosperity and growing military capability, buttressed by confidence in the guarantee by the United States to come to NATO's assistance if attacked, combined to create an atmosphere in which the threat of nuclear war or even large-scale conventional wars seemed unlikely. Especially in Europe, the Soviet Union seemed willing to seek further accommodation with the United States and its allies to reduce the possibility that nuclear war might result from accident, surprise, or miscalculation. By continuing to pursue détente with the West, the Soviet Union appeared also to believe that it could best frustrate the further evolution of strong NATO defense arrangements and reduce significantly the military threat to itself. Under the collective leadership of Alexei Kosygin and Leonid Brezhnev during 1965, no apparent change was made in the military policy course set by Khrushchev, the essence of which was to place primary emphasis on the deterrent effect of Soviet long-range nuclear missile power.

Also during 1965, the Soviet Union did not appear to regain adequate momentum in its economic growth which had begun to falter in the early 1960s, principally in the agricultural sector. The growth rate of Soviet gross national product was estimated by the Defense Department for 1965 at 4.5 percent. Progress in the consumer sector of the economy continued to fall behind expectations. Failure to increase agricultural yields forced the Soviet government to continue importing grain from the West, which in turn forced it to dip further into none-too-large gold reserves. Inability to maintain a higher rate of economic growth forced the Soviet Union during 1965 to slightly reduce its already modest foreign aid disbursements and to hold military aid deliveries at about the 1964 level. The many competing demands on the Soviet budget appeared to Department of Defense experts to be acting as a restraint on the size of its military forces. Nevertheless, according to official Soviet sources, explicit Soviet defense expenditures were expected to rise during 1965 and continue the upward trend during 1966. Also, the Soviets were expected to devote greater financial resources to military research and development, partly in reaction to the increase in United States defense expenditures and the conflict in Vietnam.

Communist China continued to make some progress toward the recovery of its economy from the disastrous Great Leap Foward (1958–1960), but the food–population balance remained an especially critical problem. Apparent failure to produce more grain during 1965 than in 1964 forced continued dependence on high-volume grain imports. The new Five Year Plan, just initiated, placed high priority on agriculture. According to the American Department of Defense, "Given reasonable weather, avoidance of extreme economic policies, and the absence of major hostilities, the Chinese economy should grow at a modest rate."[1] Despite economic set-backs and necessary compromises of domestic economic objectives, Communist China continued to support an ambitious nuclear development program while, at the same time, attempting to modernize and strengthen its entire military establishment. China's capacity to produce U-235 and to successfully explode two atomic devices suggested to some Western experts that it would soon seek to develop a thermonuclear device. Also, China was credited with being able, in the short term, to develop and test a medium-range ballistic missile and, in the longer term, to produce long-range ballistic missiles and equip them with thermonuclear warheads. Throughout 1965, China intensified its militant posture toward the United States in an apparent effort to prove the validity of the doctrine of "people's war."

Many nations in the Far East recognized the North Vietnamese aggression against South Vietnam as a threat to their own security. Stimulated by United States efforts to increase free world assistance for South Vietnam, the Republic of Korea, Australia, and New Zealand provided military assistance totalling nearly 20,000 men to United States and South Vietnamese forces. It appeared that the Philippines would also join in assisting the war effort in South Vietnam. Other nations furnished economic, medical, and humanitarian aid to the free world allies.

Elsewhere in Southeast Asia, Hanoi-supported insurgency in Laos during 1965 continued to threaten the stability and control of the Laotian government led by Souvanna Phouma. Cambodia severed diplomatic relations with the United States in May, apparently believing that the Communist Chinese would emerge victorious from the conflict in Vietnam. Thailand, on the other hand, strengthened its relations with the United States, was able to maintain internal stability and continue its economic progress, and became a staunch ally of free world forces attempting to deny a Communist victory in Vietnam. In October, a Communist-backed coup in Indonesia failed and was followed by mass popular revulsion against the Communist Party, which continued unabated during the remainder of the year. By the end of the year the influence of the Army and other anti-Communist elements appeared to be gaining.

In Japan, the Republic of China, and the Republic of Korea, there was growing concern over the apparent threat posed by Communist China. Japan continued to enjoy internal political stability and gained substantially in economic strength. Relations with the United States improved during 1965, as anti-American sentiment inspired by leftist groups in Japan tended to subside. Little prospect existed, however, that Japan would undertake any sudden increase in her defense forces to meet possible Chinese hostility. The military threat to North Korea persisted, and the possibility that Communist Chinese troops might enter the Korean peninsula could not be ignored. In recognition of the threat the United States continued to maintain two combat divisions in South Korea, and provided considerable military assistance to the 560,000-man Korean military establishment. The Republic of China felt more directly menaced by the threat from Peking. Reinforcing its bilateral security guarantee to the defense of Taiwan and the Pescadores, the United States continued to provide some military assistance to the Taiwanese forces. During 1965, sustained economic progress on Taiwan enabled the United States to terminate its economic assistance program.

On the South Asian subcontinent, India and Pakistan engaged in serious combat twice during 1965: once in April and May over the Rann of Kutch, and a second time in August and September on a much larger scale over Kashmir. These expensive conflicts seriously hampered the subcontinent's economic progress and afforded opportunities to the Soviet Union and Communist China to increase their influence in the area. The United States based its policies on continued good relations with both India and Pakistan on grounds that the fate of the subcontinent would have an important bearing on the balance of power in Asia. In pursuance of this objective the United States, since the end of World War II, had spent a total of $10 billion as an investment in the stability and security of India and Pakistan.

Ferment, instability, tension, and sporadic conflict characterized the situation in the Middle East, Africa, and Latin America during 1965. There was growing hostility between the Arab nations and Israel, posing a threat to peace and encouraging greater political and military presence of the great powers, which tended to polarize both issues and parties to the dispute. The civil war in Yemen appeared to be on its way toward settlement by the end of 1965, as a consequence of an agreement in August between the United Arab Republic and Saudi Arabia to cooperate in bringing about peace. The Soviet Union and Communist China accelerated economic and military assistance programs to nations of the Middle East and Africa in an effort to expand their influence. Generally, successes were mixed during 1965, with the greatest penetration being made in the United Arab Republic, Syria, Iraq, and Yemen, while in Africa, set-backs tended to outnumber successes. In Latin America, Cuba still posed a subversive threat to many nations of the region, but the seriousness of insurgency and terrorist attacks was successfully countered in Venezuela, Peru, and Colombia. Only in Guatemala did increased pressure from terrorist tactics appear to weaken the incumbent government. Overall, the countries of Latin America reflected a slight rate of growth on a per capita basis during 1965, advancing to 2.6 percent from 2.3 percent the year before.

Throughout 1965 Western Europe remained a picture of unprecedented prosperity and stability. According to the Department of Defense, the six Common Market countries and the United Kingdom together had a total population, a total military manpower pool, and a total gross national product well in excess of that of the Soviet Union.[2] No disagreement existed between the European members of NATO and the United States on the basic objectives of ensuring the security of Europe against Communist aggression and promoting its continued economic growth and political stability. What disagreements did arise concerned nuclear weapons policy and the future organizational structure of the alliance. The nuclear weapons policy issue focused on the role of tactical nuclear weapons in Europe and on the role the European partners would play in determining the strategic nuclear mission. Important steps were taken during 1965 at the initiative of the United States to increase the participation of all the NATO partners in the planning of joint nuclear affairs. At a meeting of NATO defense ministers in November a decision was reached "to find ways to increase Allied participation in the nuclear weapons should it ever become necessary, and to facilitate the exchange of information and data relevant to such consultation."[3]

In his annual message to Congress on January 4, 1965, President Johnson told the American people in a mood both confident and optimistic that during the past four years "we have built a military power strong enough to meet any threat and destroy any adversary. And that superiority will continue to grow so long as this office is mine. . . ."[4] He went on to say that during this period no new nation had become Communist, and the unity of the Communist empire had begun to crumble. He acknowledged that the nation still lived in a troubled and perilous world but stressed that there was no longer a single threat. The President expressed hope that the new Russian leaders shared his desire for peace and cordially invited them to visit the United States to gain impressions firsthand.

Two weeks later, on January 18, 1965, President Johnson sent a special message to Congress on the state of the nation's defenses. In his opening remarks the President said, "Today we can walk the road of peace because we have the strength we need. We have built that strength with courage. We have employed it with care. We have maintained it with conviction that the reward of our resolution will be peace and freedom. . . . I am able to report to you that the United States today is stronger militarily than at any other time in our peacetime history."[5] The President gave credit for the nation's military strength to all administrations dating from the end of World War II, and then noted, "For the past four years, the focus of our national effort has been upon assuring an indisputable margin of superiority for our defenses. I can report today that this effort has succeeded."[6] Reviewing the present status of the nation's strategic retaliatory forces, he portrayed this picture of deployed strength:

> More than 850 land-based ICBMs.
> More than 300 nuclear-armed missiles in Polaris submarines.
> More than 900 strategic bombers, half of them ready at all times to be airborne within 15 minutes.

These forces on alert, President Johnson affirmed, were superior in number and quality to those of any other nation.

Proclaiming his intention to maintain American strategic nuclear superiority, the President announced the administration's plan to continue procurement and deployment of the Minuteman II and Polaris A-3 missiles, thus greatly extending the range, accuracy, and striking power of the strategic forces. Installation of the new over-the-horizon radars would also be continued in order to give the nation almost instantaneous knowledge of ballistic missiles launched by an enemy. He announced that major new developments in strategic weapons systems would be begun during 1965, specifically,

> a new missile system, the Poseidon, to increase the striking power of our missile-carrying nuclear submarines. The Poseidon missile will have double the payload of the highly successful Polaris A-3. The increased accuracy and flexibility of the Poseidon will permit its use effectively against a broader range of possible targets and give added insurance of penetration of enemy defenses.
>
> A series of remarkable new payloads for strategic missiles. These include: *penetration aids* to assure that the missile reaches its target through any defense; *guidance and reentry vehicle designs* to increase many-fold the effectiveness of our missiles against various kinds of targets; and methods of reporting the arrival of our missiles on targets, up to and even including the time of explosion.[7]

In the closing passages of his statement President Johnson told the Congress that Secretary of Defense McNamara would soon appear before several of its committees to outline the detailed administration proposals on defense issues for the coming year. The President concluded his remarks with the following observation:

> In a world of 120 nations, there are still great dangers to be faced. As old threats are turned back, change and turmoil will present new ones. The vigilance and courage we have shown in the last twenty years must be sustained as far ahead as we can see. The defense of freedom remains our duty—twenty four hours a day and every day of the year.
>
> We cannot know the future and what it holds. But all our experience of two centuries reminds us that—
>
> "To be prepared for war is one of the most effectual means of preserving peace."[8]

Beginning on February 18, 1965, Secretary of Defense McNamara appeared before the House Armed Services Committee to present the Johnson administration's five-year defense program (FY 1966–1970) and the defense budget for fiscal year 1966. In introducing his discussion of the strategic offensive and defensive forces, the Secretary told the committee that for the first time he would include together three major programs which constituted the nation's general war forces: the strategic offensive forces, the continental air and missile forces, and civil defense. He explained that it had become clear last year because of the close interrelationship and the close interaction of the three major components of our general nuclear war posture, that "the only practical way to deal with this problem is to incorporate all three components in a single, analytical framework."[9]

The Nature of Damage Limitation

Because of its crucial importance to the overall question of national security, McNamara told the House Armed Services Committee that it would be useful to review briefly once again the nature of general nuclear war. He defined such a war as one in which the United States or its allies had been attacked by an aggressor in such a manner as to require the use of the nation's strategic nuclear forces in retaliation. He proposed to limit his discussion to situations involving strategic exchanges between the United States and the Soviet Union alone. If general nuclear war should occur, said the Secretary, attacks might be directed against military targets only, against cities only, or against both types of targets, either simultaneously or in tandem following a pause.

In a general nuclear war, McNamara explained, the United States would use such strategic offensive and defensive forces as manned bombers, strategic reconnaissance aircraft, ICBMs, SLBMs (submarine-launched ballistic missiles), anti-aircraft systems of many kinds, ABMs, anti-satellite defenses, and available civil defense capabilities. As he had explained before, the strategic objectives in general nuclear war would be: first, to deter a deliberate attack on the United States and its allies by maintaining a clear and convincing capability to inflict unacceptable damage on an attacker; second, in the event such a war should nevertheless occur, to limit damage to our population and industrial capacities. The first and highest priority capability which the United States must possess the Secretary called "assured destruction," which he defined as "the capability to destroy the aggressor as a viable society, even after a well planned and executed surprise attack on our forces." The second capability was designated "damage limitation" and was defined as "the capability to reduce the weight of the enemy attack by both offensive and defensive measures and to provide a degree of protection for the population against the effects of nuclear detonations." Although he proposed to discuss the issues of general war primarily from the standpoint of the United States, McNamara explained that "assuming . . . both sides have the same general strategic objectives, which I believe to be the case, our Assured Destruction problem is the other side's Damage Limiting problem, and our Damage Limiting problem is their Assured Destruction problem."[10]

Having told the Armed Services Committee that the nation's vital first objective was the maintenance of adequate assured destruction forces, McNamara defined them as a portion of the ICBMs, SLBMs, and the manned bombers. Such a capability, he continued, would, with a high degree of confidence, ensure that we could deter under all foreseeable conditions a calculated, deliberate nuclear attack upon the United States. It was not easy, the Secretary said, to calculate precisely what amount of damage the United States must be able to inflict on the Soviet Union in order to have a credible assured destruction capability. But, he averred, "it seems reasonable to assume that the destruction of, say, one-quarter to one-third of its population and about two-thirds of its industrial capacity would mean the elimination of the aggressor as a major power for many years."[11]

Damage-limiting forces, on the other hand, would include the remainder of the strategic offensive forces (ICBMs, SLBMs, and manned bombers), as well as area defense forces (manned interceptors and anti-submarine warfare forces), terminal defense forces (anti-bomber surface-to-air missiles and anti-ballistic missile missiles), and passive defenses (fallout shelters, warning, etc.). Strategic offensive forces would contribute to the damage-limiting objective by attacking enemy delivery vehicles on their bases or launch sites, provided, of course, that our forces could reach them before the vehicles were launched at our cities. Area defense forces would be expected to destroy enemy weapons systems before they reached their intended target areas; terminal defenses would attempt to destroy enemy weapons systems and warheads in the target area before impact. Passive defense measures (fallout shelters) would, of course, help reduce the vulnerability of the nation's population to the weapons that did impact.

McNamara stressed that once high confidence of an assured destruction capability had been attained, any further increase in the strategic offensive forces would have to be justified on the basis of its contribution to the damage-limiting objective. He set forth certain principles which he said bore importantly on any consideration of achieving a damage-limiting objective. First, the Secretary said, based on the present estimates of the forces the Soviets are expected to have during the next decade, it would be virtually impossible for the United States to be able to provide anything approaching perfect protection for its population no matter how large the general nuclear war forces we were to provide, including even the hypothetical possibility of striking first. Without question the size of expected fatalities would depend on the size and nature of an attack as well as on the capabilities of our own forces. But, McNamara reminded the committee, the Soviet Union had the technical and economic capacity to prevent the United States' achieving a defensive posture which would enable it to keep expected fatalities below a certain level. It could do this, for example, by offsetting any increases the nation might make in its defenses by increasing its offensive missile forces, and it could do so at an extra cost to itself which would appear to be substantially less than the added cost to the United States.

A second consideration pointed out by the Secretary related to the fact that each of the three types of Soviet strategic offensive systems—land-based missiles, submarine-launched missiles, and manned bombers—could, by itself, inflict severe damage on the United States, and even a very good defense against only one type of system would have limited value. Thus, McNamara explained, a meaningful capability to limit the damage of a determined enemy attack would require an integrated, balanced combination of strategic offensive forces, area defense forces, terminal defense forces, and passive defenses.

A third principle affecting damage limitation was that for any given level of enemy offensive capability, successive additions to each of our various systems have diminishing marginal value. While it was true, the Secretary explained, that in general the more forces a country has, the better it can do, beyond a certain point each increment added to the existing forces results in less and less additional effectiveness. As a consequence, the Secretary argued for a balanced allocation of resources among the various elements of the defense forces in order to assure the maximum survival of the nation's population under any conditions of an enemy attack. Therefore, the question of how much the United States should spend on damage-limiting programs could only be decided by carefully weighing the costs against expected benefits.

Pervading the entire damage-limiting problem, McNamara stated, was the factor of uncertainty, of which he mentioned three types—technical, operational, and strategic. Technical uncertainties, he said, related to the question whether a certain weapons system could be developed having the performance characteristics originally specified. Operational uncertainties arise because of the question whether a given system will actually perform as planned in the operational environment. Strategic uncertainty was probably the most troublesome, according to McNamara, since it stems from the question of what our opponent or opponents will actually do—what kind of force they will actually build, what kind of attack they will actually launch, and how effective their weapons will actually be. Because of this uncertainty it was most difficult to plan an optimum defense against one kind of attack when such a defense might not be optimum against other kinds of attack. To illustrate his point the Secretary referred to the purchase of a Nike-X defense which was optimized for an attack by ICBMs having rather simple penetration aids. Such a defensive system would include fewer high cost radars than one optimized against an attack by ICBMs equipped with advanced penetration aids.

Continuing the articulation of his strategic rationale, McNamara noted that the effectiveness of the nation's damage-limiting strategic offensive forces was critically dependent on the timing of an attack on our urban targets. Specifically, he said, "Our missile forces would be most effective against the enemy bombers and ICBMs if the attack on our urban centers were withheld for an hour or more after an attack on U.S. military targets—an unlikely contingency. Our manned-bomber forces would be effective in the damage limiting role only if the enemy attack on our urban centers were withheld for several hours."[12]

In order to reduce the technical uncertainties the Defense Department had undertaken painstaking studies and research and development tests. As a hedge against the risks of technical failure, the government was supporting parallel development approaches. To cope with operational uncertainties the Secretary reported that repeated tests were conducted in a simulated operational environment. Finally, as a hedge against strategic uncertainties, the administration was accepting less than optimum defense against any one form of attack in order to provide some defense against varied forms of attack, and by purchasing insurance—i.e., keeping open various options, such as developing and deploying a new bomber, a new interceptor, or an anti-missile defense system. How far it was wise to go in hedging against these uncertainties was one of the most difficult judgments which the Defense Department was required to make.

The Nature of Assured Destruction

McNamara turned next to a discussion of the adequacy of the nation's strategic offensive forces for assured destruction. In projecting the estimate of likely Soviet strategic offensive forces through mid-1970, he noted that any estimates were more in the nature of development and deployment patterns than a precise order-of-battle by specific weapon systems. Omitting the precise estimates because of their classified nature, the Secretary did say that the current year estimates were of the same order of magnitude as those given the previous year. A useful factor in any understanding of the assured destruction question was, according to McNamara, the tendency in all industrialized societies for population and industry to be clustered in a relatively small number of urban areas. Looking ahead to the 1970s, the concentration of population in the United States would very likely remain greater than that in the Soviet Union. However, the Secretary observed, in both countries about three-fourths of the industrial capacity will be concentrated in the 200 largest urban areas. Parenthetically, the Secretary added that even though much of Communist China's large population is distributed outside major urban areas, it remains vulnerable since most of the industrial capacity, key governmental, technical, and managerial personnel, and skilled workers are concentrated in far fewer urban areas than is the case with either the United States or the Soviet Union. Beyond the 200 largest urban areas, the percentage of population and industrial capability located in each additional increment of 200 cities falls off at a rapidly declining rate, and smaller and smaller percentages of the total population and industrial capacity would be destroyed in the event that such areas were subjected to attack. Thus, the Secretary concluded that the ability to destroy smaller and smaller urban areas would add little to our ability to deter attack.

Applying the projected Soviet strategic offensive threat for the 1970s, Department of Defense calculations showed that even after absorbing a first strike, our already authorized strategic missile force, if it were directed against the aggressor's urban areas, could cause more than 100 million fatalities and destroy about 80 percent of the enemy's industrial capacity. If the bombers of the Strategic Air Command were then to mount a follow-on attack on urban areas, the Secretary estimated that fatalities would be increased by ten to fifteen million and industrial destruction by another 1 or 2 percent. On the basis of these calculations, said McNamara, it is clear that only a portion of the projected ICBM and Polaris force without any assistance from the manned bombers would be required to inflict unacceptably high levels of destruction on an aggressor. Thus, the rationale for procuring the remaining strategic forces was that they, along with air defense forces, could limit damage if deterrence failed.

McNamara acknowledged that even though the programmed missile force alone should provide an adequate deterrent capability, it did not necessarily follow that the assured destruction job could not be done more efficiently by the bombers alone or with higher assurance with a mix of bombers and missiles. To test the efficiency of the bombers alone, the Secretary told the committee that a comparative cost and effectiveness study had been done of four alternative strategic offensive systems—Minuteman, Polaris, B-52/SRAM, and AMSA/SRAM—which could be available in the early 1970s. Each system was examined in terms of its effectiveness against a given urban-industrial complex. Employing operational factors expected for the early 1970s, McNamara affirmed that any one of the four forces alone could, with a high degree of confidence, destroy this complex even after absorbing a surprise attack. However, the Secretary emphasized, a comparison of the approximate incremental costs of the four alternative forces makes it clear that AMSA (Advanced Manned Strategic Aircraft) would be the most expensive method of accomplishing this particular goal. Indeed, McNamara stated, against improved defenses, which might be available in the 1970s, the cost of AMSA would be roughly four times that of Minuteman, the least expensive of the four systems examined.

The second question then was whether a mixed force of bombers and missiles would provide greater confidence that this nation could achieve its assured destruction objective. Two principal arguments, the Secretary said, were usually advanced to support the case for a mixed force. First, it seemed clear that as long as the United States possessed strategic aircraft an enemy could not logically make the choice of defending himself against missiles without concurrently defending himself against aircraft and their air-to-surface missiles. The converse of this argument was also true. The second point was, therefore, that in the absence of a bomber threat a potential enemy could reallocate his resources to strategic offensive forces, or to anti-missile defenses or some other military program.

Despite the arguments for retaining bombers, the Secretary of Defense declared that a persuasive case had not been made for a large bomber force. Most of the cost of an anti-aircraft defense system, he said, was quite insensitive to the size of the opposing bomber forces. Rather, the requirement for air defense was more a function of the number of targets to be defended than of the number of attacking bombers. Since an enemy could not possibly know in advance which targets United States forces intended to hit, he would logically have to defend them all. As a consequence, his expenditures for air defense were likely to be about the same regardless of whether we have a relatively large bomber force or a small one.

Continuing his testimony, McNamara compared both bombers and missiles on the basis of the percentage of the inventory of each which would predictably arrive over their scheduled target even after a Soviet first strike. The Secretary said he was confident of the excellent readiness and reliability rates of Minuteman and Polaris based on extensive testing programs. As for survival, McNamara doubted that an enemy, even by the early 1970s, would be able to destroy a significant number of Polaris submarines at sea. Also, inasmuch as an enemy missile force would have to face over 1,000 hardened and dispersed American ICBMs, land-based systems, as well, appeared to have a high survivability potential. The Secretary said he was not equally confident of the survival potential of the manned bombers. For example, if manned bombers could not become airborne within the warning time provided by BMEWS, they could be caught on their home bases by enemy ICBM or SLBM attack.

With respect to penetration of American offensive systems even if an enemy should deploy an ABM system, penetration aids and other measures should permit, said McNamara, a substantial number of offensive warheads to successfully penetrate an enemy defensive system. Aircraft, too, would face substantial penetration difficulties in the 1970s. According to McNamara, the cost of an effective anti-bomber defense appeared to be much less than the cost of a comparably effective anti-missile defense. Summarizing his findings, the Secretary concluded:

> I see little merit to the argument that bombers are needed in the Assured Destruction role because our missiles are not dependable. But I do recognize that presently unforeseeable changes in the situation may occur against which a bomber force might possibly provide a hedge. Therefore, . . . I propose to retain the option to maintain indefinitely bomber units in our Strategic Offensive Forces.[13]

Damage-limiting Capabilities of United States Forces

McNamara turned next to an appraisal of the capabilities of programmed United States strategic nuclear delivery forces to accomplish the objective of damage limitation. It must be considered feasible, he said, that despite all of our efforts to deter an enemy attack nuclear war may occur nevertheless. Thus, it is essential to possess forces whose mission in nuclear war would be to limit damage to the United States and our allies. McNamara stressed to the House Armed Services Committee that the usefulness of the strategic offensive forces in a damage-limiting role was critically dependent on the timing of the enemy attack on American urban targets. If, for example, an enemy delayed attacking American cities until sometime after striking military targets in this country, it would enable our strategic missile forces—which can reach their targets in less than one hour—to significantly reduce the amount of damage in the United States by destroying, prior to launch, a large part of an enemy's forces withheld for use against our cities. An urban attack delayed somewhat longer would enable the bomber forces to contribute to the damage-limiting task. In the event, however, that an enemy launched his initial attack against American cities, both offensive missiles and bombers would have a substantially reduced role in limiting damage. The contribution of these forces would in that case be limited to the destruction of enemy residual forces—unlaunched strategic missiles and bombers, re-fire missiles, and any other strategic forces the enemy might withhold for subsequent strikes.

Although a deliberate attack on the United States appeared to McNamara to be an unlikely probability in view of our unmistakable assured destruction capability, it must, he stressed, receive the urgent attention of the nation because of the enormous consequences it would have. Therefore, said the Secretary, he wanted to make two points clear. First, in order to rule out possible miscalculations as far as possible, McNamara underscored "that although the U.S. would itself suffer severely in the event of a general nuclear war, we are fully committed to the defense of our Allies." Second, he said, the United States did not consider the matter of damage limitation as concerning only its own population and industry. "Our offensive forces cover strategic enemy capabilities to inflict damage on our allies in Europe just as they cover enemy threats to the continental United States."[14]

After emphasizing once again to the Armed Services Committee the importance of a nationwide fallout shelter program in reducing fatalities at all levels of attack, Secretary McNamara discussed the results of a number of balanced defense postures costing varying amounts in terms of their potential for damage limitation. In conducting the studies two assumptions relating to the timing of an enemy attack were postulated. First, it was assumed that an enemy would initiate nuclear war with a simultaneous attack against American cities and military targets. Second, it was assumed that an attack against American cities was delayed long enough for forces of the Strategic Air Command to retaliate against the aggressor's military targets with long-range missiles. The results of the analysis are as follows:

TABLE I

Estimated Effect on United States Fatalities of Additions to the Approved Damage Limiting Program (based on 1970 population of 210 million)

	Millions of U.S. Fatalities	
Additional Investment	*Early Urban Attack*	*Delayed Urban Attack*
$ 0 billion	149	122
5 billion	120	90
15 billion	96	59
25 billion	78	41

SOURCE: U.S., *Department of Defense, Statement by Secretary of Defense Robert S. McNamara before the House Armed Services Committee on the FY 1966–1970 Defense Program and the 1966 Defense Budget*, February 18, 1965, p. 47.

The Secretary explained that the first $5 billion of additional investment would provide full fallout shelter protection for the entire population of the nation. For an additional expenditure of $15 billion approximately $8.5 billion would be spent on a limited deployment of a low cost ABM system, plus about $1.5 billion for new manned bomber defenses. At the $25 billion expenditure level an additional $8.5 billion would be devoted to ABM defenses (for a total of about $17 billion) and another $1.5 billion for improved manned bomber defenses.

In order to illustrate the crucial importance of a full nationwide fallout shelter program to the damage limiting role, McNamara presented Table 2 to the Armed Services Committee:

TABLE 2

Estimated Effect of Fallout Protection on United States Fatality Levels for Several Damage Limiting Programs
(based on 1970 population of 210 million)

	Millions of U.S. Fatalities			
Additional Investment	*Early Urban Attack Partial Protection*	*Full Protection*	*Delayed Urban Attack Partial Protection*	*Full Protection*
$ 0 billion	149	149	122	122
5 billion	145	120	107	90
15 billion	121	96	79	59
25 billion	107	78	59	41

SOURCE: U.S., Department of Defense, *Statement by Secretary of Defense Robert S. McNamara before the House Armed Services Committee on the FY 1966–1970 Defense Program and the 1966 Defense Budget*, February 18, 1965, p. 48.

A quick analysis of the varying levels of fatalities indicates that any damage-limiting program which excludes a complete fallout shelter system would cost at least twice as much as a program which includes such a system. At the $15 and $25 billion budget levels McNamara stated that the bulk of the additional funds would go to missile defense, and thus a high confidence in the potential effectiveness of the system would have to be assured before commitment to such large expenditure would be justified.

Secretary McNamara turned next to a consideration of the effectiveness of bombers in the damage-limiting role. One of the analyses included a comparison of the effectiveness of an advanced manned strategic aircraft with two strategic missiles—Minuteman II and an improved missile for the 1970s. Although admitting to many uncertainties with respect to both the assumptions and the planning factors used in the comparisons, the Secretary concluded, "it did demonstrate clearly one important point, namely, that there are less costly ways of destroying residual enemy missiles and aircraft than by developing and deploying a new AMSA—even ignoring the fact that enemy missile silos and bomber fields are far more likely to be empty by the time the bombers pass over than when the missiles arrive."[15]

Several tentative conclusions were offered by McNamara as deriving from the analysis of the damage-limiting problem. First, if no new defenses were provided against nuclear attack in the early 1970s, predicted enemy strategic nuclear forces would be able to inflict very high fatalities on the United States. Second, a nationwide civil defense program costing about $5 billion could reduce fatalities by about 30 million. Third, if active defense systems operated as estimated, a large, balanced damaging-limiting program costing an additional $20 billion could reduce fatalities in the United States from an early urban attack by about 40 million. Finally, no foreseeable defense program within the assumed cost constraints could reduce fatalities to a level much below 80 million unless an enemy delayed his attack on American cities long enough for strategic missile forces to play a major damage-limiting role.

Thus far in the Secretary's analysis he had not taken into account possible enemy reactions to this nation's efforts to limit damage to itself and its allies. To illustrate his point, McNamara assumed that $15 billion had already been spent to provide for a balanced damage-limiting posture which would be capable of limiting fatalities to approximately 95 million, assuming a first strike against our cities. If, then, a decision were made to spend another $10 billion to reduce fatalities to around 75 million, an enemy reaction to this decision, according to the Secretary, should be able to offset this increase in survivors in the 1970s by an expenditure of about $6 billion more on his offensive forces, or 60 percent of the cost to the United States. Furthermore, the Secretary added that at each successively higher level of U.S. expenditures, the ratio of the costs for damage limitation to the potential aggressor's cost for assured destruction becomes less and less favorable for the United States. Indeed at the level of spending required to limit fatalities to about 40 million in a large first strike against U.S. cities, we would have to spend on damage-limiting programs about four times what the potential aggressor would have to spend on damage-creating forces, i.e., *his* assured destruction forces. Despite cost disadvantages accruing to a nation undertaking a damage-limitation program, Secretary McNamara refrained from a conclusion against the United States' pursuing a major new program. The Soviet Union, he said, was much more resource-limited than this nation, and might not actually react to our initiatives as was assumed. Nevertheless, the Secretary concluded, it does underscore the fact that beyond a certain level of defense, the cost advantage lies increasingly with the offense, and this fact should be taken into account in any decision to commit the nation to large expenditures for additional defensive measures.

United States Strategic Programs for 1966–1970

As a result of the foregoing analysis, McNamara outlined six major issues which concerned the FY 1966–1970 general nuclear war programs. Briefly, these issues were: (1) the development and deployment of a new manned bomber at an estimated five-year systems cost of $8.9 to $11.5 billion; (2) the size of the strategic missile force and the issue of adding 200 additional Minuteman II missiles for a cost of $1.3 billion; (3) the overall level of the anti-bomber program; (4) the production and deployment of a new manned interceptor for an estimated cost of $4 billion; (5) the production and deployment of the Nike-X–ABM system—estimated five-year cost of $24 billion; (6) the construction of fallout shelters for the entire population at a cost to all levels of government of $5 billion.

Development of a New Manned Bomber

The first major issue addressed by Secretary McNamara was that of developing and deploying a new manned bomber for the early

1970s. He believed, he said, that the analysis of the general nuclear war problem in the early 1970s clearly demonstrated that the strategic missile force alone should provide a most persuasive deterrent to a deliberate attack on the United States. McNamara, however, thought it wise for a number of reasons to keep open the option of continuing at least some manned bombers in the strategic offensive forces indefinitely. He repeated an earlier statement that with appropriate maintenance and modification the present force of B-52s could be operated safely and effectively through the early or mid-1970s. The Secretary told the committee that about $1.8 billion had already been programmed for the strengthening of the fuselage and tail structure, the provision of structural wing fasteners, flight safety modifications, capability improvements, such as new radars and ECM equipment, and depot maintenance. Another $339 million was included in the FY 1966 budget request for these purposes. Given the present size of the B-52 force, 630 operational aircraft, and the continuing availability of two wings of B-58 medium bombers, McNamara stated that he did not think it warranted spending some $70 million over the next few years to keep two B-52B squadrons (30 aircraft) in safe operating condition. The B-52B was the oldest component of the fleet and the two squadrons were deployed to Guam to replace the retired B-47s. The Secretary proposed to phase out the B-52Bs as other newer strategic systems could take over their assignments. Apart from saving tens of millions of dollars by not continuing the B-52s, the Secretary contended it would have no effect on our strategic capability since a force of about 670 manned bombers would remain in the 1970s.

At least two other alternatives remained open to the United States, according to McNamara, which would preserve the manned-bomber option for a time following the retirement of the B-52 force. First, a strategic version of the F-111 (i.e., B-111) might be procured; second, a decision could be made to begin the advanced development work on long lead time components which would be needed for the AMSA. A strategic version of the F-111 could carry the SRAM (Short-Range Attack Missile) or bombs, or a combination of both. It would be capable of supersonic speeds at high altitudes over enemy territory and high subsonic speeds at low altitudes. The Secretary conceded that the B-111 would be more dependent on aerial refueling than the AMSA, but its range would be greater than the B-58, and its target coverage and its payload-carrying capability would be sufficient to bring under attack a very large proportion of an enemy's urban and industrial complexes. And finally, McNamara said, "Since the F-111 is already nearing production, and we plan to initiate development of the SRAM in the current fiscal year, a 'B-111' could be made available in the early 1970s at a much lower cost than the AMSA, even if the decision to commence production is postponed for another two to three years."[16]

Turning next to an assessment of the AMSA, the Secretary stated that as the aircraft was presently envisaged by the Air Force, it would incorporate the payload capabilities of the B-52 and the speed and altitude characteristics of the F-111. Its takeoff weight would be on the order of 350,000 pounds and it would require the development of a new engine and new avionics; it would also employ the SRAM. He noted that Secretary of the Air Force Zuckert had said in a memorandum transmitting the AMSA proposal to him that the Air Force intended

> . . . to complete, prior to the initiation of the Project Definition Phase, a prerequisite phase which will further refine our systems evaluation. This phase will include further evaluation of . . . (several alternatives). . . . Each system configuration will be assessed in terms of performance, cost, schedule, military effectiveness, complexity, and development risks.[17]

Considering, therefore, the high cost of an AMSA fleet ($8.9 billion to $11.5 billion), the need to develop a new engine and new avionics, the still-existing uncertainties as to the kind of bomber that should be built in the 1970s, and the remaining B-52 life which exceeded the lead time required for development of a new aircraft, the Secretary concluded that the time was not propitious to proceed with a full AMSA development. However, he conceded, it would be desirable to keep open the option for developing such an aircraft as a replacement for the B-52s when they have to be retired. Specifically, McNamara proposed to spend $39 million during FY 1966 on efforts to define the specifications and basic design, advanced avionics, and propulsion system for an advanced manned aircraft suitable for the 1970s. In addition, he recommended approval of $37 million to begin the development of the SRAM. Thus, the Secretary concluded, this four-part program would permit full development and deployment of a new manned bomber in ample time to replace the B-52s, should that decision appear to be necessary or desirable within the next few years.

The Size of the Strategic Missile Force

During 1964, McNamara said, a tentative decision had been made to increase the size of the Minuteman force from 1,000 to 1,200 missiles over a two-year period. However, on the basis of an analysis of the general nuclear war problem in the early 1970s, the Secretary was convinced that another 200 Minuteman silos were not necessary. And he stressed that it was now believed that the United States could markedly increase the "kill" capabilities of the Minuteman force through a number of qualitative improvements which appeared feasible. The Minuteman force planned for FY 1970 would have a total destruction capability of at least 30 percent to 40 percent greater than a force of the same size consisting only of Minuteman I, which would be equivalent to adding 300 to 400 missiles to a force of 1,000 Minuteman I. Furthermore, the Secretary continued, by incorporating additional improvements which now appeared possible, the destruction capabilities of the Minuteman force could be further increased, if that appeared desirable, by a factor of two compared with a force of the same size consisting only of Minuteman I.

Closely related to the size of the missile force was the issue of whether the Soviet Union would elect to deploy an effective anti-missile defense system around its urban and industrial centers. As a hedge against this possibility, McNamara told the Armed Forces Committee that work was continuing on a comprehensive penetration aids program for which approximately $1 billion had already been programmed through fiscal year 1965. A capability for employing penetration aids was already being incorporated in United States missile forces, and the Secretary predicted they would be effective against any likely defense. Inasmuch as the data derived from penetration aids research tended to contribute importantly to the prospective development of an anti-ballistic missile defense system, Secretary McNamara recommended a total funding of $168 million for FY 1966 to continue advanced development work on penetration aids and improved reentry systems.

Another measure recommended by the Secretary to counter possible Soviet anti-missile defense systems was to undertake during FY 1966 the development of a new, larger submarine-launched missile designated the Poseidon. The Poseidon would be capable of improved accuracies and larger payloads compared to the Polaris A-3, and its larger payload would permit it to carry a much larger number of penetration aids, thereby enabling it to penetrate heavily defended urban and industrial areas. Alternatively, the Secretary stressed, it could be used to attack a hardened point target with greater accuracy and a heavier warhead. The retroactive fitting (retrofit) of a part of the Polaris fleet with the Poseidon missile would greatly increase the kill capability of the submarine fleet. McNamara proposed to initiate project definition of the Poseidon missile during 1965 and requested a total of $45 million to undertake it. All in all, he estimated that around $900 million would be required to fully develop the system. Finally, the estimated cost to retrofit a force of approximately nineteen submarines was estimated by the Secretary to be roughly $2 billion, including the cost of missile development and production.

By the middle of 1966, Secretary McNamara estimated that the United States would have 800 Minuteman and 464 Polaris missiles in the operational forces. He believed, therefore, that all Atlas and Titan I missiles could safely be phased out during FY 1966 in order to reduce excessive costs of operation and maintenance. (The Atlas and Titan forces cost about $1 million per year per missile to operate and maintain, as against a comparable cost of $100,000 per missile for the Minuteman.)

The Anti-Bomber Defense Program and a New Manned Interceptor

Continuing the presentation of his posture statement to the House Armed Services Committee, Secretary McNamara turned to a discussion of strategic defensive forces. He identified as one of the major issues the determination of the proper overall level of the anti-bomber defense program. The present system of defense against manned-bomber attack was designed, the Secretary said, a decade ago at a time when it was estimated that the Soviets would build a large force of long-range aircraft. However, this had not happened and the nation instead was confronted by an ICBM and submarine-launched ballistic missile threat. Thus, the Secretary concluded, "With no defense against the ICBM and only very limited defenses against the submarine-launched ballistic missiles, our anti-bomber defenses could operate on only a part of the attacking forces. Moreover, the anti-bomber defense system itself is vulnerable to missile attack."[18] Clearly, therefore, the present anti-bomber defenses were out of balance with the other components in relation to the threat. McNamara mentioned the recent efforts to overcome the deficiency, such as providing an improved backup to the SAGE (Semi-Automatic Ground Environment) system and by dispersing the manned interceptors. Another possible improvement in the anti-bomber defense area was the production and deployment of a new manned interceptor.

In his evaluation of the need for a new manned interceptor, Secretary McNamara was emphatic that if the deployment of such an aircraft were to be considered—in the context of general nuclear war—it must add demonstrably to the overall damage-limiting effort. And, he argued, even if such an aircraft would raise the level of the damage-limiting program, it was not at all clear that a new manned interceptor system would have priority over the new advanced surface-to-air missile systems under study. Nor, he said, was it clear that the YF-12A, which had already been substantially developed, would be superior to an interceptor version of the F-111. For example, the F-111 would combine greater airborne endurance and an ability to recycle on a greater number of airfields with the fact that greater numbers could be procured for any given investment. McNamara reminded the committee that the F-111 was nearing production and could easily be combined with the Phoenix air-to-air missile to produce essentially an interceptor aircraft. The YF-12A, he acknowledged, had been under development since FY 1962 and prototypes were now available for flight test. Everything considered, the Secretary said, no decision on the production of the FY-12A was necessary in FY 1966. And he concluded, if the United States were to decide to go ahead with deployment of a YF-12A type aircraft, it would most likely produce an interceptor version of the larger SR-71 aircraft which has a substantially greater range than the YF-12A.

Production and Deployment of Nike-X

The next major issue raised by Secretary McNamara was the status of the ballistic missile defense program and particularly the question of the production and deployment of the Nike-X system. Since last year, the Secretary explained that the United States had greatly expanded its knowledge of anti-missile defense with regard to both the relative costs and effectiveness of alternative deployments and the technical aspects of the system. He stated that although the Nike-X development was progressing satisfactorily, a number of technical problems still remained to be solved. Thus, he believed it was still premature to make any commitment to production and deployment at that time, Moreover, McNamara pointed out that, in addition to the technical problems, there were even greater uncertainties concerning the preferred concept of deployment, the relationship of the Nike-X system to other elements of a balanced damage-limiting effort, the timing of the attainment of an effective nationwide fallout shelter system, and the nature and effect of an opponent's possible reaction to Nike-X deployment. Accordingly, he said, the Defense Department proposed to continue the development of the Nike-X system "on an urgent basis," and a total of about $400 million was provided in the FY 1966 budget for that purpose. Finally, McNamara said the question of the production and deployment of the Nike-X would be reexamined next year, and in his judgment the deferral of this issue until the FY 1967 budget should not delay the initial operational capability by any significant number of months beyond what would likely be achieved by starting production in the current fiscal year.

Fallout Shelters

The final major issue addressed by Secretary McNamara concerned the construction of a complete nationwide fallout shelter system. He strongly reiterated his belief in the value of such a program to a damage-limiting program and estimated the cost over five years of such a program—prorated among the federal, state, and local governments and private sources—as $5 billion. The Secretary pointed out that the executive branch had proposed an adequate fallout shelter program to the Congress for three years, but it had not been enacted. Therefore, for FY 1966, the Defense Department was proposing to concentrate on fully exploiting all of the existing potential for fallout protection and for determining with greater precision the exact nature of the residual shelter requirement.

By the early months of 1965, McNamara pointed out that a continuing survey of existing structures had identified about 127 million shelter spaces having reasonably good protection factors. Some 79 million shelter spaces in 94,000 structures were actually licensed or marked. Furthermore, he continued, by the end of FY 1965, it was estimated that 130 million spaces will have been identified and a total of 90 million spaces actually licensed or marked. The Secretary requested the inclusion of $36.3 million in funds for FY 1966 to be used for shelter surveys. Pending the completion of an analysis of possible shelter use countrywide, the Secretary did not propose additional funds for community shelter planning.

Funds appropriated through FY 1965 were deemed adequate by the Secretary to provide supplies for about 63 million shelter spaces. He asked for an additional $23.4 million for the coming fiscal year in order to procure stocks for approximately 12 million spaces. Following a brief discussion by McNamara of continuing efforts toward the establishment of a national warning system and an emergency broadcast system designed to communicate with the public in a crisis situation, he concluded his formal remarks on the strategic offensive and defensive five-year program and recommended budget for FY 1966.

The Focus of Congressional Concern

Each year since taking office in 1961, Secretary McNamara had appeared before the House Armed Services Committee, the Subcommittee of the House Committee on Appropriations, and the joint hearings of the Senate Subcommittee of the Committee on Appropriations and the Committee on Armed Services to present his estimate of the strategy, weapons systems, force postures, and costs which were best designed to preserve national security during a period covering the next five years. Following his long and comprehensive formal presentation to each of the major committees, the Secretary submitted himself to intensive questioning by committee members on all important aspects and implications of his statement. During the period from 1961 to 1963, a considerable amount of the time spent by McNamara before the major congressional committees was taken up by a discussion of alternative general war strategies open for consideration by the United States and the implications of these strategies for foreign policy and national security goals. For example, the strategy of flexible response as it applied to general nuclear war was elaborated in considerable detail by the Secretary and his assistants in the Pentagon, and critics outside the government and in Congress attacked aspects of this strategy with conviction and, often, incisiveness.

Beginning in 1964, a perceptible shift took place in the focus of the debates on the administration defense programs. Less and less were the postulates of general nuclear war strategy questioned in detail by the major congressional committees, and more and more debate tended to focus on the specific kinds of weapon systems that ought to compose the nation's strategic forces and the relative numbers of each. To a considerable extent this shift in emphasis can be explained by the progressive buildup of Soviet strategic missile forces to a point where it was widely recognized that they would soon possess a secure second-strike capability. Thus, it became more and more difficult for the Secretary of Defense or his critics to explain meaningfully general war strategy in terms of superiority, war-winning capability, counterforce, preemptive strike, or damage-limiting capabilities. Added to these growing dilemmas was the steadily increasing commitment by the United States in the Southeast Asian crisis, which tended to divert energies and interest away from strategic issues and forces to conventional war capabilities and concepts for dealing with insurgency.

During 1965, the trend away from any meaningful discussion of general nuclear war strategies by congressional committees was even more pronounced. Apart from a rather cursory interest shown by a few congressmen and senators in such issues as mutual deterrence, the need for continued American strategic superiority, and the likelihood of achieving significant damage limitation through the use of offensive forces in a counterforce role, the bulk of the questions posed to Secretary McNamara during his extended appearances before Congress tended to dwell, as they had the year before, on the need for specific kinds of strategic weapons systems, the capabilities of these systems to perform intended missions, their sizes, and particularly the issue of ballistic missile defense for the United States.

To the extent that issues of nuclear strategy were raised during Secretary McNamara's appearances before congressional committees, they tended not to provoke any sustained controversy among committee members and the Secretary. For example, during his appearance before the joint Subcommittee on Department of Defense Appropriations and the Committee on Armed Services, McNamara was asked by Senator Strom Thurmond of South Carolina whether the nation's nuclear strategy was based on the counterforce retaliatory strike or counter-city retaliatory strike. The Secretary partially evaded the question by responding, "We have the capability of destroying their population and industry, and we have the capability for destroying some but not by any means all of their strategic offensive forces."[19] He reiterated that the first priority for defense was given to the development of a force structure sufficient to destroy an enemy's urban population and industry to a level unacceptable to him. But, he said, we do not stop there. Forces are provided in addition to destroy an enemy's offensive weapons capable of striking the United States to the maximum degree practicable. Senator Thurmond then asked, "Well, are we building our forces then to implement the strategy to destroy their counterforce or cities or both?" McNamara replied that he would rather not use the term "counterforce," because, "frankly, I don't know exactly what it means."[20] A response such as this from the Secretary was indeed a far cry from the free-ranging and candid discussion of controlled counterforce general nuclear war during the first two years of his tenure in the Pentagon.

A few weeks later during the cross-examination of Secretary McNamara by the members of the House Subcommittee on Appropriations the Chairman, George Mahon of Texas, reminded the Secretary of the substantial discussion which had taken place during recent years about mutual deterrence and the possibility of a developing stalemate. He asked McNamara whether in view of this nation's disappearing nuclear advantage the United States was now more or less in a position of stalemate relative to the Soviet Union, as a result of the fact that both nations had such a tremendous military capacity. Again the Secretary's reply was a noteworthy contrast to what might have been expected several years earlier:

> Mr. Chairman, the word "stalemate" carries with it certain connotations that I would like to stay away from, so I do not wish to use that term or endorse any statement that includes it.

And then he explained:

> But I do think it is very clear that today we have forces sufficiently large to absorb fully a Soviet first strike and, after absorbing the damage of that strike, respond with a remaining force so large as to destroy the Soviet Union. But having said that, I must also say that the Soviet strike against us would cause a substantial loss of life in this country, so large as to be of great concern to us. And under those circumstances, the initiation of strategic nuclear war is not a rational policy for either power.[21]

In all probability because the Secretary chose not to enter into a discussion of the implications of nuclear stalemate, as it appeared to be an accurate or inaccurate reflection of the strategic relationship existing between the United States and the Soviet Union in 1965, there was no further examination of this issue and its implications during the House hearings.

The Debate over the Manned Bomber

Of the many major defense issues examined in detail during the appearances of Secretary McNamara before the House and Senate Appropriations and Armed Services committees, the question of the future role of the manned bomber in the nation's strategic offensive force plans was raised more often and with greater concern by both congressmen and senators than any other issue. Clearly, the case made by the Secretary during 1964 for modifying the B-52 fleet to make it capable of performing a useful mission well into the 1970s and for postponing development of a follow-on strategic bomber (AMSA) until a clear military justification existed to warrant its production and deployment had not been convincing to a number of influential congressmen whose responsibility it was to protect national security. During the 1965 hearings, the bomber issue was raised in the context of production lead time phasing to meet an anticipated 1970s threat, reliability of bombers versus missiles, defense penetration capabilities of the two systems, and, as during the 1964 debates, the probable role for the manned bomber in the future.

Secretary McNamara made his annual appearance before the House Armed Services Committee in early February 1965 to answer questions following his presentation of the long and involved defense posture statement. Early in the question period he was asked by Congressman Leslie Arends of Illinois to quickly state what he envisaged in the future for the manned bomber. The congressman also wanted to know how many studies had been going on in the Defense Department on this subject and what they revealed. McNamara said he was not certain how many studies were actually taking place. Congressman Arends rejoined that he had information that there were about 115 such studies. Clearly provoked, Secretary McNamara replied:

> Well, I am sure that the studies are cheap compared to the $1.5 billion we spent, with most of it wasted, on the RS-70. If the studies will avoid a waste of that kind, I think they represent money well spent. I don't know of anybody in the Department who thinks there have been too many studies on the subject of strategic war. In any event, the studies show a very uncertain requirement. I don't know of a single study in the Defense Department that makes clear the role of manned bombers in [deleted, but read "the 1970s"].[22]

The Congressman then asked the Secretary whether there had been a recommendation against the manned-bomber program. McNamara replied that the number of bombers being considered by any of the Defense Department studies was on the order of 200, and that this estimate was in conjunction with a missile force that through fiscal 1966 will be funded at a total strength of about 1,700 missiles, and no one of these studies indicated how 200 bombers could contribute significantly to the protection of the country in an operation that depended primarily on 1,700 missiles. The Secretary said that he understood General Wheeler and the other Joint Chiefs of Staff to believe that manned bombers should remain in the force "for the foreseeable future." Looking ahead into the 1970s with a vastly improved B-52 in the force, McNamara stated: "The clear recommendation of the Chiefs and my clear recommendation to you is that we retain the option to follow the B-52's with a manned bomber, if between now and the time when that action is required, a clear military requirement develops."[23]

While acknowledging his readiness to consider a follow-on manned bomber if a clear military requirement developed, the Secretary admitted that his views were not wholly shared by the Joint Chiefs of Staff and certainly not by the representatives of the Air Force. Congressman Arends rejoined: "I understand that there has been no recommendation against the advanced manned bomber on anyone's part down there except possibly your own?"[24] McNamara denied this was true and said the question must be turned around. The Chiefs, he said, had not recommended that a decision be made to produce and deploy a manned bomber to follow the B-52. Rather they recommended that funds be spent on the research and development of such an aircraft so that if later it was determined that it should be produced, it could be produced. General Wheeler agreed that the Secretary's evaluation was accurate, but asked to add one thing: "... that is, of course, that the Air Force takes a more extreme view as to going ahead with a manned bomber at this time—or at the earliest opportunity...."[25]

Continuing the same line of questioning, Congressman Arends asked Secretary McNamara if there was not a danger that 1972 would arrive and the nation would be without an adequate manned bomber. The Secretary replied that there was no real danger inasmuch as an Air Force recommendation to extend the life of the B-52 G and H models had been approved at a programmed cost of some $138 million, $7 million of which would be required in FY 1966. In other words, asked Congressman Arends, "at the moment we foresee going ahead with the improvement of the B-52's into the seventies?" The Secretary's reply was, "Yes." Summarizing his position, McNamara told the committee that Congress was being asked to provide funds to allow the necessary technical work to be done to insure that if later a decision was made to follow the B-52 with a new manned bomber, it could be done without any gap occurring between the end of the life of the B-52s and the deployment of the new manned bomber. The Congressman then asked whether such a decision could be made roughly in three years and still permit the United States to deploy a manned bomber on a timely basis. Secretary McNamara said that the answer depended on the type of aircraft being considered. For example, if the decision were made to produce the so-called stretched TFX, then it would be possible to wait two years before making a decision. Other types of aircraft would require a decision to be made in 1966.

In other words, Congressman Arends asked McNamara, "While there has been no determination, up to this particular time, of the real military need for an advanced bomber, it is still a possibility in the foreseeable future?" And the Secretary replied, "Not only is it a possibility but the technical work that is necessary to insure that it can be produced and deployed without a gap will be financed by the funds recommended to Congress for fiscal 1966."[26] To this the Chairman of the committee, Mendel Rivers, commented: "I think there is going to be a need, and I am glad to hear the Secretary say if there is a need he is going to have the avionics and the engine out of the woods."[27] Congressman Rivers went on to compliment Secretary McNamara on his fine statement.

During his appearance before the joint Senate Subcommittee on Defense Department Appropriations and the Armed Services Committee late in February 1965, the Secretary was asked at the beginning of the question period by Senator Stennis about the future of the manned bomber. Shortly before, McNamara had pointed out that to develop and deploy a new manned bomber would cost on the order of $9 to $12 billion. It was not necessary, he said, to make such a decision in the fiscal 1966 budget. That decision could be deferred until fiscal 1967 or fiscal 1968 and we could still be assured of being able to follow the B-52 fleet with another manned bomber without any gap occurring. Senator Stennis opened his questions by asking the Secretary how long after an affirmative decision was made on a new manned bomber it would take to put it into serial production. McNamara pointed out that the Air Force was considering two bombers for this purpose. One would be an extension or modification of the TFX, and it would take about five years to deploy a force of several hundred of these bombers. Of course, the Secretary reminded Senator Stennis, the TFX may not be the bomber the Air Force recommends. If it should be the AMSA that is ultimately recommended, requiring the development of a new engine, it would take about two years to develop the engine for demonstration testing and another six to seven years to deploy a force of 200 aircraft.

Senator Stennis was not convinced that the manned-bomber program was being given adequate priority or funding. He told Secretary McNamara, "It seems strange to me that everyone agrees that this manned-bomber concept, a new one, should not be abandoned or put aside. It should be carried forward, but still it is just not moving forward."[28] The Secretary replied that the problem was based on differences of opinion as to whether a new manned bomber should be produced and deployed at all. It was generally recognized, McNamara continued, that available information was not sufficient upon which to make a decision for or against a manned bomber. As a matter of fact, he said, "the evidence today is against an affirmative decision. But there are uncertainties; and, therefore, it is generally agreed among us that we should hedge against those uncertainties by carrying out development programs that will allow us to make a decision to produce at a later date if it then seems wise, which I don't believe it will."[29]

During his appearance before the House Armed Services Committee, McNamara was informed by Chairman Mendel Rivers, "You or one of the two of you, certainly Mr. Vance, gave me the impression that we have gotten a lot of information on the avionics and the engines at this point, so much so that we could, if need be, phase into a program definition stage (AMSA) at this time."[30] The Secretary denied this, saying that he had very recently visited the General Electric Company at Cincinnati, Ohio, which was developing the AMSA engine. He said he found the work on the AMSA engine in the stage he had anticipated it would be in. It was barely underway and was not yet at a point where the government could proceed with the program definition phase of the aircraft beyond the level of expenditure now recommended. Because of the tentative specifications established by the Air Force for the AMSA, the engine being developed for the F-111, for example, lacked adequate power to meet the AMSA specifications. Thus, the Secretary pointed out, a whole new technology for an engine was required which represented a major step forward in metallurgy and aircraft engine design. Under these circumstances, he said, it would be a serious error to pursue a program and expend funds that were not required because the engine required such a long period of development as to allow the other elements of the aircraft to be started much later.

Rivers asked Secretary McNamara to explain the difference between the Air Force request for funds for the AMSA and the funds recommended by the Department of Defense. McNamara explained:

> The Air Force requested for fiscal 1965 $15 million for the airframe, $11 million for the avionics, and $26 million for the propulsion, and $4.5 million for the SRAM missile, which is the standoff missile; and for 1966 they requested $77 million for the airframe, $14 million for avionics, $30 million for propulsion, and $37 million for the SRAM missile, that is a total of $56.5 million for 1965 and $158 million for 1966. Contrasted with $56.5 million requested for 1965 we are proposing $32.5 million; in contrast to the $158 million requested for 1966 we are proposing $76 million.[31]

John R. Blandford of the Committee staff asked the Secretary why, if the Air Force was recommending more than double the funds proposed by the Department of Defense for AMSA in fiscal 1966, they could not profitably spend it. Presumably, McNamara said, the Air Force hoped to decide on the aircraft specifications sometime in advance of the end of fiscal year 1966, at which time they would spend funds more rapidly on the airframe. However, the Secretary stressed, unless the engine specifications were clearly established at the time a decision was made to move ahead on the airframe it would be a serious waste.

Congressman Otis Pike asked McNamara whether he thought the Air Force might be aware of the Secretary's doubt that a military requirement for AMSA existed, which might have delayed the development of necesary plans and specifications. The Secretary said he doubted that the Air Force had been inhibited from submitting whatever evidence they had that a military requirement for a specific aircraft existed. He understood, he said, that the Joint Chiefs of Staff had not concluded that there was a military requirement for production. Rather they were recommending that a project definition phase be initiated even though the Air Force had not told them for what kind of an aircraft a project definition phase would be initiated. General Wheeler was asked if he cared to add anything. The General said that overall he agreed with the Secretary and had recommended in a separate view that advanced avionics and propulsion development be hastened, that the prerequisite phase proposed by the Air Force be completed as soon as practicable, and that the decision with respect to beginning the formal project definition phase be made at that time. In response to further questioning both General Wheeler and Secretary McNamara agreed that no one, including the Joint Chiefs of Staff, was recommending that a decision be made to produce a new manned bomber. Maintaining an option to produce such an aircraft in the future was the primary concern of General Wheeler and the Joint Chiefs of Staff.

Secretary of the Air Force Zuckert was asked for his opinion on the AMSA during his testimony before the House Armed Services Committee. When asked by Congressman Rivers whether he considered the AMSA a follow-on manned system, he replied:

> I don't mean to seem to quibble, but I think AMSA has to be defined. I think there has been a tendency to view AMSA as being something tangible—something that you could draw a picture of. AMSA, to me, just means an advanced manned system. I don't know whether at this point it would be a stretched version of the F-111, a 250,000-pound aircraft or a 300,000-pound aircraft.[32]

While agreeing that he was not ready to define precisely a follow-on for the B-52, Secretary Zuckert emphasized that he was in favor of vigorously pursuing a follow-on system to the B-52. He agreed that propulsion development was critical to any decision to build a new manned bomber, and added that avionics was also important. He also defined avionics as the guidance, the fire control systems, the electronic counter-measures, and generally all of the black boxes that go into making an aircraft a fighting vehicle. When asked to conjecture about a likely project definition date for the follow-on bomber, Secretary Zuckert gave as his opinion the latter part of fiscal year 1966 or early in fiscal year 1967. Finally, when pressed on the question of waiting until 1970 before making a decision to go ahead with a new bomber, the Air Force Secretary affirmed that he favored a program permitting a project definition phase in fiscal 1967 which he estimated would permit the Air Force to have an airplane by 1973.

Air Force Chief of Staff, General McConnell, testifying before the joint Senate Appropriations Subcommittee and Armed Services Committee, was asked by Senator Stennis whether the nation ought to proceed with the development of a follow-on bomber. General McConnell replied that in his opinion the decision should be to proceed, and he stated:

> . . . I have no doubt but that we will be authorized a modern manned bomber which we call the AMSA, in sufficient time to pick up the slack that will be left after the B-52's have been phased out. It is a matter of difference between the Secretary of Defense and the Air Force as to when this action should start taking place. We have been of the opinion that this action should start taking place about a year earlier than has been recommended by the Office of the Secretary of Defense.
>
> If we started it a year earlier, in other words, begin in July of this year, then we could have a capability a year earlier. We would have an operational aircraft in [deleted] and then we could have enough weapons in the inventory by [deleted] to take the place of the last B-52's which by that time should have been phased out.[33]

Somewhat later in the testimony Senator Symington asked General McConnell whether he knew the kind of aircraft he would like to have now. The General answered, "We are coming closer to it all the time. We haven't actually got it down to the point where we can give it to a contractor and ask him to give us a bid on it."[34]

Just two months later in April 1965, General McConnell made an informal proposal to the Secretary of Defense to replace the

B-52 C-F series aircraft with a bomber version of the F-111. Then in June the Air Force formally proposed to procure 210 FB-111s as a replacement for the B-52 C-Fs. In August 1965, the Joint Chiefs of Staff approved the Air Force proposal to deploy the FB-111. Following a complete review of all aspects of the proposal by the Department of Defense in the context of the overall strategic offensive-defensive forces program, the Secretary of Defense recommended, and the President approved, going ahead with the development and procurement of this aircraft, beginning in FY 1966, and phasing out the B-52 C-F aircraft on a five-year schedule proposed by the Joint Chiefs of Staff. The total anticipated investment cost of the FB-111 was about $1.9 billion. By the end of fiscal year 1971, the strategic forces could consist of 465 modernized bombers, including 210 FB-111s and 255 B-52 Gs and Hs.[35]

During the debates in Congress over the future utility of a manned bomber, the question was raised whether the bomber or the missile was more likely to survive enemy defenses in the 1970s. Congressman Mahon asked Secretary McNamara whether there was any possibility that a way might be found to paralyze our intercontinental ballistic missiles and make reliance on a manned bomber of greater importance than it otherwise might be. McNamara replied, that he believed that everyone he had talked to would agree that it is far easier to design near-perfect defenses against a manned bomber than it is to design near-perfect defenses against a ballistic missile. Even in an enemy environment, the Secretary continued, consisting of anti-missile defenses, "it is not conceivable to me that a nation which solves the problem of defending against anti-ballistic missiles would not solve the problem of defending against bombers."[36] McNamara said he knew of no one in the Department of Defense who advocated that a follow-on manned bomber be developed as a substitute for the ballistic missile because of the development of anti-ballistic missile defenses. During the Senate hearings, the Secretary was asked whether in the absence of an early decision to develop a follow-on manned bomber there was a strong possibility that improving enemy defenses would make the B-52 and B-58 force progressively vulnerable, thus creating a severe gap in the nation's bomber capability to penetrate those defenses. Secretary McNamara answered that he did not believe so, because he had no indication that any of the proposed follow-on manned bombers would have a substantially greater penetration capability against enemy defensive systems between now and 1972 or 1975 than the B-52.[37]

An important milestone in the history of United States strategic forces was reached during 1965; for the first time there were more missiles than bombers in the total forces. This historic change was attributable to the phaseout of some B-47 units and the activation of new Minuteman missile units. Air Force Chief of Staff, General McConnell, during his testimony before the House Armed Services Committee pointed out, however, that "the manned bombers still carry some 80 percent of the total megatonnage currently programmed for delivery by SAC forces and will continue to carry the bulk of these weapons through 1970."[38] Of the total of 630 B-52 aircraft, the largest portion of the strategic bomber force, the Defense Department was scheduling the phaseout during 1965 of some 40 of the early B models, leaving a total of 600 B-52s operational through the early 1970s. To meet the requirements imposed by the Vietnam war, some B-52s were modified to carry twenty-four 750-pound bombs externally, in addition to the standard load of 27 for a total of 51. A modification and strengthening program for approximately 600 B-52s, costing about $3,069 billion was planned by the administration, including $339 million for fiscal year 1966.[39]

In 1965 the Strategic Air Command still possessed units of the aging B-47. As late as 1964, B-47 squadrons were rotated continuously to bases in Spain, England, and Alaska. All such rotations to Spain and England were scheduled to terminate during 1965 and all units brought home to bases in the United States. Moreover, additional units of B-47s would be phased out of the active inventory, bringing the total since 1963 to 11 wings or 495 aircraft from a total inventory numbering originally over 1,400. According to plans, the last B-47s would phase out during fiscal year 1966. As for the B-58 medium supersonic bomber, it was planned to maintain 2 wings totalling 80 operational aircraft through fiscal year 1966, and that number would remain the same into the 1970s time period, depending on attrition.[40]

Finally, with approval by Congress of a $25 million appropriation, the funding for the XB-70 project, part of the earlier B-70 programs, would be completed for a total development cost of $1,483 million. The first XB-70 was completed in 1964 and was flown four times during the final months of the year. A fifth flight was scheduled for January 1965. A total of 180 hours flight test time was scheduled for the two-vehicle program, and McNamara believed this should be sufficient to determine the XB-70's basic aerodynamic structure and performance characteristics. It was anticipated that following completion of the initial flight test program the XB-70 could be used in connection with supersonic transports or general aeronautics research in such areas as general handling qualities of large supersonic aircraft, sonic boom measurements, etc.[41]

The Minuteman Program in 1965

In presenting the Johnson administration's defense program to the Congress in 1964, Secretary McNamara recommended a tentative five-year Minuteman program totalling 1,200 Minuteman missiles. The Minuteman program recommended to Congress early in 1965 called for a total of 1,000 missiles in 1970. The Secretary was asked by Senator Stennis of the Armed Services Committee to explain the reason for the reductions. The most important reason for the change, McNamara explained, was that the capability of the Minuteman system had been increased by the introduction into the program of improvements in guidance and other features which increased its kill capability. He could also foresee additional improvements in the future beyond those already approved if it became necessary to take advantage of them. In any event, he stressed, it would be far better, if necessary, to further increase the kill capability of the Minuteman force by introducing these added improvements in guidance, accuracy, and payload, than it would be to add to that force. A second major reason given by Secretary McNamara for the Minuteman force reductions was that a force containing 200 additional missiles would not have any material effect in reducing damage to the nation when operating in a damaging-limiting role.[42]

Congressman Mahon of the House Appropriations Subcommittee also asked Secretary McNamara to explain the administration's decision on the Minuteman force. The Congressman recalled the earlier Air Force plan calling for a Minuteman force numbering on the order of 2,600 missiles and wondered whether the reduced force proposals would provide adequate security. After explaining that the gains to be derived from qualitative improvements to the existing force, and a current evaluation of the military threat were the reasons for the decision to hold the Minuteman force at 1,000 instead of 1,200, the Secretary emphasized the current superiority in missiles enjoyed by the United States. By June 30, 1965, the nation's strategic forces would consist of 854 ICBMs on launcher and 416 Polaris missiles, a total of 1,270 ballistic missiles. In contrast, said McNamara, "their [Soviet] total missile strength targetable against us will be but a small fraction of our strength."[43]

The discussion of Minuteman capabilities continued, and Secretary McNamara was asked by Congressman George Andrews of Alabama whether the current Minuteman was a significantly better missile than the one of two years ago. The Secretary replied that it was a better missile. He also pointed out that a misunderstanding occurred on this point by using the term "Minuteman II" to describe a missile that was as different from the Minuteman I as the B-52 is from the B-47. McNamara was asked how many targets the Minuteman missile could be trained on. The early Minuteman missiles, the Secretary said, could be pretargeted on a very limited number of targets, that is, with an ability to shift from one to the other by remote control. But, he added, "The later Minuteman missiles will have capability of targeting on many more different targets with ability to shift by remote control."[44] A much more important advantage of the Minuteman II, according to the Secretary, was the reduction in the circular error probable (increased accuracy) which would increase the destructive potential of the missile by between four and eight times. Asked whether the Minuteman missile was presently capable of being so targeted, McNamara replied:

> Not in the Minuteman system, but in the Polaris system we have well-nigh complete retargeting flexibility, because the commander of the Polaris submarine has on board the submarine cards that permit him to change the target of any missile within a matter of seconds. He simply takes out one card and puts in another, and this is literally a thirty-second job. He can target any target within the range of the submarine.[45]

Again referring to the currently planned Minuteman force structure of 1,000 missiles, the Secretary stated that on the basis of what was now known, it would be, in his estimation, an "absolute waste" if the decision were made to procure additional missiles. He continued by drawing attention to the comparison of United States forces and those of its potential enemy which was in his classified statement and which indicated America's overwhelming superiority today and the maintenance of that same superiority in fiscal 1966 and 1967.

Almost inevitably the question was raised to Secretary McNamara of whether the Joint Chiefs of Staff agreed with his decision to limit the FY 1966 Minuteman force to 1,000 rather than the previous year's 1,200. The Secretary's reply to Senator John Stennis of the Armed Services Committee was a candid, "No, sir." He admitted that most of the Chiefs would have preferred to see the total left at 1,200. However, McNamara stressed, "we can increase that total to 1,200 at a later date if it seems desirable. The Chiefs recommended [that] the Minuteman force buildup should continue toward an end of 1969 objective of 1,200, and we can still reach 1,200 at the end of 1969 if it seems advisable to do so, by adding missiles at a later date."[46] Such a decision would therefore not be final at that time and would be subject to review on a year-to-year basis. Senator Stennis asked whether it was merely a matter of increasing the production rate from an active production line. The Secretary replied that it was and indicated that the retrofit program for Minuteman I would ensure a hot production facility if that became necessary.

By the end of 1964, the Navy reported that 19 Polaris submarines were on patrol in three oceans, carrying 304 missiles. According to plan, by the end of fiscal year 1965, the number of deployed Polaris submarines on combat status would increase to 26, with three in overhaul. One year later in July 1966 the Navy planned to have 29 Polaris submarines on patrol, and if production and deployment schedules held, all 41 planned submarines would be ready for sea in December 1966.[47] Each phased increment of Polaris deployment included the associated surface support ships, i.e., tenders, resupply ships, and floating drydocks, which were stationed strategically in the Atlantic and Pacific oceans.

The Poseidon Missile

During 1964 the Johnson administration did not decide to begin development of a propulsion system for the so-called Polaris B-3 missile—later renamed Poseidon. In its fiscal year 1966 program, however, the administration announced that it would initiate full-scale development of the Poseidon missile which would have payload weight and volume fully twice that of the Polaris A-3 and would incorporate improved accuracy. The Department of Defense requested an appropriation of $35 million to fund at a reasonable pace work on the long lead time items which were the propulsion system and the guidance and navigation changes.[48]

During his appearance before the Senate Appropriations Subcommittee and Armed Services Committee, Dr. Harold Brown, Director of Defense Research and Engineering, was asked by Senator Leverett Saltonstall of Massachusetts to explain the difference between the Polaris B-3 and Poseidon missiles. Dr. Brown replied that the propulsion, the payload, etc., were the same as the B-3's. Asked by Senator Saltonstall whether the Poseidon missile would have significantly greater capability to penetrate enemy defenses, Dr. Brown stressed that such capability was an important aspect of the Poseidon program. Asked by Senator Gordon Allott of Colorado what range the Poseidon missile would have in comparison to the Polaris A-3, Dr. Brown said that the Department of Defense was planning to maintain the same range (2,000-2,500 nautical miles) and take the improvements in propulsion and in the payload. In this event payload could be effectively doubled, and, if considered desirable, part of the payload could be traded off to obtain added range.[49]

As explained by Dr. Brown to the joint Senate committees, the full development program for the Poseidon missile would cost approximately $900 million. Based on the assumption that a commitment to a full-scale development program was a strong presumption of a later decision to proceed with full development of the Poseidon missile, Dr. Brown estimated that development costs would run in the neighborhood of $1 billion.

During his appearance before the House Armed Services Committee, Secretary McNamara was asked by a committee member whether there was any serious doubt about proceeding with the full development of the Poseidon missile. The Secretary explained that the Navy had not yet recommended a firm deployment program for it and that he favored deploying it. The total cost of roughly $2 billion would, said McNamara, permit the development and deployment of nineteen submarines equipped with Poseidon missiles. In explaining his request for $35 million in FY 1966 funds the Secretary stated:

> I inserted this in the budget, at the recommendation of the Navy and the Joint Chiefs, because we all believe that this is a major step forward in increasing accuracy and increasing payload. Both accuracy and payload increases will assist us in penetrating an anti-ballistic missile system if one should develop, because then we can trade off accuracy and payload for decoys or other penetration aids. As of now we don't know whether an anti-ballistic missile system will be deployed.[50]

Under circumstances in which the Soviets deployed a significant ballistic missile defense system, Secretary McNamara said he would strongly recommend the decision to develop and deploy the Poseidon missile. It was always possible, the Secretary observed, that having fully developed the Poseidon missile, an actual military requirement would not exist. He doubted such a situation would occur often, but concluded that this was one of the situations in which moving ahead with development as a prudent "insurance" measure for future deterrent capability would be justified.

The Status of the Nike-X ABM in 1965

Another key issue discussed in detail by Secretary McNamara in his annual posture statement and taken up at some length during the Secretary's hearings before the House and Senate Appropriations and Armed Services Committees, was the current status of the Nike-X anti-ballistic missile system (ABM). During fiscal year 1966, the administration asked for $400 million to continue the intensive development program on the Nike-X program. As explained by Dr. Harold Brown, effort would be concentrated during 1965 and early 1966 on the "building block" concept of Nike-X to permit maximum flexibility in deployment options and to test the effectiveness of these options against various threats.[51] During 1964, considerable knowledge of reentry had been gained primarily as a result of tests conducted at Kwajalein on the Nike-Zeus. During 1965, an intensive test and measurement program would be continued both at Kwajalein and at White Sands Missile Range to extend knowledge and technique in the discrimination area.[52]

Because of the substantial progress made on the Nike-X system by early 1965, the basic question raised by Congress concerned a possible decision by the Johnson administration to produce and deploy the system at an early date. Representative Mahon of the House Appropriations Subcommittee asked Secretary McNamara whether he still believed it was premature to make any commitment to the production and deployment of Nike-X and particularly whether technical or other considerations were controlling.[53] The Secretary replied he thought that a decision was premature for both reasons. He acknowledged that technical work was proceeding satisfactorily and the Army advised that it would be possible to begin production of the system during FY 1966. McNamara said he doubted it would be wise to proceed on the advice of the Army because development work had not progressed to the point where the system had been fully tested. Very likely, he said, if steps were taken to lay out the production process and long lead time tooling before development was completed, revisions would have to be made in the production process and tooling redesigned as design changes were introduced into the system.[54]

Apart from technical and other considerations, Secretary McNamara told the House committee that the Johnson administration had decided not to deploy Nike-X in FY 1966. The reason, he said, was that "we are not really in a position to decide that at the present time."[55] This decision could better be made in FY 1967, the Secretary stressed, and would depend considerably on whether a decision was made to deploy to meet a less sophisticated Chinese threat or a large-scale Soviet threat. On the assumption that the Nike-X development program remained on schedule, McNamara thought a production and deployment decision could logically be made in FY 1967.

Apparently sensing that a decision to deploy Nike-X would be forthcoming, Mahon asked the Defense Secretary whether the deployment of such a system would tend to heat up the cold war. McNamara said he did not think so, and elaborated as follows:

> I do not believe we could count on reducing United States fatalities from a Soviet strike in the 1970 period or toward the end of this decade below a level of about 80 million even if we did deploy the Nike-X system. I do not believe that the promise of being able to limit the potential loss of life to approximately 80 million fatalities in this country would in any way make us more willing to act aggressively than if we had not deployed that system. I do not see that it would affect our attitude toward the cold war, and I believe the Soviets would appraise our own appraisal in that same form.[56]

Secretary McNamara agreed with Mahon that if the United States succeeded in deploying a near 100 percent efficient anti-ballistic missile defense, the Soviet Union would assuredly compensate by increasing its strategic offensive power.

In response to a question by Congressman William Minshall of Ohio about the perfectibility of the Nike-X system, Secretary McNamara replied he thought it inconceivable that either the Soviet Union or the United States would likely achieve such a system in the near future. The Congressman then asked the Secretary whether any contemplated ABM system could protect against a determined enemy missile attack on an American city. McNamara stated that he did not see how, for no matter what improvements were made in an ABM system an enemy would be capable of developing penetration aids and tactics to enable him to successfully penetrate. The question arose as to whether the deployment of an anti-ballistic missile system would therefore be an exercise in futility. Secretary McNamara conjectured that a defense system could destroy a percentage of incoming warheads but not all. Perhaps defense could destroy some warheads attacking some American cities but not all warheads aimed at all American cities. This situation, said the Secretary, is simply a function of the number of warheads directed on a particular city. To illustrate his point, McNamara cited the case of Washington, D.C., which in his judgment would very likely be a high-priority enemy target. Thus, an enemy would seek to saturate such a defensive system knowing that only a single warhead must penetrate to do grave damage to the capital city.

Congressman Minshall raised the question with Secretary McNamara about the wisdom of deploying ABM defenses against Communist China. The Secretary's reply is noteworthy: "I think we could decide to develop an anti-ballistic missile system to protect us against China for a decade or two. As a matter of fact, I think this is well worth considering. That might cost $8 billion to $10 billion." On the other hand, he said, to deploy an ABM system capable of affording some protection against a large-scale Soviet attack would probably cost about $20 billion plus several billions a year to operate. In either event, the Secretary continued, an adequate fallout shelter program was an indispensable addition if ABM defenses were to be meaningful at all.

Congressman Glenard Lipscomb of California asked McNamara what would happen if Congress, and particularly the American people, would not accept the idea and would not build the fallout shelter program into the defense posture. The Secretary pointed out that by taking the postulated Soviet attack capabilities for 1970, the difference in probable fatalities between having and not having adequate fallout protection would be on the order of 100–150 million and 80–125 million fatalities. Two major considerations were implicit in this contrasting situation. First, said McNamara, should the American people vote to provide themselves with fallout shelter protection when they are fully aware that United States strategic forces today are fully adequate to deter any rational aggressor from attacking the United States? Second, is there a real difference between the effect of 80 million and 100 million fatalities on the ability of the United States to survive as a viable nation? Stated in another way, how much additional effort should the United States put into the creation of damage-limiting capability over and above a specified level of assured destruction capability? Congressman Mahon and Secretary McNamara agreed that nuclear war must be considered a possibility, that the country and human life would go on no matter how horrible such a contemplation might be, and therefore the sensible thing to do would be to take reasonable precautions. Fortunately, McNamara concluded, it was not necessary to make decisions on all the crucial issues this year. As a minimum gesture, he stressed, Congress ought to authorize some $80–$90 million dollars for the continuation of the shelter program.

The Civil Defense Program

The final major defense issue examined at length by Congress with the Secretary of Defense and his top civilian and military aides was the present status and adequacy of the nation's civil defense program. Congressman Edward Hebert of the House Armed Services Committee asked Secretary McNamara why it was that when the Joint Chiefs of Staff appeared and General Wheeler testified that a fallout shelter program was a top priority, and the Secretary concurred that it was a necessary and desirable program, yet the Defense Department had not asked Congress for the necessary funds or sent any legislation to Congress to implement that program. For three years, said McNamara, the Department of Defense presented two shelter programs to the Congress, one designed to identify, mark, and stock existing structures which might have a capability for providing protection in the event of a nuclear attack, and the other designed to add shelters to new structures, not yet built, or to physically modify existing structures. And each year, he continued, Congress cut both programs drastically.[57]

Because the controversy surrounding the entire shelter program was so intense, McNamara told the members of the House Armed Services Committee that for fiscal year 1966, he was limiting his request to $80 million which was adequate to carry on the first high-priority phase of the shelter program, i.e., identification, marking, and stocking of shelter spaces. Asked how much more the $80 million request was above last year's request, the Secretary stated that Congress in 1964 had granted only $2.3 million for shelters. According to McNamara, the cost per space for the higher priority shelter identification, marking, and stocking program was $2 to $4, in contrast to $17 to $25 per space for new construction. Asked by Congressman Hebert whether his FY 1966 shelter program recommendations were a reflection of abandoned hope that Congress could be persuaded to act favorably on his request, Secretary McNamara made it emphatically clear that he had not lost hope, but rather felt that he should concentrate his efforts on achieving short-run gains represented by the $80 million request. The previous year, he noted, so much time was spent arguing about the more expensive and controversial new construction program that the shorter run program suffered a drastic cut needlessly.

Congressman Otis Pike of New York sought to place the blame on the Johnson administration for failure to achieve satisfactory fallout shelter support from Congress. He told Secretary McNamara: "I don't think you can say that Congress turned you down and use that as an excuse not to come back, because last year and the year before, and never before have you or have the Joint Chiefs of Staff come up before this Committee or before Congress and said, 'This is a top priority item.' "[58] The Secretary rebutted strongly Congressman Pike's contention by reviewing the number of personal appearances he had made on behalf of an effective national shelter program since 1961, President Kennedy's special message stressing its importance, and the importance which he had always placed on shelters during the many discussions of a possible anti-ballistic missile program for the United States. And he concluded, "Despite all of our efforts, we lost probably 70 percent of what we asked for for this highly important identification, marking, and provisioning program."[59]

Chairman Mahon of the House Appropriations Subcommittee also questioned Secretary McNamara about the seeming pessimism implicit in the manner by which the Department of Defense was presenting its fiscal year 1966 civil defense program. McNamara explained as he had earlier to the House Armed Services Committee, that it appeared wisest and most likely of success to concentrate on the single aspect of the civil defense program calling for identifying, marking, and stocking shelters in existing structures. Because in the Secretary's judgment the broader program had already been postponed so long, he urged that the issue of designing shelters for new and existing structures be considered as a part of the overall damage-limiting program along with a new manned bomber, a new manned interceptor, additional missiles, and anti-ballistic missiles. Finally, he remarked that he thought the entire discussion could be deferred until fiscal 1967.

Congressman Dan Flood of Pennsylvania reviewed the checkered if not unsuccessful history of administration efforts to obtain support from Congress for an adequate civil defense program and then informed Secretary McNamara of a major inhibiting problem. Professing to be a strong advocate of civil defense objectives, and describing the elaborate and effective civil defense organization in his own district, he stated:

> . . . the first man I meet on South Main Street in Wilkes-Barre tomorrow morning couldn't possibly care less. I am sure he knows little about what I am telling you that actually exists in his town and country. I do not think he knows what I am talking about there. I do not think he knows these things are going on. He reads them and hears about them half a dozen times a year. But they do not sink in, and the last thing in the world that man that I met on the corner is interested in, believe me, is civil defense.[60]

Moreover, said Congressman Flood, if interest in civil defense in Pennsylvania is small, interest in all fifty states appeared to him to be even less.

Secretary McNamara was then asked by Congressman Flood to explain exactly how he defined the burdens of the Department of Defense with respect to generating public and congressional support for a strong civil defense program. He replied by saying that the responsibility for civil defense was primarily a local and state responsibility and the burden rested on the local authorities and the state authorities to make clear to the people what was required and why, and to organize the effort necessary to meet that requirement. Congressman Flood, however, got an admission from McNamara that in addition to state and local responsibilities, he did have an important secondary responsibility. How, then, the Congressman asked, does the Department of Defense propose to convince the American people that a civil defense program is an essential complement to an adequate defense program? The Secretary replied that greater efforts were needed at the congressional level—authorization and appropriations—to put through the requested programs than had been the case during the previous three to four years. McNamara added that the civil defense function had been transferred to the Army as a more efficient means of increasing services to state and local authorities. Congressman Flood rejoined that the Army-directed program was getting nowhere. Secretary McNamara disagreed, stating that just three years ago the program was defunct; now, he said, there was a plan, a program, and an organization, and people were becoming more aware of it as well as skilled in its elements.

With respect to the overall civil defense program Secretary McNamara conceded to Congressman Flood that congressional apathy was due in large measure to the program's not being well understood by the public. Emphasizing again the educational burden of state and local governments, McNamara pointed out that the current posture statement had gone farther than any previous efforts to disclose first to the Congress and then to the public the entire scope of the problem of strategic nuclear war. For example, he said, the unclassified version of the posture statement contained an extensive discussion of the whole issue, covering some thirty-two pages. And, he explained, "In this unclassified version we disclose previously classified information in order to inform the public of the advantages and contributions of a civil defense program to the damage limiting capability of this nation. We describe nuclear war. We describe the fundamental requirements to deter it. We indicate the likely results of it should it take place and describe the contribution that civil defense would make to minimizing the fatalities to this country."[61]

Congressman Flood was unimpressed with the degree of success likely to greet Secretary McNamara's efforts. The Secretary nevertheless stood firm in his belief that the unclassified material now available for congressional and public use would in time produce an educated electorate capable of making known its desire for a civil defense program similar to the one presented during the past three years by the Department of Defense.

Because the issue had been raised by defense analysts outside the government, Congressman Glenard Lipscomb asked Secretary McNamara whether "a massive civil defense program" was likely to be regarded by the Soviet Union as an indication of United States intent to initiate war against that nation. The Secretary said he thought it inconceivable that the Soviet Union would regard a civil defense program in this way, pointing out that at best the United States could expect to reduce its fatalities by having a shelter program from 100–150 million to 80–125 million, depending on the nature and timing of an attack. Thus, the argument, McNamara felt, was totally without merit. During the interchange between Congressman Lipscomb and Secretary McNamara, the Congressman apparently stated that a United States civil defense program would assuredly provoke the Soviets into increasing their strategic power and at a lower cost to them than to us. The Secretary conceded that in many situations this would be the case, but added, "It happens that the contribution of civil defense fallout shelters to our damage limiting capability cannot be offset by the Soviets through additions to their strategic offensive forces at a cost lower than that of our civil defense program."[62]

Chairman Mahon of the House Appropriations Subcommittee said that while he and other committee members embraced the objectives of the civil defense program, "there are many problems in connection with it." For example, he said, people in rural areas could feel more secure without fallout shelters than people in cities. City dwellers, Mahon continued, subjected to a direct attack would have very little warning and few would likely survive the blast and thermal effects. Secretary McNamara agreed that fallout shelters offered no protection against blast and thermal effects but suggested that a number of people outside the circle of those effects would probably die if no shelters were available. And the survivors would have a chance to reach available shelters, McNamara stressed, since it takes at least 20 to 30 minutes for the fallout radiation effects to reach the surviving people.

The extent to which Secretary McNamara was aware of the Kennedy administration's emerging plans to commit American forces on a large scale in Vietnam is uncertain, but his defense of the military budget to Congress indicated clearly that he wanted to defeat the introduction of expensive new strategic weapon systems, continue a healthy program of research and development, and emphasize in the future qualitative improvements to existing forces rather than increases in such forces. For the first time, he answered the question, "How much is enough?" by quantifying deterrence in terms of the fatalities and damage to industrial capacity that this nation's retaliatory forces should be able to inflict on an enemy's society. If accepted by Congress and the American public, the new criteria could produce a significant braking effect on those who advocated large new bomber and missile programs despite the fact that the United States enjoyed an enormous strategic superiority over the Soviet Union. Playing down the utility of a major damage-limiting program in cost and effect terms, McNamara appeared determined to hold down expenditures for strategic weapon systems in part by such diversionary efforts as a final bid to convince Congress to take civil defense seriously and to appropriate $5 billion for it. How closely calibrated the Secretary's defense proposals were to imminent Vietnam plans was then, and continues to be, unknown.

The Balance of Strategic Nuclear Forces in 1965

Intervention by the United States during 1965 in South Vietnam to prevent its being overrun by the Vietcong was strongly denounced by the Soviet Union. Both powers, however, appeared to regard the Vietnam conflict as peripheral to their vital national security interests, and fear of a possible general nuclear war, which had subsided in the detente atmosphere following the Cuban crisis, did not rise perceptibly during the year. Thus, despite the intensification of Soviet charges of United States aggression in Vietnam, the issue was kept well compartmentalized as arms control negotiations involving the two major powers and affecting Europe primarily continued in an atmosphere of marked detente.

During the celebration of the twentieth anniversary of the ending of World War II in Europe, the Soviets on May 9, 1965, paraded in Moscow a number of new strategic weapon systems. Of primary importance to Western military analysts were two new missiles claimed by Soviet leaders to be a solid-fuel ICBM and a mobile MRBM, and a large cylindrical device which was purportedly an anti-ballistic missile. None of the newly revealed systems was judged to be operational in 1965, but the appearance of the new technology did suggest that the Soviet Union was progressing in a field in which it had hitherto lagged behind the United States. The appearance of a possible Soviet ABM was not interpreted as posing any immediate threat to the existing strategic balance, but it did suggest that the Soviets were pursuing intensive research and development on a workable defense system against ballistic missiles, similar to efforts being made by the United States.

The Institute for Strategic Studies in London conjectured in its edition of *The Military Balance* for 1965 that even though Soviet public statements about their ABM described the system as designed to provide protection against American missiles, it was nonetheless possible that the Soviet Union like the United States was concerned about providing a defense against a smaller power threat, such as that of Communist China, the United Kingdom, or France. By the end of 1965, the balance of strategic nuclear power between the United States and the Soviet Union still strongly favored this nation. However, the Soviet Union made significant progress during the year toward attaining a secure second-strike strategic force, by increasing the total number of its ICBMs by 40 percent (70 missiles) and by hardening the silos of a considerable fraction of its total strategic missile force. No apparent increases were made in the number of MRBM and IRBM launchers aimed at Western Europe and part of the Far East. As was the case in 1964, the Soviets were credited with having between 700 and 750 operational launchers, having ranges from 700 to 2,100 nautical miles. In addition the Soviets had an estimated 40 submarines capable of launching 120 nuclear-tipped missiles.[63]

The United States, on the other hand, possessed 800 operational Minuteman I missiles, all in hardened silos, and 54 Titan IIs carrying the largest available United States warhead. The Navy had in commission 31 Polaris submarines carrying 496 missiles, and five more submarines were in various stages of construction. Of the 31 submarines 18 were patrolling the Atlantic, three were in the Mediterranean and four were in the Western Pacific. According to one source, in long-range missiles alone, the United States had on launcher a total of 1,417 megatons, while the Soviets were credited with 3,570 megatons.[64]

Soviet strength in intercontinental bombers late in 1965 was estimated to be about one-third of that possessed by the United States Strategic Air Command B-52 fleet.[65] Specifically, the Soviets were credited with having about 120 4-jet Bison bombers, about 80 turbo-prop Bears, and something on the order of 900 twin-jet medium bomber Badgers.[66] The Badger medium bomber was being replaced progressively by the high performance twin-jet supersonic bomber, Blinder. Also, it appeared that the Bear long-range bombers were in process of being phased out and converted to a naval reconnaissance role.[67]

In comparison, the United States possessed a total of 935 bombers, which included a total of 630 B-52s equipped with the Hound Dog stand-off missile, 80 B-58 Hustler supersonic medium bombers, and approximately 225 B-47 medium bombers, all of which were scheduled to be phased out in the near future.[68] It was estimated that the aggregate payload capacity of United States bombers totalled approximately 26,396 megatons, while the Soviets were credited with an aggregate bomber payload capacity of some 11,800 megatons.[69]

NOTES

1. U.S., Department of Defense, *Statement by Secretary of Defense Robert S. McNamara Before the House Subcommittee on Department of Defense Appropriations on the FY 1967–71 Defense Program and 1967 Defense Budget*, 1966, p. 17.

2. Ibid., p. 37.

3. Ibid., p. 39.

4. *Public Papers of the Presidents of the United States, Lyndon B. Johnson, 1965*, U.S. Government Printing Office, Washington, 1966, p. 2.

5. Ibid., pp. 62–63.

6. Ibid.

7. Ibid., p. 65.

8. Ibid., p. 71.

9. U.S., Department of Defense, *Statement by Secretary of Defense Robert S. McNamara before the House Armed Services Committee on the Fy 1966–1970 Defense Program and the 1966 Defense Budget*, February 18, 1965, p. 37.

10. Ibid., p. 38.

11. Ibid., p. 39.

12. Ibid., p. 41.

13. Ibid., p. 45.

14. Ibid., p. 46.

15. Ibid., p. 49.

16. Ibid., p. 53.

17. Ibid.

18. Ibid., p. 56.

19. U.S., Congress, Senate, Subcommittee on Department of Defense Appropriations of the Committee on Appropriations and the Committee on Armed Services, *Hearings on Department of Defense Appropriations, 1966*, 89th Cong., 1st sess., 1965, Part I, p. 274.

20. Ibid.

21. U.S., Congress, House, Subcommittee of the Committee on Appropriations, *Hearings on DOD Appropriations for 1966*, 89th Cong., 1st sess., 1965, Part 3, pp. 143–144.

22. U.S., House, Congress, Committee on Armed Services, *Hearings on Military Posture*, 89th Cong., 1st sess., 1965, p. 504.

23. Ibid.

24. Ibid., p. 505.

25. Ibid.

26. Ibid., p. 506.

27. Ibid.

28. Senate Subcommittee on Appropriations and Armed Services Committee, *DOD Appropriations, 1966*, Part I, p. 227.

29. Ibid., p. 228.

30. House, Armed Services Committee, *Military Posture Hearings*, 1965, p. 485. Secretary McNamara explained that a program definition phase was intended to allow a manufacturer to lay out the design of a system based on the general description given him, which includes such details as the desired weight of the airplane and its speed, altitude, range, and bomb load capability.

31. Ibid., p. 486.

32. Ibid., p. 1128.

33. Senate, Subcommittee on Appropriations and Armed Services Committee, *DOD Appropriations, 1966*, Part I, p. 971.

34. Ibid., p. 974.

35. Department of Defense, *FY 1967–1971 Defense Program*, pp. 61–62.

36. House, Subcommittee, *DOD Appropriations for 1966*, Part 3, pp. 134–135.

37. Senate, Subcommittee on Appropriations and Armed Services Committee, *DOD Appropriations, 1966*, p. 240.

38. House, Armed Services Committee, *Military Posture Hearings*, 89th Cong., 1st sess., 1965, p. 1117.

39. Senate, Subcommittee on Appropriations and Armed Services Committee, *DOD Appropriations, 1966*, Part 1, p. 304.

40. House, Armed Services Committee, *Military Posture Hearings*, p. 1118.

41. House, Subcommittee, *DOD Appropriations for 1966,* Part 3, pp. 289–290.

42. Senate, Subcommittee on Appropriations and Armed Services Committee, *DOD Appropriations, 1966,* Part 1, p. 304.

43. House, Subcommittee, *DOD Appropriations for 1966,* Part 3, pp. 168–169.

44. Ibid., p. 169.

45. Ibid.

46. Senate, Subcommittee on Appropriations and Armed Services Committee, *DOD Appropriations, 1966,* Part 1, p. 385.

47. House, Subcommittee, *DOD Appropriations for 1966,* Part 3, pp. 691–692.

48. House, Armed Services Committee, *Military Posture Hearings,* p. 567.

49. Senate, Subcommittee on Appropriations and Armed Services Committee, *DOD Appropriations, 1966,* Part 1, pp. 465–466.

50. House, Armed Services Committee, *Military Posture Hearings,* p. 495.

51. Senate, Subcommittee on Appropriations and Armed Services Committee, *DOD Appropriations, 1966,* Part 1, p. 223.

52. House, Armed Services Committee, *Military Posture Hearings,* p. 551.

53. House, Subcommittee, *DOD Appropriations for 1966,* Part 3, p. 355.

54. Ibid.

55. Ibid., Testimony given by General Wheeler, Chairman of the Joint Chiefs of Staff, and General John P. McConnell, newly appointed Chief of Staff of the Air Force, supported the Army view that a decision to produce and deploy the Nike-X system should be made during FY 1966 and not be deferred as Secretary McNamara recommended until FY 1967. See also Senate, Subcommittee on Appropriations and Armed Services Committee, *DOD Appropriations, 1966,* Part 1, p. 284, and House, Subcommittee, *DOD Appropriations for 1966,* Part 3, p. 890.

56. House, Subcommittee, *DOD Appropriations for 1966,* pp. 355, 356, 357, 358, 359.

57. House, Armed Services Committee, *Military Posture Hearings,* p. 499.

58. Ibid., p. 501.

59. Ibid.

60. House, Subcommittee, *DOD Appropriations for 1966,* Part 3, p. 151.

61. Ibid., p. 155.

62. Ibid., p. 156.

63. *The Military Balance 1965–1966.* The Institute for Strategic Studies (London: 1965), pp. 1, 2–3; see also U.S., Congress, House, Armed Services Committee, *The Changing Strategic Military Balance, U.S.A. vs. U.S.S.R.,* 90th Cong., 1st sess., 1967, p. 35.

64. House, Armed Services Committee, *The Changing Strategic Military Balance,* 1967, p. 35.

65. Ibid.

66. *The Military Balance, 1965–1966,* p. 3.

67. Ibid.; House, Armed Services Committee, *The Changing Strategic Military Balance,* p. 36.

68. *The Military Balance, 1965–1966,* p. 3.

69. House, Armed Services Committee, *The Changing Strategic Military Balance,* p. 36.

CHAPTER 7

Twenty Years: Perspectives

For two decades following World War II mankind survived in the nuclear age with scarcely a serious threat of a nuclear holocaust. Momentarily during both the Korean and Cuban crises it appeared that the world was on the brink of World War III, but the deterrent effect of the atomic bomb averted what otherwise might have been a nuclear disaster for much of civilized society. Thus, by the close of 1965 the world had been spared from conflict involving the major powers for virtually as long as the period of peace that separated World Wars I and II. The paradox of the nuclear age is that never have men possessed so much power yet never has that power been less useful. During much of the period of the American monopoly the atomic bomb was in short supply. As a consequence, United States superiority in the nuclear field tended to be offset by Soviet superiority in conventional arms and by the Russian Army's acknowledged ability to overrun Western Europe. Still chastened by the twin horrors of Hiroshima and Nagasaki, American political and military leaders were loath to contemplate seriously an atomic attack on the Soviet Union to preserve the nation's nuclear monopoly.

In a very few years following 1950, the Soviet Union achieved sufficient nuclear capability of its own to usher in the age of mutual deterrence. Nuclear weapons became less and less effective as instruments of diplomacy and the emphasis of defense planning shifted steadily away from planned uses of nuclear weapons in war to the deterrence of war by posing a credible threat of unacceptable retaliation. During the 1950s and the first half of the 1960s military experts sought to devise credible strategies for the exploitation of nuclear weapons to counter enemy aggression at any point in the spectrum of conflict. History offers a clear record of the failure of this endeaver at the lower end of the conflict spectrum. Mutual understanding by the Soviet Union and the United States of the sheer magnitude of destruction which a general nuclear war would inflict encouraged caution by both powers in approaching a head-on collision of vital national interests. Slowly the United States—and perhaps the Soviet Union—began to realize that even a substantial superiority in nuclear weapons and delivery vehicles could not be effectively translated into political control or diplomatic leverage.

Unceasing competition during the entire period between the United States and the Soviet Union in advanced nuclear weapons technology raised the specter of a surprise technological breakthrough by one nation or the other which could bestow a significant measure of military superiority on the successful nation. However, it appeared equally probable that new nuclear weapons achievements by one major power might be sufficiently offset by compensating new weapons or improvements in existing weapons by the other to a degree where neither side would gain a significant military advantage capable of being exploited for political and military purposes. By late 1965, there appeared to be a growing perception among Communist, nonaligned, and free-world nations that greater risks to world peace would almost certainly arise in the future unless some mutually satisfactory basis could be found from which to lower existing levels of tension and hostility, check further cycles in strategic arms competition, and devise ways of forestalling future major power confrontations out of which general nuclear war could result from accident, miscalculation or an irrational act.

Nuclear deterrence by the mid-1950s was no longer a one-way street occupied solely by the United States. The progressive buildup of Soviet strategic nuclear stockpiles and long-range delivery systems ushered in an era characterized by Winston Churchill as the "balance of terror." As a consequence, the world witnessed after the mid-1950s a major shift in Communist tactics to that of supporting conflict below a threshold where the use of nuclear weapons seemed improbable. Under the guise of supporting "wars of national liberation" the Communist leadership in Moscow and Peking pressed initiatives designed to shift the cold war battleground principally to nations in the underdeveloped regions of the world, where the risks of possible nuclear war appeared to be low and instability and frustration with the existing status quo was high. The likelihood of nuclear war between the two major powers appeared to many observers to be inevitable only in the event that conflict broke out over Berlin or in Central Europe. On the other hand, conflict in such areas as the Middle East and Southeast Asia, which often involved training specialists and technicians, weapons, and logistics support provided by the United States and the Soviet Union, seemed to be clearly perceived by both major powers as peripheral to their vital security interests. Consequently, the probability of such conflicts escalating to the level of serious major power confrontation, at which level nuclear war might be perceived as an inevitable next option, appeared quite remote as late as the mid-1960s.

Having the advantage of hindsight, it now appears quite certain that the United States during most of the period between 1945 and 1965 enjoyed a superior, and often decisive, strategic nuclear power advantage over the Soviet Union. The American Strategic Air Command, a rigorously trained and technically competent force, could in all likelihood have launched a decisive nuclear attack on the Soviet Union at almost any time during the two decades with a high probability of totally destroying Soviet resistance, while at the same time, successfully limiting damage to this country to reasonably low levels. Simultaneously, Soviet capacity to do grave damage to Western Europe grew progressively during the 1950s and early 1960s and even a near-perfect surprise attack by the United States on the Soviet Union would not likely have saved Western Europe from severe damage.

During most of this period Soviet long-range nuclear striking forces were relatively small (in both bombers or missiles), they were generally not protected by techniques of hardening and dispersal, and for the most part lacked adequate warning of a possible preemptive nuclear attack by forces of the United States and its allies. Thus, at no time during this twenty-year period did the Soviets appear seriously to regard as a rational and feasible policy a surprise or preemptive nuclear attack on the United States or its allies, despite frequent Soviet nuclear threats after the mid-1950s and repeated claims by Premier Khrushchev, particularly after Sputnik, that the Soviet Union enjoyed strategic superiority over the United States. Soviet leaders seem clearly to have perceived their strategic inferiority during the period from 1945 to 1965, but they appear also to have believed in their ability to use successfully threats and bluffs against the United States so long as such gambits were kept below some intuitive threshold, above which they believed the United States would probably feel compelled to respond with force, and perhaps nuclear force.

To a considerable extent moral and political constraints on American political and military leadership made impossible serious consideration of policies based on the threat to use nuclear weapons to contain Soviet aggression and subversion or to compel its retreat from existing positions. Of parallel importance was the fact that major gaps in this nation's information about the nature and rate of buildup in Soviet strategic power after the Korean War, a Soviet policy of tight secrecy, and its skillful use on occasions of military bluff combined to prevent American political and military leaders from attaining sufficient confidence in this nation's substantial strategic nuclear superiority to permit using it effectively on the Soviet leadership to compel them to use tactics and pursue policies acceptable to this nation and its allies.

In many respects, therefore, the twenty-year period following the end of World War II can best be characterized as the search by the United States and its allies for an adequate strategy of deterrence. Immediately following the war, the United States possessed a small stockpile of atomic bombs of relatively low yield. The idea of basing the future of American national security on a strategy of deterrence was rejected as inadequate by many professional military leaders on grounds that atomic bombs alone could not defeat the vastly superior Soviet ground forces. Only the sustained presence of massive American ground forces in Europe, they thought, would be an adequate guarantee of final victory in a major war with the Soviet Union. Consequently, the idea of continuing to base United States national security policy on a strategy of mobilization, as had been the case during World Wars I and II, received strong support from the Army and Navy well into the 1950s. Nevertheless, during approximately the first five years after the war, the American atomic bomb monopoly appeared clearly to have operated as the chief deterrent to Soviet aggression. Interservice rivalry blocked efforts to sanctify nuclear deterrence as official United States policy, and as one observer pointed out, "Deterrence was easy and uncontroversial, an accident of history, not a creature of policy."[1]

When the decision was made in 1950 by President Truman to proceed with the development of a hydrogen bomb, and there appeared to be high promise of success within a year or two, considerable discussion began within the government on the merits of embracing a strategy of nuclear deterrence as the basic plank of national security policy. The explosion by the Soviet Union of an atomic bomb in August 1949 presaged the end of an effective United States nuclear monopoly within a few years and strongly suggested that the Soviet Union in due course would also detonate a hydrogen bomb of its own. Once the Soviets were able to demonstrate that nuclear weapons could be successfully delivered against targets in the United States, any strategy this country might adopt which stressed the fighting of a nuclear war rather than the deterrence of such a war was unlikely to be credible to a nuclear opponent and very likely to be unacceptable to the American people.

Under the Democratic administration during the early 1950s a new and comprehensive general war strategy was developed jointly by the Department of State and the Pentagon which emphasized greater balance between nuclear and conventional forces. Strategic nuclear weapons systems would be depended upon primarily for deterrence of an enemy nuclear attack and conventional weapons would be used in contingencies where vital national security was not involved and where, therefore, conflict involving American forces was likely to ensue without a serious threat of escalation to nuclear war. The Korean War intervened to prevent the formal adoption of the new strategy by the Truman administration, and by the time the war ended a new administration was in power.

There followed an immediate reassessment by the Eisenhower administration of America's military posture for the prevention of general nuclear war, during which special emphasis was placed on the requirement for maintaining a healthy economy as a basic premise for defense planning. A decisive shift was made to dependence by this nation on expanded strategic nuclear retaliatory forces to deter war by the Soviet Union on Europe and the United States. At the same time, the administration committed itself to maintaining a decisive superiority in nuclear weapons and delivery systems over the Soviet Union, so that in the event deterrence failed and nuclear war resulted, the United States would be able to achieve a clear-cut military victory.

This strategic corollary to the strategy of deterrence remained Eisenhower policy until 1956 when a shift was made to a doctrine of nuclear sufficiency. From that time until the end of the Eisenhower term of office, the administration argued that the possession of superiority in nuclear weapons and strategic delivery systems could no longer prevent a catastrophe to this nation in the event of a nuclear war. The absolute growth of this nation's strategic nuclear attack capabilities and those of the Soviet Union was rapidly reaching the point where no matter which nation struck first the other would be able to retaliate with devastating power, thus relegating the notion of winning a nuclear war to the realm of fiction.

By the late 1950s, therefore, a decisive shift had been made in this nation's general nuclear war strategy to one primarily of deterrence, dependent on substantial nuclear forces-in-being, constantly on the alert and able to react with minimum warning, hardened and dispersed, and concealed in the vast expanse of five oceans. Although ominous talk of a serious American "missile gap" developed late in the 1950s (which appeared to pose a serious Soviet threat to this nation's second-strike capabilities), a general nuclear war strategy based on deterrence and retaliation remained as the official United States policy through 1965.

Secondary in importance only to United States efforts to establish a condition of stable nuclear deterrence during the twenty years following World War II, was the phenomenon of unparalleled and revolutionary technological progress, particularly in nuclear weapons and even more lethal means of their delivery. In large measure the successful aggregation of scientific talent in this country during the 1930s and 1940s coupled with the fact that the United States escaped direct damage to itself during World War II, enabled this country to build a successful atomic weapon before such a feat could be achieved by Nazi Germany or the Soviet Union. During the five-year period following the defeat of Japan, steady improvements were made in the explosive power of the atomic bomb, raising its destructive capacity from an initial level of 15 to 20 kilotons to several hundreds of kilotons. Simultaneously, the United States vastly expanded its long-range strategic air forces, trained thousands of technicians to fly and maintain them, acquired overseas bases from which to launch two-way attacks on targets in the Soviet Union, and made credible to the Soviet leaders a firm resolve to use these forces if a ground attack were launched against the recuperating nations of Western Europe. As the destructive force of the atomic bomb increased during the period from 1945 to 1950, and with it the size of the United States nuclear stockpile, deterrence resting primarily on America's monopoly of the bomb became progressively more and more credible to friends and foes alike.

Still enjoying an effective nuclear monopoly early in 1950, but conscious of important Soviet progress toward attaining its own atomic stockpile and delivery systems capable of reaching American strategic bases in Western Europe, President Harry Truman decided in January to press forward with the development of the hydrogen bomb. It was widely assumed that the Soviets were also diligently working on a thermonuclear bomb and that the United States could ill afford to risk being second in achieving such a success. Thus, within less than five years the die was cast to attempt a second exponential jump in mass destructive power, one capable of dwarfing the atomic bomb which had already achieved a revolutionary expansion in man's capacity to obliterate himself. The successful explosion of a hydrogen weapon by the United States late in 1952 removed any lingering doubts about its decisiveness in a war with an enemy like the Soviet Union which was conceded to possess superior land armies. The hydrogen bomb at long last had made it possible for one nation to destroy virtually the entire society of an adversary. The effective employment of mass land armies in future major wars involving the new "total" weapons suddenly appeared wholly improbable.

The third exponential jump in this nation's capacity to produce massive destruction was achieved beginning in the mid-1950s with the successful development, testing, and deployment of a liquid-fueled intercontinental ballistic missile. The achievement of the ICBM brought under effective nuclear threat virtually any priority target on the planet. The speed in flight of the new generation of nuclear-tipped missiles reduced to minutes the time from launch to impact on a target as distant as 5,000 to 6,000 miles. Such missiles were susceptible to dispersion and hardening which complicated an aggressor's problem in planning an attack. Overnight long-range strategic bomber forces appeared to become highly vulnerable to missile attack. Stringent new requirements arose for constant bomber alert, dispersion to a larger number of bases, long-range warning of a missile attack to guarantee minimum bomber reaction time, and invulnerable command and control systems which would enable the President of the United States and his top military commanders to maintain contact with the far-flung strategic forces under all imaginable conditions of attack.

In much less than a decade the United States perfected a solid-fuel missile capable of being deployed cheaply in hardened underground silos or aboard missile-carrying submarines, which depended for their invulnerability on the vast expanses of five oceans. The new generations of missiles achieved incredible accuracies as their guidance systems improved, so that even hardened targets became vulnerable to attack. At the same time, the requirement for large warheads was reduced as accuracies improved, thus reducing costs, permitting the deployment of larger numbers of smaller missiles, and enabling an attacker to restrict damage more effectively to an enemy's military targets. The advent of the ICBM made obsolete a great deal of the technology developed for the age of the long-range strategic bomber, and, as a consequence, set in motion an intensive as well as expensive arms race between the United States and the Soviet Union which had not ended by the end of 1965.

One of the striking phenomena of the two decades, 1945–1965, was the seeming ability of the Soviet Union either to achieve advances in weapons and delivery systems technology very soon after the United States had achieved them, thus tending to vitiate much of the military advantage conferred by the new weapons, or to develop and deploy significant new weapons systems ahead of this nation. The explosion by the Soviet Union of an atomic bomb in 1949 came much earlier than was predicted by most American experts, and the successful detonation of a hydrogen weapon so closely on the heels of the American achievement seemed even more ominous to American officials responsible for the nation's security. At times it appeared that America's widely acclaimed superiority in military science and technology might be exposed as a myth.

In 1955 the Soviets suddenly surprised the world and United States military leaders with the appearance of a new generation of long-range strategic bombers. Military and civilian officials alike argued that the Soviet Union was already out-producing the United States in modern strategic bombers and that this nation was likely to lose any claim to military superiority by the late 1950s unless dramatic increases were made in programmed strategic bomber forces. A major investigation of the "bomber gap" was made by a Senate investigating subcommittee, and a majority report was issued sustaining the notion that United States strategic superiority was in serious jeopardy. Even before the "bomber gap" furor could properly be disposed of, new reports emanated from the Soviet Union of tests of medium-range ballistic missiles, apparently designed to cover targets in Western Europe and especially American Strategic Air Command forward bases. In August of 1957, Nikita Khrushchev announced the Soviet achievement of an ICBM, which precipitated the "missile gap" controversy that lasted until late 1961.

Superficially, it was understandable why the United States was unable to sustain confidence in its scientific and technological supremacy during the greater part of the two decades. It was one thing, however, to concede that American intelligence capabilities during the period from 1945 to 1961 were simply inadequate to determine with high confidence whether the Soviet Union intended or had the capability to stockpile large numbers of nuclear weapons and deploy sufficient strategic nuclear delivery systems in a bold effort to wrest effective superiority from the United States and its allies. The United States was left with little choice but to deploy adequate numbers of nuclear-capable weapon systems in order to deny to the Soviet Union any possibility of attaining a first-strike superiority capable of threatening the nation's security. It was quite another thing, however, for the United States to continue basing strategic force requirements on outdated estimates of the Soviet threat, especially when steadily improving intelligence capabilities no longer made such dependence necessary. Yet, this is precisely what the United States did from late 1961 through 1965. Paradoxically, during the 1950s when intelligence uncertainties justified overcompensation in the deployment of American strategic nuclear delivery systems, this nation opted for a defense policy, in the face of a presumed Soviet bid for supremacy, of nuclear sufficiency. After 1961, however, when the United States was confident of its knowledge that the Soviet bid for strategic nuclear superiority was pure myth, the United States pressed hard for strategic nuclear superiority and for a very brief period actually achieved it.

Without a single major exception, the Soviet Union failed to match the progress of United States strategic air and missile capabilities at any time during the twenty-year period following World War II. Either for reasons of scientific or technical shortfalls, production difficulties, management problems, or inept political leadership, the Soviets failed to develop, produce, and deploy sufficient numbers of strategic long-range bombers or ICBMs to pose an effective challenge to this nation's strategic nuclear superiority. In retrospect a reasonable rule of thumb can be applied that the Soviet Union lagged approximately five years behind the United States in the deployment of sizeable numbers of operational strategic weapons systems such as were deployed in this nation's strategic forces. While the Soviet Union did achieve a massive strategic attack capability against Western Europe, similar in size to this nation's capability to threaten targets in the Soviet Union, and a modest capability to threaten targets in the United States, during the entire twenty years, Soviet capabilities in science, technology, nuclear weapons, delivery systems, and other related strategic hardware lagged substantially behind those of the United States. Because the Soviet Union was never able to challenge the supremacy of the United States in the important categories of strategic power, it appears new dimensions were added to an already serious Soviet inferiority complex. Soviet efforts to achieve some kind of effective nuclear parity with the United States were unsuccessful, and they scarcely even attained adequate confidence that they possessed a secure second-strike capability which could preclude a rational decision by the United States to launch a first strike or preemptive attack.

The Growth of United States Strategic Nuclear Power

The growth of American strategic nuclear power during the two decades following World War II seems to fall logically into four major chronological periods, which are worthy of some comment because of their implications. Obviously any attempt to divide history into precise periods is open to the charge of oversimplification. Nevertheless, the four periods considered here are useful in that they show certain specific trends and meanings of events, which add to rather than detract from an understanding of the twenty-year period.

1945–1953

The first period, from 1945 to 1953, was one of American nuclear supremacy or unilateral nuclear deterrence. Although it was not until late 1948 that the United States deployed its atomic-capable strategic bombers overseas in Great Britain, it seems plausible in retrospect that, given the staggering amount of damage inflicted by the war on the Soviet Union and the time required to make even a partial recovery, the rather modest atomic monopoly and capacity to deliver the weapons possessed by the United States in the immediate postwar period effectively deterred the large Soviet land armies which were maintained after hostilities ceased. Fears by the United States and its debilitated European allies of a Soviet attack aimed at taking over the strategic terrain and resources of Western Europe appear unfounded today.

There is little doubt, however, that the Soviets were determined at all costs to stake out a sphere of influence in Eastern Europe as a defensive bastion against possible future attacks on the Soviet Union. The size of the sphere of influence demanded by Stalin seemed to have been somewhat flexible in the period just before the European phase of the war ended and during the early months of 1945. But growing differences between Roosevelt and his advisors and Stalin over the postwar organization of peace in Eastern Europe hastened the coming of the Cold War with its ideological overtones. The crash buildup of American strategic power beginning in 1946 and the firm pledge by the United States of a massive infusion of economic assistance to accelerate the pace of European recovery acted as effective deterrents to efforts by the Soviet Union to abet the paralysis and prostration of European governments as a prelude to internal Communist takeover. Had the Communists succeeded in seizing political power in France, Italy, and West Germany during the immediate postwar period it is quite probable that Soviet objectives would have been attained in Western Europe without recourse to armies and the risk of American nuclear retaliation.

During the period from 1945 to 1953 the United States sought to agree on a general war strategy which reflected the realities of the nuclear age while at the same time holding onto concepts, e.g., mobilization, which had served the nation successfully during two world wars. The fact was that of the strategic options considered—nuclear containment and preventive war—this nation was unwilling to fund either of them adequately. American military planning tended to be less concerned with maintaining adequate forces-in-being with which to deter war than with the preparation of armed forces to win a major war should one occur. When the Korean War broke out in 1950, the United States was inadequately prepared to fight a conventional war on a distant front and was reluctant to bring its limited nuclear power to bear in the Far East lest the Soviet Union seize the opportunity to attack Western Europe. For a time during late 1950 and the early part of 1951, American military leaders feared the likelihood and consequences of a two-front war in the Far East and Western Europe, and the nation's forces-in-being seemed anything but adequate to meet such a challenge. As it happened, the Soviet Union, even though it exploded an atomic bomb in late 1949, failed to make sufficient progress by the time of the Korean War toward attaining a modest stockpile of nuclear weapons and delivery systems to risk challenging American power in Europe or elsewhere. Thus, as late as 1953, granting even that the Soviet Union exploded a hydrogen device in August 1953, the United States still possessed an effective nuclear monopoly of constantly growing magnitude and power, which the Soviets with their extremely limited capabilities dared not challenge.

1954–1957

The second major period, from 1954 to 1957, opened with a crest in America's strategic nuclear power advantage—represented by the large Strategic Air Command bomber force—over the Soviet Union and ended with America stunned by Soviet achievements in the long-range missile field, the portent of which was that strategic nuclear superiority appeared to be moving rapidly to the side of the Soviet Union. By 1954, the Strategic Air Command was operating from base complexes in Great Britain, North Africa, and the Far East. Rapid progress was being made on bases in Spain looking toward an early operational date. During the years prior to mid-1955, United States strategic forces consisted of B-50, B-36, and B-47 bombers; the latter were new medium four-jet aircraft capable of multiple air-to-air refuelings, enabling them to strike targets deep in the heart of the Soviet Union. The proficiency of this nation's air-to-air refueling capacity was exceptionally high and was unmatched by the Soviet Union. The strategic nuclear threat from the Soviet Union in 1954 was confined almost completely to Western Europe, even though it was conceivable that one-way missions by Soviet aircraft against targets in the United States may have succeeded in doing some haphazard damage. United States strategic bombing forces were no longer so vulnerable to Soviet attacks on overseas bases, because the Strategic Air Command was moving rapidly to balance its capabilities between the North American continent and overseas bases.

Although the United States announced a new strategy of "massive retaliation" when the nation's strategic nuclear power was at a postwar peak, the news came as a considerable shock to many free world allies, the world press, and nongovernmental defense intellectuals. Why did this country elect to increase its dependence on the threat to use nuclear weapons precisely at the time that a real long-range Soviet air power threat was beginning to emerge? Viewed in today's perspective, the most serious consequence of the Dulles manifesto of massive retaliation probably was the major deemphasis on adequate conventional ground forces to deal with conflict situations which would likely emerge once mutual nuclear deterrence became a recognized fact of international life. The manner in which Dulles couched his public statement on massive retaliation strongly suggests that the administration had failed to examine carefully the many implications of the new doctrine before announcing it to the world, and the quick retreat by Dulles and the Pentagon from extreme implications of the doctrine—i.e., that nuclear weapons were now considered to be "conventional" weapons in the United States arsenal and as such might be used appropriately in conflicts involving the grey areas of the world—reinforces this interpretation.

Hindsight, however, seems to demonstrate rather clearly that a major strategic advantage, such as that possessed by the United States in 1954 over the Soviet Union, does make credible a strategy of strategic nuclear deterrence in most situations appearing to involve major or vital security interests of the two major powers. Even though it possessed some long-range nuclear forces, the Soviet Union was in no position to challenge the credibility of the Dulles massive retaliation doctrine. The Soviet Union in all likelihood perceived the possibility that the United States under favorable conditions of attack could limit damage to itself to tolerable proportions, while this nation's superior strategic forces could destroy the Soviet society with impunity. Attacks on Dulles for the timing and implications of his strategic pronouncement tended to be highly overdrawn, even though it must be conceded to his critics that the information gap existing during the period 1954–1957 about Soviet nuclear capabilities was far more serious than in later periods, which helps explain why the world reacted with alarm and anger.

As periodically refined, the Dulles massive retaliation doctrine was basically no more than the continuation in a bilateral nuclear age of the strategy of deterrence that the Truman administration had embraced during the period of American nuclear monopoly.

Overall it worked very successfully because even though a number of local conflict situations arose, they were limited to conventional weapons, and the two major nuclear powers exercised careful discretion lest their involvement in such conflict escalate to all-out nuclear war. Thus, the strategy of deterrence worked remarkably well during the two decades following World War II; it helped to stabilize and moderate a number of potentially dangerous situations involving the United States and the Soviet Union and seems to have checked significantly Soviet aspirations to exploit situations by a resort to force.

The myth of the bomber gap lasting from mid-1955 to October of 1957, after which this issue was lost in the noise of the Soviet Sputnik, was the product primarily of existing intelligence uncertainties, a rather good job of Soviet spoofing in an effort to change the world image of its strategic nuclear inferiority and consistently bad estimating by the Air Force of Soviet bomber production and their relative capabilities as compared to America's B-52 and B-47 bombers. All in all the justification of force levels by the services during the 1950s tended to be based on very conservative estimates of the current and future Soviet military threat, and each service fought hard to retain a fixed relative percentage of the annual military budget. The fly-by of new long-range Soviet bombers in May 1955 quickly convinced many American military leaders that the Soviets were producing aircraft of equivalent performance and quality to this nation's B-52 bombers (the first of which was delivered to a Strategic Air Command unit in June 1955), that the production rate of Soviet strategic bombers was in excess of American B-52 production, and that the Soviets would press on to achieve bomber superiority by the late 1950s.

Such feelings were preeminently expressed in the Symington Air Power Senate hearings during 1956, particularly by Air Force generals Twining and LeMay, who seemed determined to prove that the Soviets were ten feet tall. By and large, the Eisenhower civilian defense officials led by Donald Quarles and Secretary Wilson took a much more moderate view of Soviet achievement and refused to be steamrollered by the Symington hearings into believing that United States defense efforts in the strategic field were too niggardly, and as a consequence this nation risked conceding its strategic nuclear superiority to the Soviet Union. The Soviet long-range strategic bomber challenge—represented by the Bear and Bison bombers—never materialized, partly one suspects because of a decision to "leap-frog" the bomber directly to medium- and long-range missiles. Soviet technology and production capacity was apparently incapable of achieving both simultaneously, and Soviet leaders seem to have believed that success in the missile field would make obsolete virtually overnight the entire United States strategic bomber force and enable the Soviet Union to achieve a decisive superiority in strategic nuclear power.

Compared to the Soviet Union the United States was late in putting a high national priority on missile development. Not until the emergence of the Killian Committee report in 1955, which conjectured that the Soviet Union might possess a decisive lead in strategic missiles by 1960, did this nation enter upon a crash missile development program. Thus, when the nation learned of the successful strategic missile test by the Soviet Union in August 1957, which was followed even more dramatically by Sputnik in October of that year, the shock and portentous meaning of the Soviet achievement hit with full force. It was not long before newspaper columnists like Joseph and Stewart Alsop and Hanson Baldwin were echoing the fears of the professional military—particularly Air Force generals—that a serious missile gap was inevitable and could be so serious as to put this nation's security in grave jeopardy.

1958–1962

The third major period, lasting from 1958 through 1962, was one during which Americans were beguiled by the specter of a seemingly inevitable missile gap. Throughout this period the United States maintained its preponderant lead in strategic bomber capabilities. Beginning in about 1959, however, defense analysts at RAND Corporation and within the Pentagon warned of the growing vulnerability of the Strategic Air Command to Soviet missile attack, especially during the period from 1960 on. General Thomas Power, Commander of the Strategic Air Command, speaking in New York early in 1960, told a public audience that because of the concentration of United States strategic power on so few air bases, the Soviet

Union might be capable of wiping out virtually all this nation's retaliatory power with as few as 300 long-range missiles. Predictions appeared in public print that the Soviets were capable of producing between 800 and 1,500 strategic missiles by about 1963 or 1964, and it was widely assumed that they would make a concerted effort to do so.

In response to what appeared to most defense experts and government officials to be the most dire threat to the security of the United States in its entire history, crash efforts were made to disperse Strategic Air Command units to a greater number of bases, a high percentage of strategic bomber aircraft was placed on constant ground alert, some aircraft were put on airborne alert, and backup supplies were stocked for a larger effort if needed, practically unlimited funds were poured into a missile warning system, and new command and control arrangements were instituted for the management of American strategic forces in nuclear war. The impression given the American public was that the United States would have to accept at least a temporary missile gap no matter how hard it strained to overcome the Soviet strategic missile lead. At issue was only the magnitude of this lead and its probable consequences for United States security should the Soviets attempt to exploit it.

On the missile gap issue, just as earlier during the bomber gap furor, significantly different estimates were made by civilian and military officials of the Eisenhower administration about the progress and implications of Soviet missile achievement. Generally, expert military opinion supported the more pessimistic forecasts of likely Soviet intentions should that nation achieve the margin of superiority being predicted. Once again many professional military leaders agreed with the more conservative estimates of Soviet intentions and capabilities; they argued that the United States must maintain strategic superiority over the Soviet Union at all costs, and they were distrustful of intelligence interpretations that tended to downgrade the probability of Soviet large-scale missile achievements in a period of just a few years.

Civilian defense officials in the Eisenhower administrations, such as Secretaries of Defense Neil McElroy and Thomas Gates, and the President himself, were consistently more optimistic about America's ability to stay abreast or ahead of the Soviet Union in overall strategic nuclear forces and pointed out that even though a small missile gap was conceivable, no deterrent gap would likely result that could offer the Soviets an inducement to launch a first strike against the United States. These leaders also pointed to the massive superiority of American bomber forces and contended that the measures taken to protect them against a surprise missile attack were adequate by themselves to deny the Soviet Union any rational basis for a first strike.

Toward the end of 1959, United States confidence in the estimates of Soviet bomber and missile capabilities had apparently improved, thanks to the information provided by the U-2 flights over Soviet soil, so that the administration undertook to shift the basis for its estimates of Soviet strategic force levels from a capabilities basis—the assumed capacity of the Soviets to produce and deploy weapon systems—to an intentions basis—the decision by the Soviet leadership to undertake a particular production and deployment of weapon systems. By doing so, administration leaders projected a much more optimistic picture of American military strength in the face of assumed Soviet progress than either congressional or military leaders, and, as a consequence, laid the basis for the emergence of a major political battleground during the presidential campaign of 1960.

Senator John F. Kennedy seized on the missile gap issue and made it a major plank in his campaign strategy. The evidence is inadequate to judge whether Kennedy sensed the falseness of the missile gap and decided to exploit the issue because the Eisenhower administration chose to deny him vital information, or whether he really believed that such a gap existed. Clearly, Kennedy was irritated because the administration deliberately chose to deny him access to sensitive information held by the Strategic Air Command at Omaha, Nebraska, and this author inclines toward the view that Kennedy was probably skeptical about the existence of a missile gap, but nevertheless seized upon it as a gift given him by the political opposition.

The Kennedy administration took office pledged to eliminate the presumed missile gap and to restore American strategic nuclear superiority. Despite an admission by Secretary McNamara in February 1961 that no missile gap existed, the administration nevertheless pressed forward with substantial increases in the strategic arsenal. Indications reaching the Kennedy leadership that the NATO allies seriously believed that the balance of strategic power was shifting in favor of the Soviet Union plus Premier Khrushchev's constant pressure on the administration to settle the Berlin issue account in large measure for the decision in October 1961 to destroy the myth of the missile gap in blunt and undeniable terms. For the next several years, the administration periodically released the score board of United States and Soviet comparative strategic nuclear strengths, and as of the end of 1965, the Soviet Union consistently was declared both numerically and qualitatively vastly inferior to this nation.

One of the major issues injected into the 1960 presidential campaign by John Kennedy was the pledge, if elected, to undertake a series of negotiations with the Soviet Union on arms control measures in an effort to reduce if not eliminate the possibility of a major nuclear war. Kennedy in fact promised to establish an agency of government to deal with arms control problems on a full-time basis. Within less than one year after his election, Kennedy kept his promise, and on September 26, 1961, the United States Arms Control and Disarmament Agency came into existence and was located in the Department of State. Given Kennedy's strong support for arms control objectives, it is enlightening to examine the impact of his and Secretary McNamara's major defense decisions on efforts to negotiate agreement on general and complete disarmament as well as more limited arms control measures with the Soviets during the period 1962 to 1965.

Recalling that by October 1961, the administration appeared to be confident of its knowledge about Soviet ICBM and bomber deployment and publicly exposed the measure of Soviet strategic nuclear inferiority before the world, it would have seemed consistent for a President and his Secretary of Defense who were publicly dedicated to arms control to seek to restrain increases in the nation's strategic nuclear delivery forces in some proportion to changed estimates of that threat. As it happened, however, major increases in United States strategic offensive forces were supported by the administration without any significant efforts at restraint. In subsequent efforts by American negotiators to find some basis for agreement on a treaty for general and complete disarmament and later for partial measures limiting strategic nuclear forces, the Soviets were confronted with a steadily increasing margin of United States strategic nuclear superiority, while at the same time they were being asked in effect to accept constraints on their nuclear forces which would have frozen them into perpetual inferiority. In retrospect there is little reason to have expected that the Soviets would accept inferiority as the basis for negotiation, particularly when this nation clearly would never have negotiated seriously on such a basis.

Apart, therefore, from the achievement of the partial test ban in 1963, all other efforts through 1965 to agree with the Soviets on major arms control arrangements, such as freezing strategic delivery forces at some agreed level and progressively reducing them, failed to make any progress whatever. This was due in large measure to the continually widening margin of strategic superiority being achieved by the United States during this period, but also to the Kennedy administration's insistence on telling the world in dramatic and detailed terms just how inferior the Soviet Union actually was. On political and psychological grounds alone, the Soviet Union could hardly have entered into serious arms control negotiations with the Western powers because of probable adverse reactions among the nations of the Soviet bloc and harmful consequences for the Soviet claim to leadership of the Communist world. When the time comes that the United States and the Soviet Union do agree on some basis for freezing and reducing existing levels of strategic nuclear forces, it is inevitable that some kind of rough balance will have been reached between the two major powers in numbers and capabilities of delivery systems. A balance will exist by virtue of each power's having different but approximately equal delivery capabilities, or some kind of roughly equal damage parity will come to be understood and accepted by both sides. That likelihood, however, seemed remote by the end of 1965.

All efforts by the United States to dramatize the extent of Soviet strategic nuclear inferiority before the world during the early months of 1962 failed to curtail Khrushchev's proclivities for the sudden and dramatic coup designed to capture the world's attention, inflate the Soviet political and military image abroad, and challenge the mettle of this nation's leadership and the courage of its people.

The Cuban missile crisis in October 1962 must be viewed as a major aberration from past patterns of behavior by Soviet leaders who ordinarily were not disposed to major risk taking. In fact, the Cuban missile crisis was a Khrushchevian anomaly and cannot be explained in any other sensible way.

In this crisis, Khrushchev was unquestionably aware of the military inferiority from which he was hedging, both nuclear and conventional. He appeared to be willing to bring the world to the brink of nuclear war in order to partially restore the badly marred image of Soviet political and military superiority which the United States was working so assiduously to destroy. Even if Khrushchev's apparent assessment of American courage had proved correct, and American leadership had equivocated and temporized and not met Khrushchev's challenge head-on, Soviet emplacement of some forty-two missiles in Cuba would not have altered significantly the existing strategic balance which already enormously favored this nation. Soviet military leaders, who apparently opposed the Cuban missile adventure, must have told Khrushchev that the moment the United States knew of the existence of Soviet missiles in Cuba this nation would act immediately on strategic warning, posture its strategic forces against possible attack, and in effect eliminate any military value of the missiles. To attack or even threaten to attack American cities in the face of certain devastation to the entire Soviet Union in return cannot be considered a rational Soviet option. The graceful way in which the United States permitted the Soviet Union to accept defeat in Cuba helped in some measure to mask the full measure of existing Soviet inferiority in late 1962.

1963–1965

The fourth and final major period from 1963 to the end of 1965 was one in which the United States continued to increase its numerical superiority and total nuclear damage ratio over the Soviet Union. However, it was also a period during which the Soviet Union began to make modest strides toward achieving a hardened, dispersed, and concealed strategic missile force which, in due time, would afford it a secure second-strike deterrent capability. Throughout this period, however, Soviet strategic missile and bomber forces remained extremely vulnerable to an American preemptive missile attack, and the only truly credible strategic threat the Soviets possessed was against Western Europe. In the absence of an equally credible strategic threat to the United States, it was difficult to imagine how the Soviet Union could effectively use its IRBM and MRBM superiority to any great political or military advantage, especially as long as the United States remained firm in its security guarantees to the NATO nations.

The Cuban missile crisis is frequently regarded as an important watershed in the postwar period; it tended to divide a period during which cold war tensions, hostility, and conflict were predominant from a succeeding period in which an atmosphere of détente began to emerge and out of which came the arms control agreements with the Soviet Union during 1963 and 1964. Viewed in the context of its strategic implications, the Soviet Union following the Cuban debacle appears to have seized on worldwide sentiment for peace and relaxation of tension to shift attention away from the inescapable fact of its military weakness. The Soviet Union desperately needed time and a period of relative calm during which it hoped to deemphasize the arms race with the United States, a production race it could not hope to win, and to engage latent hopes in this country of reaching an agreement whose effect would be to moderate the cold war and reduce the risk of possible nuclear war. Soviet willingness to enter into a limited test ban treaty in 1963 can be explained in part by Soviet fear that continued atmospheric nuclear testing by the United States might widen the margin of America's superiority even more. By pursuing more moderate policies, the Soviets also appear to have hoped to relax the solidarity of the NATO alliance and to reduce effective American power on the continent.

During the period 1963 to 1965 the Soviets began to deploy more modern strategic missiles and to harden their silos in a move to protect themselves against possible attack by United States missile forces. There appears to be some valid basis for believing that Soviet leaders after 1962 were seriously worried that the professional military in this country might persuade civilian leaders to risk a preemptive nuclear attack on the Soviet Union in an atmosphere of continuing tension, while Soviet forces were relatively small and unprotected and the probability of damage to the United States of any consequence seemed low. Soviet strategic missile forces remained extremely vulnerable to a preemptive missile strike, especially because no adequate missile early warning system was operational in the Soviet Union. Simultaneously, the expanded land- and sea-based missile program set in motion by the Kennedy administration was moving well along toward completion. Because it remained the policy of the Kennedy administration to constantly remind the Soviet Union and the rest of the world of the relative numerical and qualitative superiority of United States strategic nuclear forces, the Soviet leadership was hard put to find a way to recapture the political and military image of greatness and strength that the Soviet Union had enjoyed during the latter 1950s.

Early in 1964, the United States proposed at the Eighteen-Nation Disarmament Conference in Geneva that the two major nuclear powers agree on a limited measure of disarmament which would freeze the numbers and characteristics of strategic nuclear offensive and defensive delivery systems at some agreed level. If such an agreement could be reached, the United States believed, further expansion of the deadly and costly arms race might be avoided, and paths would be open to reductions in all types of forces from present levels. The Soviet Union rejected the United States proposal in pure propaganda terms, refusing to enter into serious technical talks on any aspects of the freeze. Subsequent efforts by the United States during 1964 and 1965 to interest the Soviet Union in a strategic nuclear freeze met the same fate as the earlier proposal. Clearly the United States freeze idea would have fixed the Soviet Union in a state of perpetual strategic nuclear inferiority, a condition they steadfastly refused to accept. Future hopes for agreement on strategic nuclear offensive and defensive arms limitations seemed to rest on this nation's willingness to permit the Soviet Union to achieve at least some approximate balance of strategic nuclear forces with those of the United States. At the end of 1965, this prospect appeared to be remote, nor was it clear whether the Johnson administration was prepared to accord a high priority to efforts leading to a possible halt in the inexorable strategic arms competition.

Balancing Military Requirements and Economic Growth

During the entire twenty years from 1945 to 1965, the United States sought to develop a coherent and enduring military strategy centered around the gargantuan power of atomic and thermonuclear weapons. With few exceptions during the postwar period, efforts within the government to develop a strategy adequate to meet the requirements for a possible general nuclear war were constrained by the need to balance economic solvency and domestic policies against necessary military force levels determined by periodic estimates of the Soviet threat. Twice during the twenty-year period strategic planning exercises took place within the Defense and State Departments designed to convert current and future foreign policy objectives and enemy threat assessments into a military posture adequate to preserve national security for the indefinite future without being constrained by some form of arbitrary budget ceiling.

The first exercise, begun in January 1950, at the initiative of the Department of State, and later designated NSC-68, was the first comprehensive statement of national strategy. As recommended to President Truman, it contained an analysis of the conflicting goals of the United States and the Soviet Union, the implications of the conflict between them, and an evaluation of their respective military capabilities. Geared primarily to the needs of the cold war, the new strategy carried a recommendation for a large-scale buildup in the nation's forces for both general and limited war. In estimating that by 1954, the Soviet Union would have a nuclear capability to launch a devastating attack on the United States, the authors of the document recognized with rare perception the need for vastly improved limited war capabilities—both conventional and nuclear—in anticipation of the arrival of a "balance of terror" when general nuclear war would no longer be a rational option. NSC-68 in important respects was the forerunner of the Kennedy strategy of flexible response, officially embraced by the United States in the years following 1961. The Korean War put aside a final presidential decision on NSC-68, and by the time the conflict had ceased, the newly installed Eisenhower administration was engaged in a thoroughgoing reassessment of United States military policy aimed at achieving a better balance between the requirements of a strong economy and strong military forces. During the remainder of the 1950s fixed ceilings on military budgets dictated a strategy for general nuclear war heavily dependent on nuclear weapons—at the expense of conventional forces—which stressed more and more the deterrence of nuclear war rather than capabilities for fighting and winning such a war.

The Kennedy victory in the election of 1960 signalled a shift away from overdependence on strategic nuclear weapons to a greater balance between conventional and nuclear forces. At the same time the President enjoined his Secretary of Defense to develop a force structure adequate to meet the nation's military requirements without regard to arbitrary or predetermined budget ceilings. McNamara launched immediately into a series of studies aimed at a complete reappraisal of America's defense strategy and a subsequent definition of the kinds of weapons systems that would best facilitate the objectives of an agreed national military strategy. The upshot of the studies was a decision by the Kennedy administration to recommend to Congress a major increase in both strategic nuclear forces and conventional forces costing many billions of dollars in additional expenditures over the next several years.

In lieu of conforming to arbitrary or fixed budget ceilings, McNamara applied the relatively new science of systems analysis to determine the comparative costs and effectiveness of competing weapons systems serving a common objective, thus aiming at eliminating waste and duplication and holding budgetary increases to manageable proportions. From 1961 through 1965 the Kennedy administration was successful in determining force structure requirements for strategic nuclear as well as conventional forces almost entirely on the basis of estimates of the enemy threat. These force structures were the product of rigorous requirements analysis, which cut fat but at the same time sought to protect the necessary muscle of the American military establishment. Not until the escalating costs of the Vietnam war began after 1965 to impinge seriously on the funding of high priority domestic programs did it become mandatory for the Defense Department to again pay close attention to budget ceilings in determining annual requirements for military forces.

If fixed budget ceilings tended to dictate the funding levels of strategic nuclear and conventional forces during the two decades following World War II, what can be said about the actual impact of military expenditures on the health and sustained growth of the American economy? Did the theory that military budgets posed a constant threat to economic solvency and needed to be carefully tailored to some preconceived ceiling seem to fit the economic facts of the postwar period? Both the Truman and Eisenhower administrations followed fiscal policies that placed arbitrary spending limits on military programs on an apparent premise that the stability of the American economy depended on avoiding stresses on an essentially fragile framework. It is noteworthy that during neither the Truman nor the Eisenhower administrations did military force programs have to compete with ambitious domestic programs aimed at improving education, medicine, jobs, cities or the lot of racial minorities. The civilian defense and financial advisors to both presidents consistently advocated conservative economic practices which stressed the avoidance of tax increases as well as deficit spending. There is slight evidence to indicate that budget and treasury officials helped to develop acceptable executive defense programs on the basis of a systematic theory of economics. Military budgets were primarily the product of politics and the exercise of power on the part of interest groups both within and outside the government. Thus, upper limits on the size of defense budgets were not determined so much by the limit the economy was able to sustain, but by how much the American people could be persuaded to support.

Except for the period of the Korean War, and for a brief period following the Sputnik missile crisis, military expenditures during the first fifteen years following World War II had little or no serious impact on the American standard of living or on the steady pace of economic growth. Contrary to the fears of the conservative economic and fiscal managers that overspending on military forces by the United States posed as great a threat to the nation's security as the Soviet Union, it appears in retrospect that military expenditures, which were actually quite modest during this entire period when viewed as a percentage of gross national product or in absolute dollar terms, could actually have been twice as large without jeopardizing either the healthy improvement of the American standard of living or the health and steady growth of the national economy.[2]

Military expenditures as a percentage of gross national product varied during the period from 1945 to 1960 from a high during the

Korean War of 13.5 percent to a low of 4.5 percent during the height of demobilization in 1947–1948. It is significant that during the years following the Korean armistice, military expenditures fluctuated in a narrow range between 9 percent and 10 percent of the gross national product, which reflected in part the acceptance by American military planners of the forces-in-being concept and a growing rejection of mobilization as a basis for meeting possible future military crises. Particularly after Korea, while military expenditures were not insensitive to adverse estimates of the Soviet military threat, such expenditures tended to lag significantly behind "crises" estimates by key public officials of an encroaching Soviet strategic nuclear threat to the security of the United States. Civilian leadership in the Eisenhower administration played a major role in holding down increases in military expenditures in the face of putative bomber and missile gaps, and the fact that increased expenditures could be absorbed only so rapidly by the economy also tended to place a practical limit on actual increases for military outlays.

Toward the end of Eisenhower's second term substantial increases were authorized for expansion and protection of strategic offensive and defensive forces to offset the possibility that the Soviet Union might make good on its ICBM threat. Some of these programs were well underway at the time the Kennedy defense team came into office. In the main the Eisenhower strategic nuclear programs were continued by Kennedy and McNamara and in many instances, such as the Minuteman and Polaris missile programs, forces were substantially augmented. Hand in hand with recommended increases in defense expenditures—for strategic nuclear and conventional programs—by the Kennedy administration came a new breed of economic and fiscal managers dedicated to the proposition that larger defense outlays need not necessarily pose a threat to economic stability and growth, cause serious inflation, depress economic growth rates, or hinder standards of living. The Kennedy philosophy held that the nation could afford whatever expenditures were necessary to guarantee the national security. And because of the rigorous application of new budgeting concepts developed mainly by economists at the RAND Corporation, as well as the introduction of the techniques of operations research or systems analysis, it became apparent initially that arbitrary budget ceilings were not to be controlling. However, the new analytical tools used for determining annual weapons systems requirements were soon applied by McNamara's civilian analysts in such a manner that programmed military forces bore a significant relationship to domestic economic requirements and to annual growth in gross national product as well.

Critics of the Kennedy-McNamara defense programs were hard put at first to master the complexities of the new budgeting and systems analysis techniques, and many of them were initially deferential to the new Pentagon defense-planning techniques because of agreement that previous management of military force planning was both inadequate and imprecise. They were willing to give McNamara and his Whiz Kids a fair chance to demonstrate their talents. During the first five years of the McNamara revolution in the Pentagon the majority of informed opinion generally agreed that long overdue management improvements and cost-saving measures were successfully implemented by the three services and the Joint Chiefs of Staff, even though agreement was far from unanimous among the services, on Capitol Hill, and among nongovernment critics about the wisdom of certain McNamara decisions on specific weapon systems and on the nation's increasing involvement in the Vietnam conflict.

According to democratic theory, the policies of government, including defense policy, are shaped by public opinion. During the period from 1945 to 1965 to what extent did public opinion actually positively or negatively affect the magnitude and cost of military programs? With minor exceptions during the entire period public opinion favored large military forces, generally larger than those espoused by the administration in power. Public opinion polls consistently reflected a public attitude in favor of maintaining existing levels of defense expenditures or supported increases in such expenditures, particularly if the increases were being advocated by the executive branch. Because of the growing complexity of military technology, alternative military strategies, and foreign policy commitments during the postwar period, the public tended more and more to acquiesce in executive leadership and rarely expressed informed views to congressmen or other government decision-makers. As a consequence, the battles over defense expenditures and military forces and strategies raged primarily between the executive and Congress, or within the Pentagon between the services and the Secretary of Defense. Overall, public opinion sided with the executive, but there were times when congressional voices claimed at least momentary public attention, particularly when special investigations of military preparedness indicated that the United States was not spending enough on military forces to maintain a safe margin of superiority over the Soviet Union. Generally, however, executive will prevailed, because Congress was reluctant to accept responsibility for thrusting on the President larger military expenditures than either he or his military advisors were advocating. Only in those cases in which the executive recommended reduced military outlays for military forces and Congress raised a strong voice of protest, did public opinion express itself forcefully enough in general terms to persuade the administration to support higher levels of military effort.

During the entire two decades there were no major instances of serious debate by Congress on the issue of reducing defense expenditures, and with great consistency House and Senate votes on military appropriations bills reflected near unanimity. The lack of serious public debate by Congress during final airing of military appropriations bills added to public apathy and abetted a general public withdrawal from serious interest in the nature and purposes of military programs and their relationship to foreign policy objectives. Having abdicated from the contest, the American public had little choice but to have faith in the wisdom and integrity of defense experts in the executive branch and Congress to define and carry out a national security program which related military forces to a reasonable estimate of an enemy threat and which fully took into account at the same time unsatisfied domestic sector needs.

The McNamara Strategy of General Nuclear War

During roughly the first years of McNamara's stewardship of the Pentagon, serious attempts were made by the Secretary and his defense intellectuals to innovate new ideas for a strategy of general nuclear war which reflected either the actual or anticipated military relationship between the United States and the Soviet Union. It was during this period that much public discussion was devoted to a controlled response or counterforce strategy, which stressed the employment of offensive bomber and strategic missile forces primarily against enemy long-range attack forces, the avoidance of initial attacks on enemy cities as an inducement to an enemy to refrain from attacks on American cities, and the possibility of successfully using offensive and defensive forces to limit damage to the United States regardless of whether this nation's forces struck first or second. In addition to these strategic innovations the President and the Secretary of Defense assured the world that the United States enjoyed a meaningful superiority in strategic nuclear power over the Soviet Union and would continue to do so in the predictable future. Nuclear superiority implied a capability to achieve both predetermined political and military goals without undue risks to the security of the United States.

McNamara officials addressing key audiences advocated the discreet use of nuclear force, secure command and control of strategic bombers and missiles, and a counterforce general war strategy designed to limit to the maximum nuclear damage to the United States and touted the virtues of strategic superiority as a checkmate to aggressive Soviet policies. McNamara cogently presented the same case before congressional committees, in public forums, and at the annual gathering of the NATO membership. The entrancing logic of the McNamara strategy initially attracted a wide segment of the informed defense community, but other informed critics soon attacked the premises of the new strategic innovations as unattainable, uninteresting to the Soviet Union, expensive, and potentially provocative since a possible first strike was implied. Beginning in about 1963 a perceptible shift began to take place in McNamara's rationale for a viable strategy of deterrence and general nuclear war.

Particularly in the unclassified and publicly available posture statement, which the Secretary of Defense presented annually to the House Armed Services Committee and in the testimony given by McNamara before the House and Senate Appropriations and Armed Services committees, there began to appear a noticeable shift away from emphasis on a strategy of counterforce, the values of nuclear superiority, and the appropriateness of a city avoidance option. McNamara pointed out that the Soviet Union was rapidly achieving an adequate secure second-strike force, which the United States would not, under any foreseeable circumstances, be able to destroy to such an extent that this nation could escape from a nuclear war with little or no damage. McNamara was more and more skeptical that the United States could add significantly to its security by attempting to maintain a margin of superiority over the Soviet Union in numbers of delivery systems, arriving warheads, megatonnage, or quality of weapons systems, since both the Soviet Union and the United States would soon possess sufficient damage-inflicting capacity to destroy each other even after receiving a first strike. Looking into the foreseeable future at the anticipated weapons systems likely to be available to this nation or the Soviet Union, McNamara could not foresee that predictable military technology was likely to give a meaningful superiority to either the Soviet Union or the United States. Continued efforts to maintain some form of superiority were certain to be more and more expensive and probably would be counterproductive in terms of a stable balance of power, efforts to achieve some workable form of arms control, and the achievement of political aims.

During the period from 1963 to 1965 McNamara became less and less enamoured of the notion that the United States could significantly limit damage to itself in a nuclear war through the employment of strategic bombers and missile forces. The likelihood that either the Soviet Union or the United States might rationally decide to launch a preemptive or first nuclear strike diminished as each developed a large and secure second-strike strategic nuclear force. Although there might have been some significant advantage to the United States during this period in resorting to a preeemptive strike against the Soviet Union under circumstances of dire provocation or major challenge to this nation's national security, information gaps as to actual Soviet long-range strategic capabilities and strong political constraints on American leaders virtually ruled out any possibility that the United States might initiate war on the Soviet Union.

As was stated earlier, the United States did enjoy a marked and meaningful strategic nuclear superiority over the Soviet Union during most of the period under study, but chose to use it as an instrument for peace, détente, and arms control. In his public statements the

Secretary of Defense moved progressively away from a discussion of fighting a nuclear war to greater and greater emphasis on deterring the possible outbreak of such a war. In other words, the idea of significantly limiting damage to the United States during general nuclear war gave way to an overriding need to maintain an assured destruction capability of such size that no single enemy or combination of enemies could possibly make a rational decision to attack this nation. Although imprecise, McNamara's definition of assured destruction was that combination of forces capable, under any imaginable circumstances of attack, of inflicting between 20 percent and 30 percent casualties on the Soviet population and destroying between 50 percent and 60 percent of its industry.

The McNamara analysis of the facts of strategic nuclear life was, of course, not accepted entirely by the Joint Chiefs of Staff, service leaders, and many congressmen and senators on Capitol Hill responsible for defense programs and budgets. The idea that the United States might not be able to maintain its strategic nuclear superiority over the Soviet Union indefinitely and achieve a meaningful victory in nuclear war, if such were thrust upon us, was anathema to many professionals having a responsibility for the security of the United States. An influential segment of the defense community argued for ever greater efforts in research and development on advanced strategic weapons systems and nuclear warheads and urged that the President and Congress approve substantial increases in existing force levels of bombers, offensive and defensive missiles, and missile-launching submarines.

While agreeing that America must never be second in the field of research and development on new weapons technology, Secretary McNamara refused, and the President sustained him, to accede to demands by Congress, the Joint Chiefs of Staff, and other members of the defense community for major increases in the strategic force levels that President Kennedy had approved early in his first term. Rather, McNamara began to talk increasingly about the wisdom of seeking properly verified arms control agreements with the Soviet Union designed to slow the pace of the arms race in strategic weapons and ultimately to reduce stockpiles from their already awesome levels. If such arms control agreements could be achieved, McNamara believed, it might become possible once again to limit damage in this country resulting from a nuclear war which offensive and defensive forces were no longer able to achieve. Thus, by the end of 1965, the battleground for future years was shaping up between those who advocated maintaining United States strategic nuclear superiority indefinitely and at all costs and those who believed that the likelihood of maintaining strategic nuclear superiority that had any real meaning was very slim, not worth the expected cost, and likely to upset a relatively stable military balance and be disruptive of efforts to achieve arms control arrangements with the Soviet Union and other nations.

Looking beyond 1965, a number of possible trends in the dynamic strategic nuclear environment deserve some conjecture because of factors and forces already discernible at the end of 1965. Even though it appeared that the United States might become deeply enmeshed in the Vietnam conflict following its heavy commitment of forces during 1965, the desire for further accommodation by the Soviet Union with the United States in the field of arms control did not seriously abate. New opportunities for the control of nuclear weapons proliferation and possibilities for reaching agreed limits on the future size and composition of strategic nuclear forces appeared somewhat promising despite the oftentimes painfully slow pace of progress. Developments in nuclear weapons technology continued unabated, however, and it appeared that within a very few years a new generation of offensive and defensive weapons would surely emerge from the research and development stage and be ready for deployment, if Defense, the executive, and Congress gave their blessing. The deployment of a new generation of strategic weapons systems would in all probability raise a host of new implications for the security of the United States, its free world allies, and other nations of the world.

By the end of 1965, the Soviets were clearly accelerating the deployment rate of hardened and dispersed strategic ballistic missiles. How fast and how long the new rate of deployment would continue seemed to bear importantly on future United States decisions about whether to deploy new and added numbers of its own strategic weapons systems. The Soviet Union was also thought to be making substantial progress toward achieving a Polaris-type submarine, it appeared to have achieved a breakthrough in the anti-ballistic missile area, and Soviet missile tests indicated success in the solid-fuel missile field, possibly leading to the deployment of a land-based, mobile ICBM. Simultaneously, the United States was making steady progress on its own anti-ballistic missile system, and it had in advanced stages of research and development sophisticated decoys for existing missile systems as a hedge against a successful Soviet ABM, as well as multiple independently targeted reentry vehicles (MIRVs) which might be available near the end of the decade to vastly improve the accuracy and penetration capabilities of the nation's strategic missile systems. In the absence of an understanding or agreement between the Soviet Union and the United States to forego the next round of increases in the quantity and quality of strategic weapons systems, what implications might this situation raise for world security?

Taking into account all imaginable weapons system options likely to be available to the Soviet Union and the United States during the five-year period after 1965, it seemed unlikely to many observers that either nation would achieve a surprise breakthrough in strategic weaponry of a magnitude sufficient to give it a superiority as decisive as that possessed by the United States during the period of its nuclear monopoly. At best, it appeared that one nation might gain some modest, albeit temporary, advantage over another in weapon invulnerability, weapon accuracy, penetration capability, assured defense, or positive warning of enemy attack.

Since it was probable that a momentary advantage gained by one nation in a particular weapons development would be offset by achievements in other areas by another nation, it seemed difficult to foresee how a modest advantage could be translated into either political or military gains. On the other hand, the extremely conservative way this nation historically had perceived the intentions and technological prowess of the Soviet Union seemed destined to produce serious distortions in the image of the actual strategic military balance existing at any one time between this country and its major adversary. Gaps in this country's information about the nature and extent of certain Soviet weapon developments and deployments, and uncertainties about Soviet intentions in pursuing ideological or foreign policy goals could very well lead in the future to an overcompensating reaction by the United States. Such a situation could very well generate an action-reaction cycle in which both the Soviet Union and the United States would unnecessarily increase their strategic nuclear delivery capabilities in order to offset what one thought the other was doing, although it could not be sure. In the absence of certainty about what either the United States or the Soviet Union was doing in the field of strategic weapons, both nations have tended historically to accept a conservative estimate of each other's intentions and capabilities and have overcompensated substantially in the number of weapons systems deployed to meet a presumed threat by the other. The new generation of weapons systems, characterized by the ABM, MIRV, and mobile ICBM, seemed certain to accentuate this possibility.

A number of consequences may flow from a cycle in an arms race which is generated by serious misperceptions on the part of both the United States and the Soviet Union about the type and rate of each other's deployment of particular strategic offensive and defensive nuclear weapons systems. For one, there are always greater risks of destabilizing an existing strategic balance which has become relatively stable over a period of time because the major powers have come to understand and have confidence in their estimates of the size and capabilities of each other's strategic forces. A strategic balance which is no longer perceived as stable increases the possibility that conflict might occur. It is also possible that certain kinds of qualitative improvements in strategic weapons systems, such as MIRV or ABM, might convey an impression to the nation lagging behind that its adversary is striving to achieve a first-strike capability. Such fear is bound to increase tension, damage possibilities for détente and arms control agreements, and may very well increase the possibility of war because of miscalculation or accident. And in the final analysis it makes no economic sense for nations willingly to continue spending billions of dollars on new and greater numbers of weapons systems when the prospect of either side achieving significant gains in its security appear so marginal.

Thus, as the United States and the Soviet Union faced the final half of the 1960s, the options open to them in the strategic nuclear weapons field seemed quite clear. Unless both nations independently decided that no significant increases in overall military security were likely to result from a continuation of the strategic arms race and, as a consequence, engaged in serious talks about ways and means of stopping the buildup in strategic weapon stockpiles, it appeared that a major new cycle in the strategic arms race was inevitable with all its uncertainties, its instabilities, its risks of war, its awesome costs, and the probable undermining of hopes for further détente. Using past history as a guide for predicting trends in the future, the probability seemed poor that nations would strive concertedly for agreement to halt the arms race in new and more deadly strategic weapons systems, in lieu of allowing that race to continue inexorably. On the other hand, it was conceivable, at least, that events both domestic and foreign might conspire to force a major reevaluation of priority resource allocations by the United States and the Soviet Union, which could lead both nations to take initiatives aimed at heading off what otherwise could well be an arms race lasting for decades.

NOTES

1. Samuel P. Huntington, *The Common Defense* (New York: Columbia University Press, 1961), p. 298.

2. For a discussion of this issue, see Warner R. Schilling, Paul Y. Hammond, and Glenn H. Snyder, *Strategy, Politics and Defense Budgets* (New York: Columbia University Press, 1962), pp. 1–53, 214–235 and Huntington, *Common Defense*, pp. 277–283.

CHAPTER 8

Epilogue: Impacts of Vietnam and SALT on Nuclear Strategy

The decision taken by the United States in July 1965 to escalate the war in Vietnam in order to stave off an inevitable Communist victory was to have a substantial influence on Congress's, the executive's, and Secretary of Defense McNamara's attitudes and options regarding the selection, funding, and deployment of advanced strategic nuclear offensive forces during the years from 1965 to 1969. The deeper the nation's immersion in Vietnam, the more McNamara consumed his prodigious energies in the details of the conflict, constantly seeking to salvage an acceptable administration face-saving termination of the war. Defense budgets totaling almost $50 billion prior to escalation in Vietnam rose sharply to approximately $66 billion, $73 billion, $75 billion, and $82 billion from FY 1966 to FY 1969.[1] At the same time military expenditures on major strategic nuclear forces declined significantly during the period from 1965 to 1968 relative to what they had been in the early 1960s and would be after President Nixon took office.[2]

Apparently, McNamara was substantially convinced by 1965 that the United States had bought a much larger strategic nuclear force early in the Kennedy Administration than was warranted by the existing Soviet threat or was prudent for the long run as offering much hope of arresting a costly arms race between the two superpowers. The margin of United States strategic nuclear superiority over the Soviet Union grew so large by the mid-1960s that only unlikely self-denial on the part of the Soviet Union in trying to catch up could, in McNamara's judgment, halt the "mad momentum of the arms race." As early as 1963, the Secretary began to question the value of superiority as a means of gaining either military advantage or diplomatic leverage over a nation like the Soviet Union, which already possessed substantial strategic nuclear offensive power. He argued that possession of secure, second-strike strategic nuclear forces by both the United States and the Soviet Union augured best for a long-term stable relationship and posed the least likely threat of a catastrophic nuclear war. Furthermore, McNamara became philosophically a strong supporter of efforts to bring the arms race under control through formal or tacit agreement, thus reducing further the possibility of nuclear war and creating a more favorable climate for the improvement of Soviet-American relations.

Under Premier Khrushchev's leadership, the Soviet Union made no serious bid during the early 1960s to match the United States in numbers or diversity of strategic missiles and bombers. Soviet ICBMs initially were deployed in "soft" sites, making them vulnerable to preemptive attack and casting serious doubt on whether the Soviet Union possessed a credible second-strike retaliatory force. By the time of Khrushchev's removal from office in late 1964, the Soviet Union progressively was hardening its 250 land-based missile sites, although the United States had nearly four times the number of strategic missiles.[3] Undoubtedly an important precipitating factor in Khrushchev's overthrow was his refusal to accede to military demands for substantial increases in strategic hardware with which to challenge the widening American lead. By early 1965, United States intelligence sources detected a major step-up in the rate of Soviet strategic missile deployment which virtually coincided with the United States decision to make a major ground force commitment in Vietnam.

From the very outset of our military commitment the cost of the Vietnam conflict proved to be substantially higher than that forecast by the Johnson administration. As budgetary pressures mounted, the President progressively shifted defense priorities away from strategic offensive and defensive forces to those conventional forces required to prosecute the war in Southeast Asia. At the urging of Secretary McNamara, proposals by the Joint Chiefs of Staff for major new strategic weapon systems (i.e., ABM, advanced manned strategic bomber, Poseidon, and Minuteman III) were rejected or simply deferred. McNamara's personal reservations about the value, cost, and attainability of meaningful superiority seem to have disposed him to accept some measure of strategic weapons parity with the Soviet Union, while continuing the search for means to halt and stabilize the arms race by negotiation or executive agreement. Given the attitudes of key congressmen, many of whom held important positions on the Armed Services and Appropriations committees, and the power of pressure groups such as defense industry and professional military spokesmen, neither the President nor the Secretary of Defense was willing to risk the political capital needed to sell the American public on the wisdom of holding back expenditures on new strategic weapon systems in favor of accepting some measure of equality with the Soviet Union. The value of sustained military superiority over our principal Communist adversary was deeply entrenched among Americans who genuinely believed that United States nuclear superiority during the postwar period was largely responsible for the unbroken peace and should be sustained indefinitely, costs permitting.

Vietnam war costs soon rose, however, from \$12–\$13 billion to \$20–\$25 billion or more annually, and the Johnson administration declined to propose tax increases to finance the war on a pay-as-you-go basis. Consequently, increased war costs and competing domestic priorities combined to steadily narrow the defense options available to the nation's leaders. As early as 1965, Secretary McNamara sought to block Pentagon urgings for the funding of an advanced strategic bomber and a new ICBM and ABM system by essaying for the first time to quantify how much defense was enough to deter any rational decision by the Soviet Union to attack the United States, and how much damage we could expect to inflict on Soviet population and industry after absorbing the full weight of a surprise attack.

In explaining the new criteria of assured destruction, McNamara argued that surviving strategic nuclear forces capable of destroying between one-quarter and one-third of the Soviet population and about two-thirds of its industrial capacity should "deter under all foreseeable conditions a calculated, deliberate nuclear attack upon the United States."[4] Any additional forces in excess of those needed to maintain assured destruction would, McNamara reasoned, have to be justified on the basis of their capability to limit damage to the United States if deterrence failed. The probable effectiveness of damaging-limiting forces was tied closely to the timing and nature of an enemy attack, and McNamara believed it unlikely that the Soviet Union would withhold initial attacks from United States urban centers in favor of counterforce attacks on strategic bomber bases, missile silos, critical defense industry and major command and control centers. McNamara was also aware that insistence by this nation on possessing large damage-limiting forces tended to undermine the assured destruction capability of Soviet forces, thus constantly generating pressures on both sides to deploy new or additional numbers of existing strategic weapon systems.

Since United States strategic nuclear forces in 1965 were substantially larger and more versatile than their Soviet counterparts, McNamara appeared to favor restraining any significant changes in the Soviet-American strategic force relationships in order to avoid triggering action-reaction responses and to invest any savings in the insatiably expensive Vietnam conflict. Finally, McNamara realized clearly that the Soviet Union was capable of increasing the rate of its ICBM, bomber, and SLBM force deployment to a point where it would be politically and economically impractical for the United States to respond unless the Soviet Union made a clear bid for superiority.

Faced with growing Pentagon and congressional pressures to deploy new offensive and defensive forces, McNamara steadfastly rejected proposals to weaponize the AMSA (Advanced Manned Strategic Aircraft), to add 200 Minuteman II missiles to the land-based ICBM force of more than 1,000, and to go ahead with the deployment of the Nike-X ABM system. Although arguing that the existing missile force (Minuteman and Polaris) was adequate of itself to deter a deliberate attack on the United States, the Secretary acquiesced in the military position of retaining some manned bombers in the strategic offensive force indefinitely. Another McNamara tactic aimed at postponing decisions to deploy new and expensive weapon systems, such as AMSA and Nike-X, was to stress qualitative upgrading of existing systems (B-52, Poseidon, and Minuteman III), to argue that persistent technological problems militated against a premature decision to produce a system (Nike-X), and to consent readily to continue a questionable system in research and development on grounds that the expected threat at a future time period did not yet require a budgetary decision to deploy.

As American involvement in Vietnam intensified, McNamara cast more and more doubt on the efficacy of continuing to increase the size and character of damage-limiting forces. He credited the Soviet Union with the economic and technical capacity to prevent this nation from achieving a posture that could hold its fatalities below some tens of millions. During 1966, China's Cultural Revolution offered McNamara sufficient pretext to postpone an ABM deployment decision while at the same time he developed a fallback rationale for a future China ABM costing an estimated \$8–\$10.5 billion if ultimately a decision was made to deploy. In so doing, he stoutly opposed deploying an ABM defense against a future Soviet threat on grounds of the high cost and the ease with which the Soviet Union could negate it by deploying additional offensive forces. He further postponed a final decision on AMSA, by agreeing to the recommendation of the Joint Chiefs that a B-52 fleet of 255 aircraft be augmented by 210 FB-111s. In addition to recommending accelerated engineering development of the Poseidon missile at a total projected cost of \$1.3 billion (no decision was made on the size of a future retrofit program), McNamara revealed that enough major improvements were being made in the performance of the Minuteman missile to warrant designating it the Minuteman III. He announced that initial procurement of the missile—ultimately to be equipped with a MIRV warhead—would begin during FY 1967.[5]

The United States began the year 1967 with better than three times the number of ICBMs and SLBMs possessed by the Soviets, plus a lopsided advantage in intercontinental bombers.[6] Thus, the United States enjoyed a very substantial superiority in overall combat effectiveness. McNamara estimated that even granting a Soviet first strike against this nation in 1972 more than one-half of the forces programmed for that period would survive and remain effective. Unless, therefore, some surprising Soviet force deployment program or technological breakthrough occurred, there was no doubt about the sanctity of our assured destruction capability during the next five years.

By the fall of 1966, there was growing concern within the Johnson administration that the United States and the Soviet Union might well be embarking on a new high-intensity and expensive round of strategic arms competition. It appeared that the stepped-up deployment rate of Soviet strategic weapons systems (ICBMs and SLBMs) since the removal of Khrushchev was based on a firm decision to challenge American superiority which had existed during the entire postwar period. In addition the administration announced new evidence that the Soviet Union was deploying an anti-ballistic missile defense system around Moscow.[7] Increased pressure from Congress and the military was put on the Johnson administration either to counter the Soviet ABM deployment by deciding to deploy the Nike-X, or to approach the Soviets on the idea of arranging talks on mutual ABM limitations.

In November 1966 at the Texas White House, the President made the decision to approach the Soviet Union secretly on the idea of ABM limitation talks. Simultaneously, he also decided to announce in his forthcoming budget message his determination to defer a decision to deploy the Nike-X contingent on Soviet willingness to discuss ABM limitations. In a subsequent message early in 1967, the President stressed that in the absence of talks he would reconsider the decision to deploy an ABM system. The effect of Johnson's decision was to placate, briefly at least, both the advocates of new weapons deployment and those urging the path of negotiations. It is also clearly stated in the 1967 Defense posture statement that the President agreed with McNamara's firm opposition to deploying an ABM system against the Soviet Union, since it would seriously jeopardize the success of any future arms control talks, and even more seriously would cost in the range of $20–$40 billion for a capability almost certain to heat up the arms race and result in a relatively ineffective system. The Secretary stressed:

> It is a virtual certainty that the Soviets will act to maintain their deterrent which casts such grave doubts on the advisability of our deploying

> the Nike-X system for the protection of our cities against the kind of heavy, sophisticated missile attack they could launch in the 1970's. In all probability, all we would accomplish would be to increase greatly both their defense expenditures and ours without any gain in real security to either side.[8]

While temporizing on ABM, the administration took a number of actions in the strategic weapons area which in the long run would prove more controversial and potentially ominous in arms race terms than the ABM. Significantly, the decision was taken to recommend production and deployment of the Poseidon missile, which would markedly improve the range as well as accuracy of the Polaris weapon system. The Minuteman III, on which a deployment decision had been made the previous year, was now to become a larger component of the total Minuteman force. Most important, however, was the decision to initiate the development of new multiple independently targetable reentry vehicles (MIRV) specifically designed to penetrate targets defended by ABM defenses.[9] Finally, it was revealed that the components for the Nike-X ABM, such as the Sprint and Spartan interceptor missiles and the supporting radar and computer components, were not yet fully tested, and in some cases, i.e., Spartan, were still on the drawing boards. Any decision in coming months to deploy ABM would necessarily be political since feasible deployment was at least three to five years in the future.

By fall 1967, the Soviet Union had not responded to United States overtures for defensive arms limitation talks, despite strong personal efforts by the President and Secretary McNamara at the Glassboro summit conference in June. Because a decision on whether to deploy ABM turned primarily on political considerations (the 1968 election) and not on the military requirement to offset a growing Chinese or Soviet threat, President Johnson was put in the position of having to make a decision no later than the budget message of January 1968. To run the risk of further postponing a decision in favor of ABM deployment would in all probability subject the President to Republican arguments that he was permitting a serious national security gap to develop because of accelerated Soviet offensive and defensive force deployment.

In a puzzling address in San Francisco on September 18, 1967, McNamara announced the President's decision to proceed with a limited ABM deployment.[10] Carefully marshaling arguments against deployment of a large scale ABM—at a price near $40 billion—and forthrightly presenting his own assessment of existing strategic nuclear power relationships between this nation and the Soviet Union, McNamara strongly affirmed that the United States possessed a clear superiority in nuclear strength over the Soviet Union but denied that it possessed a credible first-strike capability. He regretted the absence of accurate information in early 1961 about the size and nature of Soviet strategic nuclear forces that induced the United States to over-compensate and to deploy forces during the 1960s in excess of actual need. He stressed that "unlike any other era in military history, today a substantial numerical superiority of weapons does not effectively translate into political control, or diplomatic leverage."[11] Expressing a substantial consensus within the administration, McNamara rejected a deliberate arms race with the Soviet Union, arguing that the action-reaction phenomenon made it foolish and futile.

> What we would much prefer to do is to come to a realistic and reasonably riskless agreement with the Soviet Union, which would effectively prevent such an arms race. We both have strategic nuclear arsenals greatly in excess of a credible assured destruction capability. These arsenals have reached that point of excess in each case for precisely the same reason: we each have reacted to the other's build-up with very conservative calculations. We have, that is, each built a greater arsenal than either of us needed for a second-strike capability, simply because we each wanted to be able to cope with the "worst possible case."
>
> But since we now each possess a deterrent in excess of our individual needs, both of our nations would benefit from a properly safe-guarded agreement, first to limit, and later to reduce, both our offensive and defensive strategic nuclear forces.[12]

The limited ABM deployment (Sentinel) proposed by McNamara would serve a threefold purpose: (1) to protect American cities against a relatively small and unsophisticated Chinese attack expected by the mid-1970s; (2) to add, if necessary, a measure of protection to our Minuteman sites against a future Soviet attack; and (3) to protect against the contingency of an accidental launch of an ICBM by any of the nuclear powers. Although there was scarcely any public evidence that Chinese progress toward achieving an ICBM capability justified the administration's decision, McNamara argued that the lead times for the proposed limited ABM and anticipated Chinese ICBM capabilities were the same.

The ABM concession thus momentarily placated the demands of key congressmen and defense officials for a new weapons system which, if expanded on a "building block" basis over the next five to ten years, could conceivably pump tens of billions of dollars into a nervous and outsized defense complex. McNamara made the strongest possible case against deploying ABM to meet expected Soviet threats, but he did not prohibit the Army from deliberately selecting radar and missile-launching sites close to major cities, thus providing the system with the growth potential to become a large anti-Soviet system. At the very least, the President could rest contented that he had removed the defense gap issue from the 1968 election should he choose to run.

Those advocates within and outside the government who favored efforts to halt further cycles in the arms race by seeking to arrange a formal or tacit agreement with the Soviet Union were at least partially satisfied that the proposed ABM deployment would not necessarily bring into play the action-reaction phenomena. A healthy environment for strategic arms limitation talks appeared to exist. The question never seriously addressed during the debate, however, was why ABM deployment against a Chinese threat was necessary when most Sinologists judged the Chinese to be at least as rational as the Soviets, and when nuclear deterrence had worked so effectively for over a decade between this nation and the Soviet Union.

The year 1968 proved to be a year of surprises: President Johnson declined to run for the presidency, Secretary McNamara departed his Pentagon post, and on the very eve of announcing that the United States and the Soviet Union had agreed to hold strategic arms limitations talks, Soviet forces led an invasion into Czechoslovakia, thus postponing indefinitely the long sought after talks. Intensive planning was conducted by the Johnson administration during the early months of 1968 to develop the negotiations position the United States would take if and when the Soviet Union agreed to hold strategic arms limitation talks. Not until June 27 did the Soviet Union finally announce that it was ready to begin discussions on the mutual restriction and subsequent reduction of offensive and defensive missile systems.[13] On July 1, when the Treaty on the Non-Proliferation of Nuclear Weapons was opened for signature, President Johnson announced that the United States and the Soviet Union had agreed to enter in the nearest future into discussions on the limitation and the reduction of *both* offensive and defensive strategic nuclear delivery systems. Subsequently, the President sought and apparently got an agreement with the Soviets to launch the Strategic Arms Limitation Talks (SALT) at a summit meeting in Moscow with Kosygin. High expectations were shattered the very next day when Soviet troops invaded Czechoslovakia.

The fall presidential campaign, as anticipated, elicited fundamental differences between candidates Richard Nixon and Hubert Humphrey over Soviet foreign policy objectives and the wisdom of engaging in talks on strategic arms limitations so soon after the Czechoslovakian affair. Since the Soviet Union continued to deploy both strategic offensive and defensive systems at a rather high rate, Nixon charged that the Democrats were guilty of creating a "security gap." He rejected a defense posture based on strategic parity with the Soviet Union and promised to restore clear-cut superiority of American military power.[14] Following his election, Nixon opposed Democratic recommendations to urge the Soviets to initiate talks immediately, and apparently refused to accept any responsibility for whatever initiatives the Johnson administration might take. The change of administrations and possibly word of Nixon's negative reaction to early talks may have persuaded Moscow to remain silent until January 20, 1969, when the Soviet Foreign Ministry announced that the Soviet Union was ready to start a serious exchange of views on a mutual limitation and subsequent reduction of strategic nuclear delivery vehicles, including defensive systems.

In what proved to be Robert McNamara's farewell statement as Secretary of Defense, he reviewed events, problems, and achievements of his seven-year tenure in the 1968 posture statement. Asserting that the cornerstone of our strategic policy must remain that of deterring a deliberate attack on either the United States or its allies, he said that the first priority was to maintain an assured destruction capability, defined as "the clear and present ability to destroy the attacker as a viable 20th Century nation and an unwavering will to use these forces in retaliation to a nuclear attack upon ourselves or our allies.'' He rejected the value of maintaining a significant damage-limiting capability as adding significantly to our deterrent.[15] After debunking the notion that gross megatonnage was a reliable indicator of destructive power, McNamara asserted that United States strategic forces were superior to those of the Soviet Union; but he cautioned that such "superiority" was of little significance in terms of national security.[16] No matter how skillfully the Soviet Union or the United States might plan a first strike, the inescapable fact in 1968 as well as in the foreseeable future was, said McNamara, that such an attempt would result in mutual suicide.

Perhaps the most portentous aspect of McNamara's farewell statement was the contradiction between the strong support given to the principle of strategic arms limitation talks, and the decision by the Johnson administration to press forward with the deployment of MIRVs on Poseidon and Minuteman III missiles. The Secretary rationalized extensive MIRV deployment as a hedge against possible large-scale Soviet ABM deployment in the 1970s. At the same time, he acknowledged that the Galosh ABM missile deployment around Moscow was proceeding at a moderate pace, and he announced as the consensus of the intelligence community that the so-called Tallinn system (being deployed across the northwestern approaches to the Soviet Union) had no significant ABM capability. McNamara did not even imply that the sharp step-up in America's planned offensive and defensive forces might well trigger the very action-reaction phenomena he had so eloquently argued against. Even more perplexing, the Secretary asserted that the accuracy of Soviet missiles was still substantially inferior to our own and there was no evidence that the Soviet Union was developing a new advanced intercontinental bomber. Nothing alluded to by McNamara suggested that the Soviets were engaging in strategic offensive and defensive programs which seriously threatened our assured destruction capabilities. Consequently, it is difficult to imagine how Soviet leaders could avoid interpreting the MIRV decision as a deliberate American escalation of the strategic arms race. Since MIRVs were theoretically capable of extreme accuracy, they connoted to some a counterforce capability. Furthermore, the Soviet Union could legitimately question whether the United States was embarked on a new quest for strategic superiority or indeed whether it was seeking a first-strike capability. It remained to be seen how the Nixon administration would react to the Johnson defense programs, having made a much tougher assessment of Soviet intentions and capabilities during the campaign.

The first real glimpse into the Nixon administration's attitude toward the SALT talks and its preferred strategic nuclear doctrine came on January 27, 1969, during the President's first major news conference. The President said that he favored strategic arms talks, but he sought to link agreement to participate with progress in reaching political settlements in the Middle East and Vietnam. Soviet response to this Nixon proposal was swift and extremely negative. Almost as quickly, the President modified his position and agreed to hold talks compartmentalized from other political issues.

During the same press conference a reporter asked the President about his pledge during the campaign to restore America to a position of uncontested nuclear superiority. The President sidestepped the issue, arguing that it was a case of semantic misunderstanding and explaining he would prefer to settle for "sufficiency" than either superiority or parity.[17] He offered no definition of sufficiency analogous to the criteria defining assured destruction, and even though four criteria for strategic sufficiency were agreed upon as part of a National Security Council study, those criteria were not made public officially until March 1971 in Secretary Laird's posture statement. The Nixon administration appeared to be firmly opposed to specifying the number of strategic nuclear forces deemed adequate to deter a rational aggressor from attacking the United States. As events proved, the doctrine of sufficiency offered almost no basis for reaching decisions affecting force size and composition consistent with the doctrine's implied acceptance of at least rough parity in strategic nuclear forces with the Soviet Union. And in fact, one of the criteria raised serious doubts that the administration was prepared to settle on a strategic force posture which did not contain some degree of "superiority."

The sufficiency criteria enunciated by the Nixon National Security Council included:

> maintaining an adequate second-strike capability to deter an all-out surprise attack on our strategic forces.

providing no incentive for the Soviet Union to strike the United States first in a crisis.

preventing the Soviet Union from gaining the ability to cause considerably greater urban/industrial destruction than the United States could inflict on the Soviets in a nuclear war.

defending against damage from small attacks or accidental launches.[18]

By and large, there is no obvious difference between the deterrence criteria established by the Johnson and Nixon administrations, other than perhaps that Nixon's advisors insist on avoiding the issue of "how much is enough." An idea of what was meant by sufficiency can only be gleaned from a careful reading of the annual defense posture statements and testimony by key defense officials before the Armed Services and Appropriations committees. Through mid-1971 the Nixon administration remained in a transition phase, holding the line against the deployment of new strategic weapon systems and in effect ratifying the definition of sufficiency as some degree of parity. One aspect of the Nixon sufficiency criteria is puzzling, however: that of preventing the Soviet Union from attaining the capability to inflict considerably greater urban/industrial destruction than the United States could inflict on the Soviet Union in a nuclear war.

The Nixon administration has endorsed a second-strike defense posture having the unquestioned capacity of inflicting an unacceptable level of damage on an aggressor. Nevertheless, administration spokesmen have repeatedly accused the Soviet Union of deploying large megaton SS-9 ICBMs for the ostensible purpose of achieving a first-strike capability against this nation's Minuteman ICBMs rather than as a prudent move toward real parity with United States strategic forces. In addition the administration has refused to accept the thesis expounded by many nongovernmental defense intellectuals that the deployment of MIRVs on Minuteman III and Poseidon missiles vastly improves the target coverage of our strategic forces, offers potential improvements in the accuracy of each warhead—which would nullify, partially at least, any meaningful advantage of superior Soviet megatonnage capability—and perhaps most important of all, tends to convey to the Soviet Union that the United States is embarking on a program which for several years will open a substantial "warhead gap" in its favor. MIRV deployment, then, may be precisely what is inducing the Soviet Union to continue deploying ICBM missiles, not for reasons of seeking a first-strike advantage, but merely to maintain a condition of sufficiency with the United States resembling parity. Taken at face value, the President appears committed to maintaining a significant degree of qualitative or quantitative superiority over Soviet strategic force capabilities in order to have a reasonable prospect of achieving rough parity of destruction from a second-strike posture.

The Nixon administration has also chosen to stress the growing vulnerability of our land-based ICBMs and bombers to Soviet SS-9s, SS-11s, SS-13s, and SLBMs, rather than the actual invulnerability of our strategic deterrent, which is reinforced by the triad force posture, and particularly by the size and invulnerability of the Polaris-Poseidon fleet, which alone possesses more than sufficient retaliatory power to deter an attack on the United States. While it remains a moot issue at what point in the future there may come a dramatic breakthrough in anti-submarine warfare capabilities, prospects do not appear bright for the predictable future. Any decision, therefore, to deploy new strategic weapons systems on the basis of the uncertain future of Polaris-Poseidon invulnerability is not warranted by lead-time requirements or the size and character of Soviet strategic forces under deployment or operational in mid-1971. To the credit of the administration, considerable deference has been shown to the SALT talks, which the President and his top advisors would clearly like to have succeed.

On March 14, 1969, the President announced, somewhat surprisingly, his intention to continue the deployment of ABM designed (1) to protect United States land-based forces against a direct attack by the Soviet Union, (2) to defend the American people against the kind of attack the Communist Chinese could likely launch during the next decade, and (3) to protect against the possibility of accidental attacks from any source.[19] The modified ABM was called Safeguard; it differed from the Sentinel primarily in that it was somewhat reduced in scale and was not placed close to cities. The President insisted that the Safeguard program was not provocative and that the Soviet Union should not view it as a prelude to an offensive strategy threatening the Soviet deterrent. He also described the system as providing an incentive for a responsible Soviet weapons policy and for the avoidance of upward pressures on American and Soviet strategic arms budgets. To placate his critics the President promised to review the ABM annually, and to tailor any future requests for funds to actual need.

The Nixon ABM decision triggered one of the most spirited and searching debates in the Congress on a major defense item ever witnessed during the postwar period. The issue was joined early by academic defense intellectuals—scientists, former defense officials, and social scientists—who testified preponderantly against the ABM before Senate and House Committees, wrote technical, highly analytical articles in major newspapers and periodicals generally critical of the ABM decision, and appeared in public forums and on television to carry their message to the American public. As events turned out, Americans had reached a state of disillusionment with the war in Vietnam, were shocked by public disclosures of cost overruns on major weapons systems, and were seriously questioning defense claims on shrinking budgets at a time when urgent programs in the public sector competed for funds. Above all, ABM critics pointed out, the United States and the Soviet Union were approaching rough parity in strategic weaponry—connoting a more stable strategic balance—and appeared to be on the verge of beginning talks on limiting the incessant arms race. Quite apart from the technical doubts raised about the ABM system, most critics wanted to postpone a decision to deploy ABM in order to preserve a favorable environment for arms talks and to determine whether restraint on our part would be reciprocated by the Soviet Union.

As the debate moved toward a vote in Congress, the administration made clear its determination to refuse any compromise and to fight for Safeguard to the bitter end. The balance of forces in the Senate for and against the ABM grew extremely close by mid-summer, giving confidence to the opponents and forcing the Nixon administration to exert pressure on wavering senators and congressmen to support its position. The deciding vote, taken on August 6 in the Senate, resulted in a victory for the administration by virtue of a tie vote. The House sustained the Senate by a wider margin. The opponents of ABM had received a severe setback, since they clearly recognized that once ABM deployment was approved it would be extremely difficult to arrest its progress in the future.

One of the more interesting, if not portentous, aspects of the so-called ABM debate was the failure of the ABM critics to insist throughout the debate on coupling both ABM and MIRV and to attempt to seek a compromise position with the Nixon administration affecting both systems. To be sure there were those, like Senators Edward Brooke and Clifford Case and many nongovernment defense intellectuals, who argued that any decision to deploy MIRV should be postponed for a reasonable period as a stimulus to getting the SALT talks started and as a commitment to their eventual success. In effect, however, the ABM critics did not insist on maintaining the close relationship of ABM and MIRV at all stages of the debates in order to wrest some form of concession to slow the MIRV program in return for a strictly limited or ''thin'' ABM system. The consequence was, of course, that the crucial—and much more potentially destabilizing—MIRV issue was lost in the noise of the ABM debate, and the only serious compromise made on MIRV to date has been the President's pledge to refrain from improving the accuracy of the independently targetable warheads which an enemy might regard as connoting a first-strike capability. Obviously from a Soviet point of view President Nixon's assurance that the United States would not continue a MIRV testing program designed to improve its accuracy was insufficient as a basis for a decision by Soviet leaders to refrain from any further adjustments in strategic force postures. The most likely explanation of Soviet missile deployment patterns since the SALT talks began is that they feel a need to increase their force size to reach effective parity with United States strategic forces, and possibly even to offset United States MIRV deployment which adds a substantial capabilities improvement to United States strategic missile forces.

In retrospect the arguments opposing the deployment of ABM against a small and relatively unsophisticated *Nth* country ICBM threat or the possibility of an inadvertent or irresponsible attack in the future make sense only in an arms control constraint context. On the premise that a Sentinel or Safeguard ABM, if deployed as planned, would entitle the Soviet Union to deploy a similar system under a SALT agreement, the asymmetrical radar deployments favoring the Soviet Union would raise the specter of a future clandestine ABM missile deployment which, in the absence of intrusive inspection, could result in a sudden and serious degradation of this nation's assured destruction capability. This argument, highly important to the SALT negotiations on possible agreed levels of ABM, was generally subordinated in the public debate to technical, political, arms race, and "how much is enough" issues.

To argue as the critics did that a limited ABM system, which was patently incapable of seriously eroding a massive Soviet assured destruction capability, was inherently destabilizing and could not effectively be constrained once deployment began from growing to become a major threat to the Soviet Union was sheer sophistry. By almost any measurement American and Soviet strategic offensive forces were, as of mid-1969, far in excess of the requirement for credible second-strike deterrence. Critics of the ABM variously employed overkill tactics against the ABM and tended to underestimate their political clout with Congress and the American public in their determined bid to block any ABM deployment. By their own logic, the deployment of a thin ABM system would tend to erode some of the overkill capability in Soviet offensive forces, was unlikely to be opposed by a defense-biased Soviet leadership, and could have been used as an effective argument against any precipitous deployment of new strategic weapon systems.

Furthermore, it is by no means clear in retrospect that a thin ABM deployment decision would complicate the SALT talks, thus diminishing their chances for success. Indeed, the primary issues delaying the success of a partial SALT agreement appear to be mainly focused on the manner in which offensive systems would be limited. Arguments that a thin ABM system would be destabilizing, undermine United States credibility with allies, or hopelessly postpone improved relations with Communist China were made unconvincingly or not at all. The ABM proposed by the Johnson administration—and badly reoriented by the Nixon administration under political pressure—was attacked by Congressional and academic critics in the thick of the debate as much because they sensed the possibility of a first major victory over the executive on a major weapons system as on the merits of the issue. In any event by attacking the ABM frontally and administering only glancing blows at the MIRV deployment program, the key issue affecting the SALT talks in the short and longer range was defaulted, with little prospect of altering the decision in the future.

The fact that MIRV critics have not been able to generate much serious public interest, since the crucial ABM debate, in restraining further MIRV testing and deployment for a reasonable period, pending progress in the SALT talks, supports the contention that they simply missed a vital opportunity. All of the arguments concerning the destabilizing nature of MIRV (first-strike implications), its arms race–generating tendencies, its negation of the principle of sufficiency or parity, and its prematurity either in terms of the Soviet ABM, or SS-9 and SS-11 threat were far more important than the arguments levelled against ABM. Both the Johnson and Nixon administrations consistently refused to acknowledge publicly the arms race–producing significance of major qualitative improvements in strategic forces such as are being achieved in the Minuteman III and Poseidon missile programs, preferring always to argue solely in terms of comparative numbers of launchers and vehicles, megatonnages, or simply deliverable warheads. Reassurance by the Nixon administration to its domestic critics and the Soviet Union that the United States would continue deploying MIRVs but would refrain from improving the guidance systems that could convey a first-strike intention was simply unbelievable, because it was amply clear to everyone that the United States possessed the technology to improve substantially the accuracy of the MIRVs if it chose to do so, so that the Soviet Union was forced to accept at face value the President's pledge, which existing national verification methods could not corroborate.

The Nixon administration, while officially embracing the doctrine of sufficiency, has lost some credibility by continuing a major MIRV deployment program, while at the same time castigating the Soviet Union for deploying additional SS-9, SS-11, SS-13 and SLBM systems, which by impartial standards of comparison have not exceeded parity with the United States. Thus, as of mid-1971 no reasonable argument can be made that the Soviet Union is striving for strategic superiority when, in fact, the United States took steps beginning in mid-1968 to widen the deterrent gap in its favor, thus in all likelihood stimulating the Soviet Union to greater offensive deployment efforts merely to stay abreast of major United States force improvements.

Clearly, the MIRV eventually will prove to be a major obstacle if SALT talks continue indefinitely, although any preliminary agreement is likely to ignore MIRV altogether. Properly conceding the Soviet technological capacity to weaponize MIRV in three to five years, the United States stands to become the ultimate victim of its own insatiable appetite to deploy new weapons systems. Soviet throw-weight advantage in its SS-9 missile forces once MIRVs are installed will appear extremely threatening to this nation and inevitably generate new pressures to deploy more strategic forces, such as laser, ABM, mobile land-based missiles, bombers, and undersea long-range missile systems (ULMS). The cost will be high; such deployment will generate Soviet responses and in all probability make a long-range major SALT agreement virtually impossible. As of mid-1971, MIRV deployment was never justified as a response to Soviet ABM deployment, or even the likelihood of such deployment, given deployment lead times favoring the MIRV. It must be viewed as significantly improving United States targeting capability against a wide variety of Soviet targets, as helping to keep the United States ahead of the Soviet Union in the quantitative and qualitative arms race, and as providing this nation with a temporary yet important accuracy leverage if future events demand it.

From January until early June 1969, the Nixon administration was engaged in a major reassessment of the Johnson SALT negotiating position assembled for talks which appeared certain in August 1968. During this period Soviet high officials declared their readiness to discuss limitations on strategic offensive and defensive weapon systems and prodded the new administration to give its consent. On June 19, President Nixon said in a news conference that the administration was completing its strategic review and the United States had informed the Soviet Ambassador that talks could begin sometime between July 31 and August 15. On July 10 Soviet Foreign Minister Andrei Gromyko announced that the Soviet Union was prepared for SALT. For unknown reasons further delays prevented a joint announcement until late October that the talks would begin in Helsinki on November 17.

The initial talks at Helsinki and Vienna were exploratory, each side probing the other on the definition of subject matter and the nature of the issues to determine whether a basis existed for proposing an outline agreement on which more specific negotiations might proceed. In the jargon of the negotiators, the talks proceeded in a businesslike fashion devoid of ideological or polemical content. In August 1970, on the United States' initiative, the talks moved from an analysis of broad issues to a discussion of specific measures. According to President Nixon, the American delegation proposed to the Soviet Union possible approaches involving both numerical and qualitative limitations on strategic offensive and defensive forces, including MIRVs, a position very similar to the one developed by the Johnson administration during 1968.[20] A subsequent proposal introduced by the Soviets diverged from ours in important respects, including a major difference on the definition of strategic forces. The Soviet Union defined strategic offensive weapons as those capable of attacking its territory, including United States forces in Europe and carrier-based aircraft. A second major disagreement arose over whether a separate agreement limiting only ABMs should be negotiated as a prelude to a wider agreement at some future date. The President has said publicly that his position was to "strive for an initial agreement which is as broad and comprehensive as possible. It must deal with the interrelationship between offensive and defensive limitations."[21]

President Nixon's objective in the SALT is to achieve a verifiable agreement in which neither side gains any unilateral advantage and in which a stable strategic equilibrium is achieved. The administration is also on record as supporting strategic sufficiency, which ostensibly concedes to the Soviet Union the right to attain rough parity in strategic offensive and defensive forces. In fact, however, neither the Johnson nor Nixon administrations appeared comfortable with a condition of strategic parity as confirmed by frequent public condemnation of Soviet efforts to equal United States strategic capabilities and by the deployment decisions taken over the past several years, which seem certain to be interpreted by the Soviet Union as a bid by this nation to maintain a significant degree of superiority.

A consistent theme of Secretary Melvin Laird and his Chief of Research, John Foster, has been that the sustained deployment of

SS-9 ICBMs by the Soviet Union in numbers approaching 400 could seriously jeopardize the survivability of the nation's land-based Minuteman and Titan II missile force, and presumptively enable the Soviet Union rationally to consider a first strike against the United States in imaginable future crisis situations. As of mid-1971, however, the Soviet Union had deployed less than 300 SS-9s, and gave little evidence of a determination to push on toward the critical level of 400 as projected frequently by Laird and Foster. The accusation against the Soviet Union appears at the minimum to be premature—particularly in light of probable initial success in the SALT talks affecting SS-9s—and at best is purely a technical argument, which completely ignores political and other constraints on the Soviet leadership.

By implication the Pentagon leaders contend that decisions on strategic force deployment must be made on the basis of examining each leg of the triad (Polaris, Minuteman, and bombers) separately to ensure that none of the three is vulnerable to possible attack. Any technical argument that can be raised which proves that one triad leg—i.e., the Minuteman missile force—is becoming vulnerable to a Soviet first strike is all that is needed to generate Pentagon requests for new weapons systems or hardening and dispersal improvements of existing missile systems. Consequently, the fact that the Polaris submarine force of forty-one boats—capable in future years of possessing up to ten warheads per missile on thirty-one boats[22]—was virtually invulnerable to the technology of the early 1970s, and by Secretary Laird's own admission would likely remain so for from five to seven years, made little difference in defense planning calculations even though the Polaris force alone contained far more nuclear capability than anyone has described as minimally essential for pure deterrence. In addition Laird and Foster consistently avoided telling the American public about important strategic warning improvements in the offing that would seriously complicate Soviet planning for an attack on this nation, and neither had added, as of mid-1971, a word about the substantial force improvements this nation is getting from the MIRV program. In public testimony during 1971, Deputy Secretary of Defense David Packard told the Senate Foreign Relations Subcommittee on Arms Control, International Law and Organization that the Soviet SS-9 missiles in their present configuration did not pose either a numerical or an accuracy threat to this nation's land-based missile force.[23] Thus, on any other than pure technical grounds, the argument to isolate one leg of the triad for purposes of defining vulnerability rather than to consider them together and to make judgments accordingly is wholly specious. It is simply not demonstrable that, as Secretary Laird stated in his 1972 defense posture statement, the MIRV programs for the Minuteman and Polaris forces are "essential to preserve the credibility of U.S. deterrent forces when faced with the growing Soviet strategic threat."[24]

The question of what and how much to tell the American public about the facts of the strategic nuclear balance existing between the United States and the Soviet Union from year to year was handled quite differently by the Kennedy-Johnson and the Nixon administrations. From 1963, Secretaries of Defense McNamara and Clifford gave to the American public in their annual posture statements an accurate and complete account of the shifting balance of nuclear power between the two superpowers. During that period, the United States was vastly superior to the Soviet Union in effective strategic nuclear striking power, and the philosophy was embraced within the administration that public confidence would be sustained by providing full knowedge, and, in turn, the Soviets would both be encouraged to develop secure second-strike forces of their own and would not miscalculate the size and capabilities of American strategic power because of the exercise of secrecy.

In the Nixon administration, there has been a significant change in the previous policy of giving the American public full and accurate information on the changing Soviet threat. The President pledged during his campaign to restore the nation to a position of strategic nuclear superiority, which it sustained during the entire postwar period. The new defense team rejected the McNamara definition of assured destruction in precise quantitative terms and sought a new doctrine to supersede it. When, in early 1969, Nixon was asked whether he would keep his campaign pledge to restore American strategic nuclear superiority, he said that he favored sufficiency, a term first employed during the Eisenhower administration. Sufficiency connoted to some the notion of strategic parity, since the new administration very early committed itself to the success of

SALT. However, as the criteria of sufficiency were made public and a new strategy called "realistic deterrence" was announced by the Pentagon, it was virtually impossible to distinguish the new strategy from the old. There are several apparent reasons for this. Secretary Laird, a consummate politician fully conversant with the habits of Congress, was confronted with growing public disillusionment with the Vietnam conflict, changing congressional attitudes toward defense spending, a growing vocal liberal minority strongly championing the SALT, and a clear bid by the Soviet Union to attain at least parity in strategic weapons with the United States. Confronted with such a diverse set of constraints, defense officials have not seen fit to inform the American public either accurately or completely about the strategic nuclear balance existing between the two superpowers in the early 1970s. For example, public statements are replete with numerical comparisons of United States and Soviet forces, but very little is said about significant qualitative differences, which mainly favor the United States. This is unfortunate because the administration has postponed deployment decisions on new weapons systems (through 1971) and has instead funded qualitative improvements in existing weapon systems, such as MIRV on Minuteman III and the Polaris–Poseidon. Although the second-strike deterrent capabilities of this nation have never been more secure, taking into account both qualitative and quantitative measurements, Pentagon officials have consistently detracted from U.S. strengths to the American public, our principal allies, and potential adversaries, which is psychologically disturbing and factually misleading.

One of the most controversial positions adhered to by the Nixon administration has been the so-called "bargaining chip" rationale for continuing to deploy Safeguard while the SALT talks are proceeding satisfactorily and to argue similarly against restraint on MIRV deployment. During his appearance before the Subcommittee on Arms Control, Secretary Packard contended, "It is my view that if we had not proceeded on the ABM program as we did . . . we would not be talking in Helsinki today." Moreover, Packard continued, failure to authorize construction at two additional Safeguard sites for a total of four "would put the likelihood of moving ahead to an agreement [in SALT] in great jeopardy."[25] Paul C. Warnke, a former defense official in the Johnson administration, took sharp issue with Packard, arguing that "what provides the opportunity for a SALT agreement is the mutual desire to avoid a new, costly and risky round of arms deployments."[26] Thus, he said, it was the *possibility* not the *act* of deployment that provided an incentive to the Soviet Union to negotiate, and any fast paced deployment of MIRV and ABM was likely to be self-defeating and expensive.

On the specific administration point that ABM was an essential bargaining chip in the SALT, Professor Marshall Shulman, testifying before the Arms Control Subcommittee, pointed out that not only did MIRV and ABM deployment tend to weaken the position of moderates in the Soviet Union who favored efforts to reach a SALT agreement, but such deployment virtually assured that the Soviet leadership will feel obliged to match us step for step since it could not afford as a policy imperative to be pressured into an agreement on unfavorable terms. In the field of nuclear weapons in particular the bargaining chip tactic virtually insured greater dynamism of the arms race. The wisest course for the United States to follow, Shulman continued, would appear to be that of debating the deployment of major weapon systems on their intrinsic merits rather than to use them as bargaining pressures, since the Soviet Union easily understood our tactic and discounted it as a transparent device.[27]

On May 25, 1971, President Nixon appeared in the White House press room and announced:

> The governments of the United States and the Soviet Union, after reviewing the course of their talks on the limitation of strategic armaments, have agreed to concentrate this year on working out an agreement for the limitation of the deployment of antiballistic missile systems [ABMs]. They have also agreed that together with concluding an agreement to limit ABMs, they will agree on certain measures with respect to the limitation of offensive strategic weapons.
>
> The two sides are taking this course in the conviction that it will create more favorable conditions for further negotiations to limit all strategic arms.[28]

By and large President Nixon's initiative was warmly applauded by the American public. The effect of the working agreement appeared clearly to loosen somewhat the tight linkage that had existed between offensive and defensive weapons systems since the talks began. Administration officials stressed, however, that the linkage of the two systems had not changed. One informed observer explained a possible agreement as limiting rival ABM systems to a Moscow system which would be matched by the two United States Safeguard sites in North Dakota and Montana. Indications were that both numerical and qualitative limitations on ABM would be agreed to. In all probability such an agreement involving ABM would be in treaty form. Very likely there would be a joint declaratory statement by the United States and the Soviet Union to limit numbers of land-based strategic missiles to an agreed ceiling. This understanding would, from this nation's point of view, be aimed at curtailing Soviet SS-9 deployment at somewhere near the 300-missile level—a level most analysts agree would not pose a serious threat to the United States land-based missile force. Verification of the ABM agreement and missile ceilings would be accomplished by respective national capabilities.

Apparently any prospective agreement would contain no immediate limitation on submarine-launched missiles or bombers, and no qualitative controls would be placed on MIRVs. In effect neither the United States nor the Soviet Union would be prevented from qualitatively upgrading existing strategic offensive forces under a preliminary agreement. If negotiations continue as expected after an initial understanding is reached, it is conceivable that either some qualitative controls will later be agreed upon or, alternatively, that both sides will agree to accept reductions in certain types of forces, thus achieving a similar objective.

The major obstacle barring progress of limiting offensive systems involves so-called forward-based systems, which consist of United States nuclear-capable fighter-bombers deployed in Europe, and carrier-based aircraft deployed worldwide. The Soviet Union insistently argues that any systems capable of striking Soviet territory from such bases of operation are strategic; yet it rejects United States insistence that Soviet IRBMs and MRBMs would have to be included. The United States, conscious of its commitments to the defense of NATO, insists that fighter-bombers in West Germany, for example, are clearly tactical and should be excluded from the definition of strategic weapons. By late 1971, it appeared that the Soviet Union had agreed to set the issue aside temporarily in the interest of permitting the discussions to move toward agreement.

Early in 1971 the Nixon administration announced that it was embracing a strategy of "realistic deterrence" which it characterized as "a new approach to national security planning concepts and a reformulation of older concepts."[29] The new strategy appears to be an amalgam of the Nixon Doctrine and the criteria of sufficiency, therefore integrating political and military requirements as the basis for determining those strategic nuclear and conventional forces adequate to guarantee the security of the United States. Like all administrations before it, the Nixon administration stressed the need for capabilities that enhanced effective deterrence from attack at all conflict levels. In the conflict spectrum below general nuclear war, however, the administration declared a need for adequate war-fighting capability—in limited nuclear and conventional options—to successfully deter possible Soviet and Chinese adventures. No attempt was made at defining with any degree of precision what the Nixon administration actually meant by sufficiency, or realistic deterrence, which in effect ignored a fundamental problem.

In his assessment of the Soviet strategic nuclear threat, Laird stated that as of the end of 1970 the Soviet Union had some 1440 operational launchers. But, he added, construction on new silos has slowed during the past year. Thus, if sufficiency is defined as meaning rough parity, the Soviet missile level posed no threat to the United States' second-strike capability, especially in view of the United States' lead in bomber and SLBM forces. Laird pointed out that the Soviet Union had tested MRVs many times since August 1968, but he offered no evidence that there had been any MIRV testing and cast doubt that the Soviet Union had MIRV-equipped missiles operational as of early 1971. Even regarding the presumed accuracy of the SS-9 missile, Laird conceded that substantial accuracy improvements could be made by about 1975–1976, thus placing at risk undefended Minuteman silos. The SLBM fleet, according to the Secretary, had reached seventeen operational Polaris-type subs, fifteen more were being readied and the Soviet Union at current production rates was likely to reach parity with us sometime in 1974. As for strategic bombers, the Soviet force numbered around

200, 50 of which were configured as tankers. Although a new swing-wing bomber was undergoing tests—probably as a replacement for the obsolescent medium-range TU-16—there were no signs of deployment. Soviet ABM deployment around Moscow was apparently progressing slowly.[30] In sum, the Soviet Union was engaging in something akin to an arms "crawl" with this nation as of mid-1971 and certainly in existing numbers and configuration Soviet strategic offensive and defensive forces posed no serious threat to the Nixon criteria of sufficiency. Secretary Laird said as much himself in his posture statement:

> Recent analyses of strategic force effectiveness indicate that planned strategic forces should continue to provide an adequate deterrent for the near term. We do have reliable and survivable strategic retaliatory forces, and their capabilities for retaliation today can not be denied by nuclear attack.[31]

As an offset to Soviet strategic nuclear weapons deployment, Laird proposed that during FY 1972 this nation spend $1.278 billion on Safeguard, expanding it to two additional sites for a total of four. Equipping of Minuteman III and Poseidon missiles with MIRVs was to continue at a high rate. In addition the administration advocated engineering development of the B-1 intercontinental bomber, which it described as designed "to enhance survivability in all modes of operation through faster reaction, increased resistance to overpressure, faster flyout times, higher speeds and lower altitudes during penetration, reduced infra-red and radar cross sections and greatly increased ECM abilities as well,"[32] Substantial sums were also recommended for a short-range attack missile (for the B-52 and B-1 bombers) and a new undersea long-range missile system, as well as a subsonic cruise armed decoy. Continued development was urged on an airborne warning and control system, and deployment of a new satellite strategic surveillance system. By almost any standard of measurement, qualitative or quantitative, the Nixon force recommendations were much more ambitious than their observable counterpart Soviet programs, and if all were eventually weaponized this nation would probably have a significant qualitative advantage over the Soviet Union. In accordance with the administration rationale, in the absence of a SALT or other agreement constraining the proposed programs, all of them would be allowed to proceed in an orderly fashion—Congress permitting—to be used if needed as bargaining chips.

Indeed the proposed strategic forces program appeared to sustain the critics of United States defense programs who said that during most of the postwar period technology has tended to dictate strategy, not vice versa. Put another way, the relationship of such programs to a reasonable definition of sufficiency is hard to imagine, and in fact appears to be masking a clear desire to perpetuate some degree of United States superiority in strategic nuclear forces. Only if one views the Nixon Doctrine, the criteria of sufficiency, and a strategy of realistic deterrence as a *process* which will become clearer and more explicit with the passage of time can one hope to understand the administration's objectives. As of late 1971, no significant deployment decisions had been made on new strategic weapons systems, thus prolonging a transition phase begun in 1969.

In conclusion, several observations are essential to put into clearer perspective the principal events, trends, and policies during the period from our heavy commitment in Vietnam (mid-1965) through mid-1971, which importantly shaped the nation's major security programs. To this observer one of the most persistent myths embraced by defense and top political leaders in the United States is the notion that superiority in nuclear weapons and delivery systems conveys to the possessor meaningful political or military leverage. During the period of virtual United States nuclear monopoly, which ended in any real sense prior to the mid-1950s this nation indeed might have successfully carried out a nuclear surprise attack on the Soviet Union without suffering serious damage to itself. Obviously, however, the weight of political judgment in this nation was opposed to such an attack. By the late 1950s and early 1960s the Soviet Union clearly possessed sufficient intercontinental bomber forces and, presumably, ICBMs to deter the United States from any rational decision to attack preventively. Interestingly enough, as greater disillusionment over the value of nuclear superiority captured many government leaders and defense intellectuals in the mid-1960s, no adequate political rationale could be found to carry the message to the American public. There were haunting memories of the election of 1960 and Kennedy's assertion against Nixon of a "deterrent gap," which partly inspired the 1967 Johnson ABM decision, and which averted serious pressure on McNamara and Johnson to make a frontal assault on the myth of nuclear superiority. McNamara's testimony before Congress and several of his major speeches and public interviews bespoke his personal doubts about superiority, and he even hinted that parity of nuclear forces between the United States and the Soviet Union would produce the most stable relationship short of effective arms control agreements.

Paradoxically, one of the consequences of the Vietnam conflict was that the rapidly escalating costs permitted the administration to hold the line against pressures from Congress and the Pentagon to deploy new and expensive strategic weapons systems. The critics of parity/sufficiency were effectively silenced by the twin forces of insatiable Vietnam costs and growing domestic priorities to such an extent that the Soviet decision to achieve rough parity with the United States in nuclear strategic forces was, until the election of 1968, largely acquiesced in. And despite the Nixon campaign assertion in 1968 that the Soviet Union was rapidly eroding the margin of American superiority, and his pledge to maintain our overwhelming superiority, the cost of Vietnam and urgent domestic programs again have compelled him and Secretary Laird to strive for the success of SALT and to defer, as of mid-1971, the deployment of the B-1, the ULMS, and an improved ICBM. In part this explains why the President clarified his position in favor of "sufficiency" early in his administration while refusing to disavow his campaign pledge of continued superiority. He could see no better or more realistic alternative.

A second observation on the period from 1965 to 1971 is that the public dialogue on the evolving Soviet strategic nuclear threat has opened up a serious credibility gap in the defense sector. Having embraced early in the administration the criterion of sufficiency—strongly implying rough parity—Nixon defense officials have consistently impugned the Soviet Union for deploying strategic weapons systems, although most Soviet analysts agree that the deployment is probably intended to achieve strategic parity with the United States. In addition the MIRV and ABM decisions effected by Johnson and sustained by Nixon may in themselves be partly responsible for Soviet insistence on deploying more SS-9, SS-11 and SS-13 strategic missiles than the United States has in its combined Minuteman and Titan forces, thus conveying an impression of a Soviet bid for superiority or a first-strike capability. In any event there is no firm evidence as of mid-1971 to indicate that the Soviet Union is in quest of a strategic capability in excess of parity, and the existing United States–Soviet Union strategic balance although asymmetrical conveys no meaningful political or other advantage to either party. In order to reduce the existing credibility gap administration spokesmen should be more cautious in prematurely releasing highly tentative evidence of Soviet intentions publicly and take greater pains to avoid overstating Soviet threats as a means of bargaining for higher annual defense appropriations, to influence the outcome of the SALT talks, or to blunt dovish attitudes among congressmen and academic defense intellectuals. The consequences of our future relations with the Soviet Union are far too important to be made the victims of inaccurate or premature reporting, and, in light of the complexity of the issues involved, the American public is very easily misled or hopelessly confused by the often incomplete and contradictory public dialogue.

A related aspect of the so-called Nixon administration defense credibility gap revolves around its insistence on comparing only the quantitative aspects of the strategic nuclear balance. It would appear clearly inconsistent with the implications of the doctrine of sufficiency to fail to report candidly to the American people the qualitative advantages this nation enjoys over the Soviet Union in such key weapons areas as MIRV, missile guidance accuracies, phased array radar, computers, Sprint ABM missiles, Polaris-Poseidon submarines, and strategic bomber technology, and the comprehensiveness and reliability of our command and control and warning capabilities. These are superior factors of which many Americans are only generally aware, but which undoubtedly are common knowledge to Soviet leaders and importantly influence their own strategies and war plans. Only on one occasion, in the sole defense posture statement (1969) issued by Clark Clifford, was a candid effort made to explain United States qualitative weapons superiority over the Soviet Union. His report got little press attention and nothing of its kind has been repeated by the Nixon administration. In fact, the United States enjoyed, as of 1971, a very significant qualitative edge over the Soviet Union in essential strategic weapons areas, which should afford this nation ample basis for exercising restraint in adding numerically to its existing forces pending reasonable efforts to achieve balanced and fair agreements in the SALT talks, or clear evidence of Soviet determination to push us into another lap of the arms race.

Looking ahead to the late 1970s and early 1980s and conjecturing about comparative technological rankings of the Soviet Union, the United States, Japan, and Western Europe, the future for the Soviet Union appears to be the most uncertain. Barring a major internal upheaval or severe depression in the Western world (Japan included), present trends in military-related technology seem to indicate that an overly rigid Soviet economic structure and stultifying system of incentives foredooms that nation to a second-rank position behind the United States, Japan, and Western Europe. One apparent reason for the Soviet Union's apparent readiness to expand cordial relations with the United States and Western Europe in the 1970s is that it feels it necessary to trade détente for an improved expectation of availing to itself the fruits of Western technology, lest the Soviet domestic economy and massive defense effort simply fail to meet anticipated challenges from the West. So long as party strictures require a high degree of centralization and minimal free markets, the Soviet Union will find itself in serious jeopardy of failing to be the world's prime example of a superior socialist system in such domains as science, technology, productivity, and human values. The twenty-fourth Soviet Party Congress seems to have set the Soviet Union on a clear path toward ultimate failure to meet the future challenges from an already technologically superior West.

Closely related to the process of accurately informing the American public about all important aspects of Soviet strategic nuclear capabilities and probable intentions is the adequacy and sophistication of the strategic analysis performed. In this author's judgment, objective analysis of Soviet decision-making dialogue, factional disputes within the Soviet political-military structure, and Soviet efforts to signal policy intentions to the United States have been submerged too often in a cold war ideological framework which, at least since the mid-1960s, has more and more ceased to characterize Soviet behavior patterns. Official Soviet publications in recent years have revealed important insights into the internal debate among political, military, and scientific factions over foreign policy, defense and domestic sector priorities, and SALT.[33] Thus, in future years it should be possible to compare United States and Soviet military capabilities and to realistically assess high-level Soviet attitudes on defense, foreign policy, and arms control issues as a basis for reaching consensus in this country on foreign and defense policy positions.

As a consequence of our reluctance to carefully examine, analyze, and use the increasing body of evidence on Soviet decision-making processes, the United States has had to base its defense policy and force-level decisions on a premise of a greater-than-expected Soviet threat. To some extent in recent years this policy has fallen into disuse because this nation has been disposed to accept a condition of de facto parity in strategic weapons systems with the Soviet Union. Historically, however, the United States has consistently over-estimated the Soviet strategic nuclear threat during the entire postwar period and has just as consistently deployed strategic forces in excess of any reasonable requirement for a second-strike retaliatory capability. In part, also, our strategic forces are tributes to the successes of pressure groups and their arguments for maintaining a safe margin of superiority over the Soviet Union, regardless of the high cost and uncertain political value. In equal measure, however, they are simply the consequence of poor homework on the part of Congress and the executive, which resulted consistently in approved defense programs amply insured against any possibility that the greatest imaginable Soviet threat might materialize.

One can only hope that broad acceptance of rough parity in strategic weapons systems characterizing today's (1971) strategic balance, plus the growing ability of American analysts to understand the internal Soviet debate and its probable meaning for Soviet security policy, will temper the disposition of this nation's leadership prematurely to deploy new weapons systems before hard evidence exists that the Soviet Union is doing so. In all probability it was the premature American decision to deploy large numbers of strategic weapons systems during the 1960s that eventually led to the major Soviet challenge that today our leadership decries as a Soviet bid to gain strategic nuclear superiority over the United States.

Each side has ample cushion in its existing strategic forces to act as a hedge against surprise deployments by the other, and each would have ample deployment lead-time, if needed, to offset whatever the other may do. In the interim neither side would stand to gain a first-strike position vis-à-vis the other. American political and military leaders must strive in the future to subordinate strategic weapons decisions to clearly defined strategic objectives and to forgo tendencies to permit weapons technology to shape the strategy this nation will follow in the 1970s and 1980s.

One final observation relates to official American attitudes toward pursuing arms control agreements with the Soviet Union designed to complement or offer an alternative to traditional defense policy. Debate within the national security establishment on every major arms control proposal from the test ban to SALT has tended to limit the scope of each proposal on grounds that arms control agreements should be virtually risk free before they are entered into. Obviously, it is inconceivable that any arms control agreement could be risk free. Equally as obvious, there are numerous risks nations run when they are parties to persistent arms races, not the least of which is an increased risk of nuclear war. Most Americans have become conditioned to arms race risks either because of trained resignation to whatever fate may befall them, or in a naïve belief that the more arms this nation has the more it is secure against aggression. The fact is, however, in future relations of this nation with the world's major powers, absolute security will never be an option; rather, available options will entail various sets of risks, which will have to be carefully assessed in order to determine whether it is in the net interest of the United States to accept them. It is essential, therefore, that the American public be given a clearer and more dispassionate understanding of the comparative risks of entering into a specific arms control measure as contrasted with alternative arms race costs and risks if no arms control measure is agreed to. Even though all risks can not be fully quantified, serious weight should be given to the safety cushion already built into our military force structure which acts as insurance against cheating or technological surprise. Such a cushion virtually ensures that future enemy technological surprise or clandestine cheating will result at worst in the acceleration of an arms race and not the initiation of war. Such comparative risk assessments are made routinely within the arms control community, but surprisingly little has been said publicly about the results.

NOTES

1. U.S., Department of Defense, *Statement by Secretary of Defense Clark M. Clifford on the 1970 Defense Budget and Defense Program for FY 1970–1974*, January 15, 1969.

2. Johan Jorge Holst, "Parity, Superiority or Sufficiency? Some Remarks on the Nature and Future of the Soviet-American Strategic Relationship," *Adelphi Papers*, no. 65 (London: The Institute for Strategic Studies, February 1970), p. 31.

3. *The Military Balance 1965–1966* (London: The Institute for Strategic Studies, 1965), p. 40.

4. U.S., Department of Defense, *Statement of Secretary of Defense Robert S. McNamara before the House Armed Services Committee on the FY 1966–1970 Defense Program and 1966 Defense Budget*, February 18, 1965, p. 39.

5. Ibid., p. 63.

6. U.S., Department of Defense, *Statement of Secretary of Defense Robert S. McNamara before the House Armed Services Committee on the FY 1967–1971 Defense Program and 1967 Defense Budget*, February 1966, p. 41.

7. Ibid., p. 40.

8. Ibid., p. 53.

9. Although the initial rationale given for MIRV deployment was the need to improve our force capabilities to penetrate Soviet ABMs protecting Moscow and potentially other major cities, conflicting testimony given before Congress by the Chief of Staff of the Air Force and civilian officials of the Department of Defense during 1970 left a clear impression that attainable accuracy improvements for Minuteman III and Poseidons equipped with MIRV would provide a substantial portion of our strategic forces with a hard target or counterforce capability. Under pressure from Congress—led by Senator Brooke—Secretary of Defense Laird and the White House gave public assurances that the MIRV warheads planned for both Minuteman III and Poseidon missiles would not possess a hard target kill potential and were designed strictly to offset Soviet SS-9 deployment and anticipated increases in Soviet ABM capabilities. The Nixon administration also gave its pledge to the Soviet Union that tests of a more accurate MIRV would be foregone in the interest of assisting a successful outcome of the SALT talks.

10. For the text of the address, see U.S., Congress, Joint Committee on Atomic Energy, *Hearings on the Scope, Magnitude, and Implications of the U.S. Antiballistic Missile Program*, 90th Cong., 1st sess., Nov., 1967, Appendix 4, pp. 105*ff*.

11. Ibid., p. 108.

12. Ibid., p. 109.

13. U.S. Congress, House, Subcommittee on National Security Policy and Scientific Developments of the Committee on Foreign Affairs, *Hearings on the Diplomatic and Strategic Impact of Multiple Warhead Missiles*, 91st Cong., 1st sess., 1969, p. 296.

14. Chalmers M. Roberts, *The Nuclear Years, the Arms Race and Arms Control 1945–1970* (New York: Praeger, 1970), pp. 92–93.

15. U.S., Department of Defense, *Statement by Secretary of Defense Robert S. McNamara on the FY 1969–1973 Defense Program and the 1969 Defense Budget*, January 22, 1968, p. 47.

16. Ibid., p. 52.

17. Richard Nixon, *A Report to the Congress on U.S. Foreign Policy for the 1970's: A New Strategy for Peace*, February 18, 1970, p. 121.

18. U.S., Department of Defense, *Statement by Secretary of Defense Melvin R. Laird before a Joint Session of the Senate Armed Services and Appropriations Committees on the Fiscal Year 1971 Defense Program and Budget*, February 20, 1970, p. 62.

19. Department of Defense, *1970 Defense Budget and Defense Program for Fiscal Years 1970–1974*, pp. 46–47.

20. Richard Nixon, *United States Foreign Policy for the 1970's: Building for Peace, The President's Report to Congress* (Washington, D.C.: Government Printing Office, Feb. 25, 1971), p. 365.

21. Ibid., p. 366.

22. *The Strategic Balance 1971–1972* (London: The International Institute for Strategic Studies, 1971), p. 2.

23. Murray Marder, "Extension of ABM is Urged," *The Washington Post*, July 14, 1971, p. 1.

24. U.S., Department of Defense, *1971 Defense Program and Budget*, p. 66.

25. Marder, "Extension of ABM," p. 1.

26. Ibid.

27. Marshall D. Shulman, *Statement before the Senate Foreign Relations Subcommittee on Arms Control, International Law, and Organization*, July 14, 1971, *Congressional Record*, July 16, 1971, E7851–53.

28. *The Washington Post*, May 21, 1971, p. A8.

29. U.S., Department of Defense, *1971 Defense Program and Budget*, p. 17.

30. Ibid., pp. 45–47.

31. Ibid., p. 63.

32. Ibid., p. 68.

33. Lawrence T. Caldwell, "Soviet Attitudes to SALT," *Adelphi Papers*, no. 75 (London: The Institute for Strategic Studies, February 1971).

Note on Sources

The focus of this study is the buildup of United States and Soviet strategic nuclear power following World War II, the strategies designed to utilize this power, and the impact of arms control initiatives and the Vietnam conflict on United States and Soviet perceptions of the utility of that power during the 1970s. The study is both historical and analytical in approach, and thus seeks to trace events in the postwar period as accurately as possible, while conjecturing about the implications of policy choices, future trends in nuclear weapons technology, and strategic ideas likely to shape importantly the nation's future national security.

Even within the limited scope of this study, the useful literature is so copious and variously rich that it is possible to include only a selection of primary and secondary sources which, in the author's judgment, are intellectually rigorous, reflect well the viewpoints of participants closest to the scene, and appear to be an accurate representation of events as they probably happened. For reasons of convenience, as well as merit, the literature is subsumed under four major headings: nuclear monopoly, 1945–1953; massive retaliation, 1954–1960; flexible response, 1961–1968; nuclear sufficiency, 1969–1971.

Nuclear Monopoly, 1945–1953

In the immediate postwar period, a substantial debate took place among defense analysts over the effects of strategic bombing during World War II, some contending that strategic bombing was vastly overrated, others arguing that, because heavy strategic bombing came late in the campaign, its effects on such highly industrialized economies as Germany and Japan were considerable and in the long run probably would have been decisive. The best appraisals of the strategic bombing campaigns against Germany and Japan are found in U.S., Strategic Bombing Survey, *European War,* Reports Nos. 1–207 (Washington, D.C.: U.S. Government Printing Office, 1945); U.S., Strategic Bombing Survey, *Pacific War,* Reports Nos. 1–107 (Washington, D.C.: Government Printing Office, 1946); Bernard Brodie, *Strategy in the Missile Age* (Princeton: Princeton University Press, 1959); Fred C. Ikle, *The Social Impact of Bomb Destruction* (Norman: University of Oklahoma Press, 1958); Eugene M. Emme, ed., *The Impact of Airpower* (Princeton: Van Nostrand, 1959). Brodie's analytical and thorough study remains the standard work in the field.

The debate on the beginnings and nature of the cold war is characterized by revisionist extremists, such as Gar Alperovitz, D. F. Fleming, W. A. Williams, and David Horowitz. Moderate revisionism characterized by the writings of Martin F. Herz, *Beginnings of the Cold War* (Bloomington: Indiana University Press, 1966); Louis B. Halle, *The Cold War as History* (New York: Harper and Row, 1967); Adam Ulam, *Expansion and Coexistence: The History of Soviet Foreign Policy, 1917–1967* (New York: Praeger, 1968); Herbert Feis, *From Trust to Terror: The Onset of the Cold War, 1945–1950* (New York: W. W. Norton, 1970), achieve varying degrees of balance between the communist conspiratorial school and the devil theorists.

For the best overall survey of the period 1945–1953, the standard work remains Samuel P. Huntington, *The Common Defense: Strategic Programs in National Politics* (New York: Columbia University Press, 1961). In addition, there is value in Alfred Goldberg, ed., *A History of the United States Air Force, 1907–1957* (Princeton: Van Nostrand, 1957), and Albert C. Weidenbusch, "A Short History of the Department of Defense" (Master's thesis, University of Omaha, 1962).

More specialized works in the fields of armed services politics, defense budgets, congressional roles in defense funding, and the evolution of nuclear strategy include Warner R. Schilling, Paul Y. Hammond, and Glenn H. Snyder, *Strategy, Politics and Defense Budgets* (New York: Columbia University Press, 1962); Edward A. Kolodziej, *The Uncommon Defense and Congress, 1945–1963* (Columbus: Ohio State University Press, 1966); Perry McCoy Smith, *The Air Force Plans for Peace, 1943–1945* (Baltimore: Johns Hopkins Press, 1970): Vincent Davis, *Postwar Defense Policy and the U.S. Navy, 1943–1946* (Chapel Hill: University of North Carolina Press, 1966); Bernard Brodie and Arnold Wolfers, eds., *The Absolute Weapon: Atomic Power and World Order* (New York: Harcourt, Brace and Co., 1946); Glenn H. Snyder, *Deterrence and Defense* (Princeton: Princeton University Press, 1961); Arnold Wolfers, "Superiority in Nuclear Weapons: Advantages and Limitations," *The Annals* 290 (November 1953): 7–15; Dean G. Acheson, *Present at the Creation* (New York: W. W. Norton Co., 1969).

Massive Retaliation, 1954–1960

The George Kennan policy of containment was distorted by John Foster Dulles in early 1954 through his pronouncement that henceforth the United States would seize the initiative at such times and places that its interests were involved by the exercise of a threat of massive retaliation. Dulles's speech before the Council on Foreign Relations in New York City is useful: "Evolution of Foreign Policy," January 12, 1954, Department of State Press Release No. 8. Criticism of the speech was immediate; the most perceptive came from William W. Kaufmann, "The Requirements of Deterrence," Memorandum No. 7, Center of International Studies (Princeton: Princeton University, 1954); and Bernard Brodie, *Strategy in the Missile Age* (Princeton: Princeton University Press, 1959).

The doctrine of massive retaliation spawned a new generation of civilian strategists and defense analysts. Among the seminal studies of the period are: Henry A. Kissinger, *Nuclear Weapons and Foreign Policy* (New York: Harpers, 1957), and his *The Necessity for Choice* (New York: Harpers, 1960); Richard Leghorn, "No Need to Bomb Cities to Win War," *U.S. News–World Report* (January 28, 1955): 78–92; Herman Kahn, *On Thermonuclear War* (Princeton: Princeton University Press, 1960); Paul Nitze, "Atoms, Strategy and Policy," *Foreign Affairs* 34 (January 1956): 188–198; Robert E. Osgood, *Limited War* (Chicago: University of Chicago Press, 1956); Thomas C. Schelling, *The Strategy of Conflict* (New York: Wiley, 1966); Maxwell D. Taylor, *The Uncertain Trumpet* (New York: Harper & Bros., 1959); T. F. Walkowicz, "Counterforce Strategy," *Air Force* (February 1955): 25–30; Albert Wohlstetter et al., *Selection and Use of Strategic Air Bases, RAND* Report, R-266 (April 1964), and his "The Delicate Balance of Terror," *Foreign Affairs* 37 (January 1959): 211–234; U.S., Congress, House and Senate, Joint Economic Committee, *National Security and the American Economy in the 1960's,* by Henry Rowen, 86th Cong., 2d sess., January 30, 1960; U.S., Congress, Senate, Committee on Foreign Relations, *Developments in Military Technology and Their Impact on U.S. Strategy and Foreign Policy,* pursuant to S. Res. 336, 85th Cong., and S. Res. 31, 86th Cong., December 6, 1959.

A substantial number of ideas on nuclear strategy emanated from the private research organizations, which began in the late 1940s and flourished during the 1950s. See Bruce L. R. Smith, *The RAND Corporation: Case Study of a Nonprofit Advisory Corporation* (Cambridge: Harvard University Press, 1966); Gene M. Lyons and Louis Morton, *Schools for Strategy: Education and Research in National Security Affairs* (New York: Praeger, 1965); Joseph Kraft, "RAND: Arsenal For Ideas," *Harpers* (July 1960): 69–76; Paul Dickson, *Think Tanks* (New York: Atheneum, 1971).

Until the mid-1950s, the annual testimony of defense officials before the House Armed Services Committee, and the Subcommittee of the Committee on Appropriations, and the Senate Armed Services and Appropriations Committees, tended to be sparse on such issues as new weapon systems, strategy, and budget proposals. The apparent threat from the Soviet Union to overtake the United States in strategic power brought Congress to life. See U.S., Congress, Senate, Subcommittee on the Air Force of the Committee on Armed Services, *Study of Air Power,* 84th Cong., 2d sess., April–June 1, 1956, Vols. I and II; U.S., Congress, Senate, Preparedness Investigating Subcommittee of the Committee on Armed Services, *Inquiry into Satellite and Missile Programs,* 85th Cong., 1st and 2d sess., 1957 and 1958, Parts 1, 2, and 3. From 1957 to the early 1960s, exceptional coverage of United States defense policy was provided in an annual volume by Charles H. Donnelly, *United States Defense Policies* (Washington, D.C.: Government Printing Office). Consult also Charles H. Donnelly, *The United States Guided Missile Program* (Washington, D.C.: Government Printing Office, 1959).

The presidential campaign of 1960 is treated adequately in John F. Kennedy, *The Strategy of Peace* (New York: Harper and Bros., 1960); Arthur M. Schlesinger, Jr., *A Thousand Days* (Boston: Houghton Mifflin Co., 1965); Theodore C. Sorensen, *Kennedy* (New York: Harper and Row, 1965); Theordore H. White, *The Making of the President, 1960* (New York: Atheneum House, 1961).

Flexible Response, 1961–1968

John F. Kennedy's victory in the election of 1960 presaged a fundamental change in the strategy for national defense from massive retaliation to flexible response. Innovations in strategic ideas which were gestated during the Eisenhower years were given life by the civilian defense intellectuals who assumed key positions in the Department of Defense. An adequate and perceptive treatment of Robert S. McNamara, the man and Secretary of Defense, is found in Henry L. Trewhitt, *McNamara: His Ordeal in the Pentagon* (New York: Harper and Row, 1971). The best summary description of the "Prelude to Revolution" and the early stages of McNamara's Pentagon management remains William W. Kaufmann's *The McNamara Strategy* (New York: Harper and Row, 1964).

The intellectual underpinning of the strategy of flexible response can be found among the following: *The Statements of the Secretary of Defense before the House Armed Services Committee on the Five Year Defense Program and the Annual Defense Budget,* issued annually by the Department of Defense. Commonly called the *Posture Statement,* it contains both an analysis of recommended force programs and individual weapon systems. During the early Kennedy period when new strategic programs were unfolding, it is useful to consult the annual presidential State of the Union messages. No effort to understand the McNamara Pentagon would be complete without a selective reading of the Secretary's and the Joint Chief's annual testimony before the House Subcommittee of the Committee on Appropriations, *Hearings on DOD Appropriations for the years 1964 to 1968;* the House Committee on Armed Services, 1961–1968; and joint hearings before the Senate Subcommittee on Appropriations and the Armed Services Committee, 1961–1968; and the *Congressional Record* during the annual summer debates on the defense appropriations bill.

To understand the theory behind the defense strategy embraced by the McNamara strategists during his early tenure, consult: Michael Brower, "Controlled Thermonuclear War," *The New Republic* (July 30, 1962); Morton H. Halperin, "The 'No Cities' Doctrine," *The New Republic* (October 8, 1962): 16–20; Stewart Alsop, "McNamara Thinks About the Unthinkable," interview with Secretary of Defense Robert S. McNamara in *Saturday Evening Post* (December 1962); Michael Brower, "Nuclear Strategy of the Kennedy Administration," *Bulletin of the Atomic Scientists* (October 1962); Stewart Alsop, "Our New Strategy: The Alternative to Total War," *Saturday Evening Post* 236 (December 1, 1962); John T. McNaughton, "Address before the International Arms Control Symposium," University of Michigan, Ann Arbor, Michigan, December 19, 1962; Alain Enthoven, "U.S. Defense Policy for the 1960's," Address before the Loyola University Forum for National Affairs, Los Angeles, California, February 10, 1963; Robert S. McNamara, "Address at the Commencement Exercises," Univeristy of Michigan, Ann Arbor, Michigan, June 16, 1962.

Studies on the Cuban missile crisis are legion. Among the more useful are: Arnold L. Horelick and Myron Rush, *Strategic Power and Soviet Foreign Policy,* R-434-PR (Santa Monica: The RAND Corporation, 1965); Elie Abel, *The Missile Crisis* (Philadelphia: J. B. Lippincott and Co., 1966); Roger Hilsman, *To Move a Nation* (New York: Doubleday and Co., 1967); Arthur M. Schlesinger, Jr., *A Thousand Days* (Boston: Houghton Mifflin, 1965); Theodore C. Sorensen, *Kennedy* (New York: Harper and Row, 1965); R. F. Kennedy, *Thirteen Days: A Memoir of the Cuban Missile Crisis* (New York: W. W. Norton, 1967); Arnold L. Horelick, "The Cuban Missile Crisis: An Analysis of Soviet Calculations and Behavior," *World Politics* (April 1963): 363–389.

Because of confusion surrounding the nature of the missile gap in early 1961, an understanding of how the missile gap evaporated by the fall of the same year can be found in Stuart Symington, "Where the Missile Gap Went," *The Reporter* (February 15, 1962): 21–23; *U.S. News-World Report,* "Why It's Russia's Turn to Worry About a 'Missile Gap' " (December 3, 1962): 45–48; The Institute for Strategic Studies, *The Military Balance* (annual) (London, England); Roswell L. Gilpatrick, Speech before the Business Council, Hot Springs, Virginia, October 21, 1961, DOD Office of Public Affairs Release # 1173–61; Edgar M. Bottome, *The Missile Gap: A Study of the Formulation of Military and Political Policy* (Rutherford: Fairleigh Dickinson Press, 1971).

Secretary McNamara's management of the Pentagon polarized critics and defenders. Overall assessments of the McNamara years, as well as case studies of his major weapon decisions, are available in profusion. The more balanced and perceptive accounts include Michael H. Armacost, *The Politics of Weapons Innovation* (New York: Columbia University Press, 1969); Alain C. Enthoven, *How Much is Enough: Shaping the Defense Program, 1961–1969* (New York: Harper and Row, 1971); James M. Roherty, *Decisions of Robert S. McNamara* (Coral Gables: University of Miami Press, 1970); Henry L., Trewhitt, *McNamara: His Ordeal in the Pentagon* (New York: Harper and Row, 1971); Robert Art, *The TFX Decision: McNamara and the Military* (Boston: Little Brown & Co., 1968); Adam Yarmolinsky, *The Military Establishment: Its Impacts on American Society* (New York: Harper and Row, 1970); Morton H. Halperin, "The President and the Military," *Foreign Affairs* 50 (January 1972): 310–324.

Following World War II, Congress rubber-stamped defense budgets proposed by the executive in almost monotonous fashion. This cycle was not seriously interrupted until 1967 when the question of ABM deployment precipitated an intense and comprehensive debate over the political–military merits of the proposed system. A cross-section of opinion would include: Robert S. McNamara, "Address before United Press International Editors and Publishers," San Francisco, California, September 18, 1967, DOD Release # 868–67; Benson D. Adams, "McNamara's ABM Policy,

1961–1967," *ORBIS* (Spring 1968): 200–225; Abram Chayes and Jerome B. Wiesner, eds., *ABM: An Evaluation of the Decision to Deploy an Antiballistic Missile System* (New York: The New American Library, 1969); Johan J. Holst and William Schneider, Jr., *Why ABM? Policy Issues in the Missile Defense Controversy* (New York: Pergamon Press, 1969); D. G. Brennan, "The Case For Missile Defense," *Foreign Affairs* 47 (April 1969): 433–448; J. I. Coffey, "The ABM Debate," *Foreign Affairs* 45 (April 1967): 403–413; R. W. Garwin and H. A. Bethe, "Antiballistic Missile System," *Scientific American* (March 1968): 3–13; Ralph E. Lapp, "A Biography of the ABM," *New York Times Magazine* (May 4, 1969): 29*ff.*; R. L. Rothstein, "The ABM, Proliferation and International Stability," *Foreign Affairs* 46 (April 1968): 487–502; J. J. Stone, "The Case Against Missile Defenses," *Adelphi Papers*, no. 47 (April 1968) (London: Institute for Strategic Studies); U.S., Congress, Senate, Subcommittee on Military Applications of the Joint Committee on Atomic Energy, *Hearings, Scope, Magnitude, and Implications of the United States Antiballistic Missile Program*, 90th Cong., 1st sess. (Washington: U.S. Government Printing Office, 1968); U.S., Congress, Senate, Subcommittee on International Organization and Disarmament Affairs of the Committee on Foreign Relations, *Hearings, Strategic and Foreign Policy Implications of ABM Systems*, 91st Cong., 1st sess. (Washington: U.S. Government Printing Office, 1969), Pts. 1 and 2: U.S., Congress, House, Subcommittee of the Committee on Appropriations, *Hearings, Safeguard Antiballistic Missile System*, 91st Cong., 1st sess. (Washington: U.S. Government Printing Office, 1969); U.S., Congress, Senate, Committee on Foreign Relations, *Hearing, Intelligence and the ABM*, 91st Cong., 1st sess. (Washington: U.S. Government Printing Office, 1969); U.S., Congress, Senate, Subcommittee on Arms Control, International Law and Organization of the Committee on Foreign Relations, *Hearings, ABM, MIRV, SALT, and the Nuclear Arms Race*, 91st Cong., 2nd sess. (Washington: U.S. Government Printing Office, 1970).

Finally, the McNamara story would not be complete without consulting his own *The Essence of Security: Reflections in Office* (New York: Harper and Row, 1968).

Nuclear Sufficiency, 1969–1971

During its first two years in office, the Nixon administration proclaimed its strategic goal as one of sufficiency and its military strategy to be realistic deterrence. A central issue in the debate over the meaning of sufficiency and realistic deterrence is whether in fact there are any real differences between the Nixon strategy and that of the Kennedy-Johnson administrations described as flexible response. An important innovation introduced by the Nixon administration which sheds some light on the declared strategic posture is U.S., Department of Defense, *U.S. Foreign Policy for the 1970's, A Report to the Congress by Richard Nixon* (Washington: U.S. Government Printing Office, 1970 and 1971). Complementing the President's statement are: U.S., Department of Defense, *Statement by Secretary of Defense Melvin R. Laird Before a Joint Session of the Senate Armed Services and Appropriations Committees on the Fiscal Year 1971 Defense Program and Budget*, February

20, 1970, mimeographed by the DOD; and U.S., Department of Defense, *Statement of Secretary of Defense Melvin R. Laird Before the House Armed Services Committee on the Fiscal Year 1972–76 Defense Program and the 1972 Defense Budget,* March 9, 1971, mimeographed by DOD; U.S., Congress, House, Committee on Armed Services, *Hearings on Military Posture,* 91st Cong. 1st and 2d sess. and 92d Cong. 1st sess. (Washington: U.S. Government Printing Office, 1969–1971); U.S., Congress, House, Subcommittee of the Committee on Appropriations, *Hearings on Department of Defense Appropriations for 1970, 1971 and 1972,* 91st Cong., 1st and 2d sess., and 92d Cong., 1st sess. (Washington: U.S. Government Printing Office, 1969–1971); U.S., Congress, Senate, Committee on Appropriations, *Hearings, Department of Defense Appropriations,* 92d Cong., 1st sess. (Washington: U.S. Government Printing Office, 1971); U.S., Congress, Senate, Committee on Armed Services, *Hearings on S. 939 (H.R. 8687),* 92d Cong., 1st. sess. (Washington: U.S. Government Printing Office, 1971).

The Strategic Arms Limitation Talks (SALT) by the end of 1971 had entered a critical phase. Most analysts predicted that agreement would likely result but the more prolonged the negotiations the greater the prospect of a limited agreement. A brief discussion of the SALT origins is contained in Chalmers M. Roberts, *The Nuclear Years: The Arms Race and Arms Control, 1945–70* (New York: Praeger, 1970). The best sources of information on the highly confidential talks have appeared in the *New York Times* and the *Washington Post,* primarily by William Beecher and Chalmers Roberts respectively. The U.S. Arms Control and Disarmament Agency published in its periodic *Disarmament Document Series* and its annual *Documents on Disarmament* useful chronologies and public statements on the SALT. Considerable vital information is also contained in the Nixon administration's reports to the Congress on *U.S. Foreign Policy for the 1970's,* cited above. For Soviet interest in the SALT, consult Lawrence T. Caldwell, "Soviet Attitudes to SALT," *Adelphi Papers,* no. 75 (London: Institute for Strategic Studies, 1971).

On arms control in general, see: George W. Rathjens, *The Future of the Strategic Arms Race Options for the 1970's* (New York: Carnegie Endowment for International Peace, 1969); Herbert Scoville, Jr., *Toward a Strategic Arms Limitation Agreement* (New York: Carnegie Endowment for International Peace, 1969); Roman Kolkowicz, "Strategic Parity and Beyond Soviet Perspectives," *World Politics* (April 1971): 431–451; Benjamin S. Lambeth, "Deterrence in the MIRV Era," *World Politics* (January 1972): 221–242; Herbert F. York, *Race to Oblivion: A Participant's View of the Arms Race* (New York: Simon & Schuster, 1970); J. I. Coffey, *Strategic Power and National Security* (Pittsburgh: University of Pittsburgh Press, 1971).

INDEX